A Review of Managing Quality and a Primer for the Certified Quality Manager Exam

Also available from ASQC Quality Press

Insights to Performance Excellence 1997: An Inside Look at the 1997 Baldrige Award Criteria
Mark L. Blazey

Goldratt's Theory of Constraints: A Systems Approach to Continuous Improvement
H. William Dettmer

Business Process Benchmarking: Finding and Implementing Best Practices
Robert C. Camp

Principles of Quality Costs: Principles, Implementation, and Use, Second Edition
ASQC Quality Costs Committee; Jack Campanella, editor

Measuring Customer Satisfaction
Bob E. Hayes

Understanding and Applying Value-Added Assessment: Eliminating Business Process Waste
William E. Trischler

The Quality Toolbox
Nancy R. Tague

To request a complimentary catalog of publications, call 800-248-1946.

A Review of Managing Quality and a Primer for the Certified Quality Manager Exam

Thomas J. Cartin
Donald J. Jacoby

ASQC Quality Press
Milwaukee, Wisconsin

A Review of Managing Quality and a Primer for the Certified Quality Manager Exam
Thomas J. Cartin and Donald J. Jacoby

Library of Congress Cataloging-in-Publication Data
Cartin, Thomas J.
    A review of managing quality and a primer for the certified
quality manager exam / Thomas J. Cartin, Donald J. Jacoby.
        p.   cm.
    Includes bibliographical references and index.
    ISBN 0-87389-358-1 (alk. paper)
    1. Quality control.   2. Total quality management.   3. Quality
control—Examinations, questions, etc.   I. Cartin, T. J. (Thomas
J.), 1924–   .   II. Jacoby, Donald J., 1948–   .   III. Title.
TS156.C3644   1997
658.5'.62—dc21   97-2864
                                                                    CIP

10 9 8 7 6 5 4 3 2 1

ISBN 0-87389-358-1

Acquisitions Editor: Roger Holloway
Project Editor: Kelley Cardinal

ASQC Mission: To facilitate continuous improvement and increase customer satisfaction by identifying, communicating, and promoting the use of quality principles, concepts, and technologies; and thereby be recognized throughout the world as the leading authority on, and champion for, quality.

Attention: Schools and Corporations
ASQC Quality Press books, videotapes, audiotapes, and software are available at quantity discounts with bulk purchases for business, educational, or instructional use. For information, please contact ASQC Quality Press at 800-248-1946, or write to ASQC Quality Press, P.O. Box 3005, Milwaukee, WI 53201-3005.

For a free copy of the ASQC Quality Press Publications Catalog, including ASQC membership information, call 800-248-1946.

Printed in the United States of America

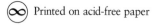 Printed on acid-free paper

Quality Press
611 East Wisconsin Avenue
Milwaukee, Wisconsin 53202

Contents

Preface xi
Acknowledgments xvii

1. QUALITY STANDARDS.................................   1
    A. Total Quality Management (TQM)   1
    B. Theory of Variation (Common and Special Causes)   9
    C. Continuous Process Improvement (CPI)   11
    D. Cycle Time Reduction.................................   15
    E. Supplier Quality Management   17
    F. Customer Service   22
    G. Quality Awards/Standards Criteria
       (Baldrige, ISO 9000, GMP)   24

2. ORGANIZATIONS AND THEIR FUNCTIONS...........   39
    A. Organization Assessment..............................   40
    B. Organization Structures (Matrix, Hierarchical)   46
    C. Quality Functions Within the Organization...............   51
    D. Communication Within the Organization.................   53
    E. Change Agents and Their Effects on Organizations   58
    F. Management Styles (By Facts and Data, Coaching,
       Other Leadership Styles)   63

G. Business Functions 71
   1. External: business climate, safety, legal and regulatory,
      warranties, technology, environmental 71
   2. Internal: human resources, engineering, sales and
      marketing, finance, research and development,
      purchasing, safety 73

3. QUALITY NEEDS AND OVERALL STRATEGIC PLANS . . . 79
A. Linkage Between Quality Function Needs and
   Overall Strategic Planning 82
B. Linkage Between Strategic Plan and Quality Plan 83
C. Quality Function Mission 87
D. Priority of Quality Function Within the Organization 90
E. Metrics and Goals That Drive Organizational
   Performance 92
F. Formulation of Quality Principles and Policies 97
G. Resource Requirements to Manage the Quality Function . . . 98

4. CUSTOMER SATISFACTION AND FOCUS 103
A. Types of Customers (Internal, External, Intermediate,
   End-User) 104
B. Elements of Customer-Driven Organizations 105
C. Customer Expectations, Priorities, Needs, and Voice 106
D. Customer Relationship Management and Commitment
   (Complaints, Feedback, Guarantees, Corrective Actions) . . . 109
E. Customer Identification and Segmentation 111
F. Partnership and Alliances Between Customers
   and Suppliers 113
G. Communication Techniques (Surveys, Focus Groups,
   Satisfaction/Complaint Cards) 115
H. Multiple-Customer Management and Conflict
   Resolution 118
I. Customer Retention and Loyalty 120

5. CONTINUOUS IMPROVEMENT 123
   A. Improvement Tools 123
      1. Quality Control Tools 123
      2. Quality Management Tools 143
      3. Plan-Do-Check-Act (PDCA) 145
      4. Quality Function Deployment (QFD)................. 146
   B. Cost of Quality 149
   C. Process Improvement.................................... 153
      1. Reengineering 158
   D. Trend Analysis.. 162
   E. Measurement Issues...................................... 164
      1. Reliability and Validity 164
      2. Sampling Plans and Other Statistical Analysis
         Techniques 167
      3. Specifications, Calibration, and Process Capability....... 175
   F. Concurrent Engineering 183
   G. Total Productive Maintenance 186

6. HUMAN RESOURCE MANAGEMENT 193
   A. Leadership Roles and Responsibilities 194
      1. Conflict Resolution 196
      2. Professional Ethics.................................... 199
   B. Quality Staffing Issues................................... 202
      1. Selection 203
      2. Performance Evaluation................................ 205
      3. Professional Development.............................. 208
      4. Goals and Objectives 209
   C. Quality Responsibilities in Job/Position Descriptions 210
   D. Employee/Team Empowerment........................... 211
   E. Team Formation and Evolution 214
      Teams and Other Work Groups 217
   F. Team Management 219
      1. Facilitation Techniques 222
      2. Performance Evaluation................................ 223
      3. Recognition and Reward............................... 224

7. TRAINING AND EDUCATION 229
    A. Importance of Top-Down Support and Strategic Planning
       for Quality Training...................................... 231
    B. Training Subgroups and Topics 233
       1. Facilitator Training and Selection 237
    C. Training Needs Analysis................................. 240
    D. Post-Training Evaluation and Reinforcement.............. 244
    E. Training Tools 245
       1. Lectures, Workbooks, Case Studies, On-the-Job
          Training... 246
       2. Use of Technology in Training (Videos,
          Computer-Delivered Instruction, and Others) 247

8. PROJECT MANAGEMENT 251
    A. Planning and Monitoring................................. 254
       1. Integrated Quality Initiatives 257
       2. Short- and Long-Term Quality Plans and Objectives..... 258
       3. Feedback Loops...................................... 260
       4. Performance Measures and Timelines.................. 262
          a. Resources 264
          b. Methodologies...................................... 264
       5. Relevant Stakeholders................................. 270
       6. Benchmarking.. 270
       7. Budgeting.. 273
       8. Cost-Benefit Analysis (CBA) 275
    B. Implementation 275
       1. Management Support and Organization Roadblocks 276
       2. Short-Term (Tactical) Plans 278
       3. Cross-Functional Collaboration 278
       4. Continuous Review and Enhancement of
          Quality Process 279
       5. Documentation and Procedures 281
    C. Project Closure 281

Appendix A: Control Chart Test Patterns and
              Control Limit Formulae 285
Appendix B: Certified Quality Manager Body of Knowledge...... 289
Appendix C: ASQC Glossary of Terms 293

Index.. 319

Preface

Everyone doing his best is not the answer. It is necessary that people know what to do. Drastic changes are required. The responsibility for change lies with management.

Statistical methods are not enough. He that starts with statistical methods alone will not be here in three years.

These quotes, from W. Edwards Deming's *Out of the Crisis*, highlight what modern quality management is all about. In the first statement, the changes refer to the knowledge required and the way organizations must now be structured and managed. The second statement means that a mechanistic approach won't succeed. Statistics and statistical thinking are an integral part of the modern approach, but every aspect of organization theory and management is involved. The scope of this book's table of contents indicates the breadth of organization involvement required. Everything has to change: the way organizations are managed, management and employee skills, and a primary focus on customer satisfaction as an organization's reason for being. Profits and competitive position are a result of that focus.

The implications of what is now required in the way of skills and knowledge for the quality practitioner are also recognized by ASQC in its certification program for quality managers. This book is organized to cover the same subject matter as the published body of knowledge for that certification. It is a body of knowledge that should be shared by all management.

The perspective of this book is the authors' synthesis of reference readings and more than 50 years of combined experience in teaching, consulting, and industrial management positions in engineering, manufacturing, and quality functions.

The traditional quality control function in industry rarely achieved effective quality control. At least not at an acceptable price. This was not because the knowledge to do so wasn't available, but because of the prevailing management concepts of who was responsible for quality and how it was achieved. The responsibility was mostly delegated to a functional quality organization that relied, to a great extent, on appraisal (inspection and testing) as the main control. At the same time, quality control was also viewed as an expense to be minimized. This led to a common assumption that high quality was costly. It was never clear how much inspection was enough.

Around 1930, Walter Shewhart clearly described how to produce high quality. He determined that using statistical methods to measure performance would provide information for control and improvement. He also alluded to the other aspects of what is now referred to as a total quality (TQ) approach. Deming was a Shewhart disciple who did not find American management receptive to the concept of variation and process control, but he was influential in convincing Japanese industry to adopt it, with obvious success.

In the 1980s and 1990s, beginning in industry, many organizations began their journey toward higher quality and customer satisfaction. Many are succeeding, but many have failed and many are still only talking about it.

The service area does not have a tradition of a quality control function or managing using TQ, but many are adapting to it. The principles of TQ prescribed in this book are totally applicable to the service area, business, government, and education.

Intended Audience

Organizations vary so widely in size, type, scope, and function that it isn't practical to provide a book that will describe every situation. The application of TQ principles or fundamentals described in this book can offer guidance to industry, government, education, and nonprofit organizations. The references listed include many special quality management books for different needs.

A small organization may be organized differently from a large one, but similar tasks are usually performed. Therefore, managers using this book must understand the principles and then select the information and references that best fit their needs and tailor them to their organization.

Organizations also vary widely in their level of quality maturity. Many concentrate on achieving registration to the international quality system standards (ISO 9000 series), and some use the Baldrige Award criteria for self-improvement. Many organizations are not yet involved in adopting the new quality management paradigm; some are examining it with serious interest, some are in the early stages of implementation, some failed in their first attempt and are looking for new direction, some are emphasizing reengineering, and some are merely curious. Also, there are people joining team-managed organizations who are not familiar with what it is all about. There are many small-business managers who are being pressed by their customers, or competition, to adopt some variation of a total quality organization. And finally, there are students or quality professionals preparing for quality certification examinations. The authors hope that this book will help these individuals understand the scope and complexity of modern quality management and the basics of the subject matter. This book may also serve as the outline and text for a course in quality management, such as the one offered by ASQC, with the instructor adding specific reading assignments and case studies.

Scope

The number of subjects covered in this book indicates the breadth of organization involvement when an organization adopts a policy to focus on customer satisfaction and continuous improvement to become a product or service leader. This book is fundamentally an introduction and guide. It is not a tutorial, nor is it written to provide an in-depth understanding of every subject. That can only be achieved by extensive study.

The subject of total quality management has been addressed by a flood of books, articles, and research in the late 1980s and 1990s. Thus, extensive references are provided for further reading. The best source for such material is the ASQC Quality Information Center at ASQC head-quarters in Milwaukee, Wisconsin.

It is the intent of the authors to identify the elements of managing quality in all the organization functions that must participate if the term *total* is to be meaningful. This holistic approach is one of the most significant changes in the role of quality in leading organizations. Another is the need for management leadership, as is the need for different managing skills.

Reference was made earlier to the traditional role of quality control. Now, as J. M. Juran describes it in his *Quality Control Handbook,* the quality function is what the entire organization does to ensure that it provides ever-improving products and services. There is still a role for the quality specialist and manager, however; it will vary with different kinds of organizations. The specialist's role is mentioned throughout the text.

Terminology affects interpretation and understanding. Much of the language in studying quality has both general and specific interpretations. The authors have tried to be clear about this in the discussions. For example, modern quality management is referred to by several different acronyms, such as total quality control (TQC) and total quality management (TQM), which are the oldest and most common. Many organizations and specialties have selected their own. The acronym TQ will be used to identify the quality activities of an organization having these prime elements.

- Focus on customer satisfaction

- Continuous improvement

- Organizationwide involvement

- Team management

Organization of the Book

The book format follows that of the ASQC Certified Quality Manager body of knowledge, with two exceptions. The theory of variation is in Chapter 1, because it is basic to the TQ management thinking, and the subject of project management is last, in Chapter 8, because all of the material that precedes it applies to successful project management.

Project management usually requires managing work using TQ tools and techniques.

There are eight chapters and two appendices. The eight subjects represent the key activities and responsibilities of management that must be understood to manage a TQ organization. They must also be understood by all members of an organization for them to participate intelligently and effectively in the improvement activities.

A limitation of any book is that subjects have to be separated into a clear and understandable format. In studying and practicing quality management, however, the different subjects are interrelated and interdependent. So the authors have to depend on the readers reading all the chapters and making the connections as they progress. They have tried to limit repetition and give each chapter something of a stand-alone quality and use cross-referencing where useful.

Chapter 1 is a discussion of what are considered quality standards in quality management. The authors have moved theory of variation into this category. Deming considered it fundamental to proper management thinking. Under the subheading TQM is a discussion of the growing recognition that perhaps the most important factor in becoming a TQ organization is the need to recognize that the traditional organization structures and methods of operating must give way to a fast-acting, team method of managing. This is also basic to understanding what process management is and how it differs from traditional functional management.

The Baldrige Award and ISO 9000 are two popular quality standards. An overview of their content is included, and they are referenced throughout the book. The Baldrige Award is recognized as a valuable framework for achieving significant organizational improvement. The ISO 9000 standards have gained worldwide recognition as a basis for developing a quality system.

Chapter 2 addresses organization functions and relationships in TQ. Chapter 3 describes the importance of quality planning, setting objectives, and performance measurement at every level. Chapter 4 focuses on customers and the factors involved in achieving their satisfaction in an environment of rising expectations, with the world as the marketplace. Chapter 5 describes the tools, techniques, and methodologies employed in managing continuous improvement. Chapter 6 looks at the complex and critical issues involved in managing the most difficult organizational factor of all, human resources. Chapter 7 discusses training and education, reflecting on the important role it must take when organization structures and relationships are changing along with new skills, management philosophies, policies, and techniques. Chapter 8 discusses the elements in successfully using project management, a popular vehicle to manage work and change.

Appendix A contains statistical control chart formulas and control chart test criteria. They support the material in Chapter 5. The glossary in Appendix C presents ASQC's list of terms common to quality management.

The most comprehensive list of quality reference material available for purchase is in the ASQC Quality Press Publications Catalog. *Quality Progress* magazine publishes peer-reviewed articles on all aspects of quality. Back issues are available on CD-ROM. A wide variety of quality information is also available through the Internet. The January 1995 issue of *Quality Progress* identifies some sources, with their World Wide Web addresses.

The *Quality Progress* web site address is http://qualityprogress.asqc.org and is a good source of quality management information.

Acknowledgments

The genesis of this book was rather unusual. In an attempt to provide our members with some form of preparation for the pilot Certified Quality Manager exam, as chair of the Baltimore Section of ASQC I took it upon myself to form two study groups. Reasoning that the best way to learn a subject is to prepare to teach the subject, each member of each study group was assigned responsibility to teach one module of the exam. Some of the members of the study groups shared the compilation of materials with friends from ASQC who are natural-born publicists (Gene Underwood) and, as a result, the Baltimore Section was contacted by Quality Press and asked to refine these materials for publication.

To my Baltimore board, which has supported me in this leap of faith, as well as many other leaps: Thank you. These past two years have been absolutely some of the best. To the original study group members, whose names are listed below: You did good work! To the writers, Tom Cartin and Don Jacoby, who took the dream and made it a reality: Thanks.

And last—but not least—to all of you who will ever use this book: Best wishes for a satisfying career. May you truly make a difference for the better in all that you attempt.

E. Elizabeth Reigel
Chair, Baltimore Section of ASQC
1994–1996

The study group members were

Rick Coberly	Todd Forsythe	Kevin Gilson	Joel Glazer
Alan Glasby	Sid Lewis	Joe Ludford	Francis Nielsen
Howard Swartz	Rick Townsley	Frank Vojik	Bob Weaber
Brian Wilhelm	Sandra Winters	Augy Ziegler	

The authors also wish to acknowledge the very valuable final editing work of Beth Reigel. The book's quality was improved through her efforts.

Thomas J. Cartin
Donald J. Jacoby

Chapter 1
Quality Standards

1.A. Total Quality Management (TQM)

The term *quality management* has a history going back more than 50 years. Its theoretical foundation was the development of probability mathematics in the early 1920s. Shewhart[1] used those concepts to develop statistical quality control charts. The high volume and close tolerance requirements of World War II provided the need for a wide application of statistical techniques to control quality. The nature and purpose of war production products, including interchangeability of parts, made the economic control of quality a critical and life-preserving issue. This initiated the wider use of control charts, but even then the emphasis was on inspection and sampling, not process control. That emphasis continued after the United States switched to civilian production and became supplier to the world. Cost and schedule, not quality, were the focus of management attention. The use of control charts and process control virtually disappeared, except in the process industries. Even in the postwar defense industries it was uncommon. The only significant statistical quality technique used was inspection sampling, and it wasn't uncommon to use sampling plans with an acceptable outgoing quality level of 3 percent defectives. The Department of Defense (DOD) developed the first widely used quality control inspection and quality system specifications for its suppliers, but the emphasis was on inspection by contractor inspectors and those of the DOD. It was a focus on the mechanics, tactics, and symptoms, not the root (system) causes or the proper quality objectives and strategies. Until about the mid-1980s, quality management meant the management of the quality control activities in industry.

Armand V. Feigenbaum[2] is credited with coining the term *total quality control* and describing a quality system to provide it. This system can be found in his book *Total Quality Control*. General management ignored the book, however, treating it as a book for quality specialists.

U.S. management's interest in quality from a modern perspective began in the 1970s, when managers visited Japan in large numbers to find out how it could become so competitive yet deliver high quality at lower costs. Many were also stimulated by Columbia Broadcasting Company's television show "If Japan Can Why Can't We?" the question referring to higher quality at lower cost. Many came away with the idea that Japan's secret was quality circles. Thousands of companies started them. They didn't listen to Deming[3] or Juran,[4] who were still preaching that success lay in using the elements of what has become TQM. They continued with the prescriptive, canned approach instead of understanding concepts and applying uniquely tailored corrective actions.

Quality circles peaked and faded as the primary quality improvement technique. During this period management continued to manage much as it always did: as vertical, functional organization structure with top-down direction. But Deming was beginning to get through to some CEOs, and they began to understand that the way they managed had to change. Deming's four-day seminars for upper management began to have an effect; in essence, he began to describe the core of what has become TQM. The successful penetration of U.S. markets by Japanese companies caused the awakening of companies like the Ford Motor Company, which began the journey toward managing with the customer foremost in mind and adopting the policy of continuous process improvement. As the full implication of TQM became apparent, managing quality became more comprehensive, as the breadth of the subject matter of this book indicates. The movement grew, and leading companies like Hewlett-Packard, Xerox, AT&T, and Procter and Gamble are now deeply committed to managing using TQM principles. But TQM is complex, in its early stages, and still evolving. It is a long process; it involves changing the traditions, attitudes, and activities of the entire organization; and we are still learning what it takes to do it well.

Other evidence of TQM's value (and complexity) is presented by T. B. Kinni.[5] His listing and discussion of America's best manufacturing plants identifies nine major areas of similarity, organized into three core strategies—customer focus, quality, and agility—and six supporting competencies that help achieve those strategies—employee involvement, supply management, technology, product development, environmental responsibility and safety, and corporate citizenship.

The question is, why do TQM at all? It is hard work, disruptive, and costly. The answer is that organizations that are buffered or protected in some way, without competitive pressures, seem to be the last to change. Changes in the marketplace make it obvious to many that businesses can't be conducted in the same old way.

- The marketplace is worldwide and changing rapidly and unpredictably. One has only to consider what is happening in the telecommunications and medical care arenas to see this.

- Survival in a rapidly changing and unpredictable environment requires organizations that are flexible, fast reacting, and structured differently with a different culture.

- Hierarchical organizations developed in mostly stable, slow-changing, highly predictable markets can't compete. When frequent, fast, new action is needed, they are encumbered by their own bureaucracies and ingrained attitudes and behavior.

The Need for Change

TQM is a radical change from traditional management. Deming and Juran, Peter Drucker,[6] and Alvin Toffler have all said that change is needed in order to survive. But the degree and nature of the changes are not fully understood by many organizations. The perception seems to be that TQM is a formula they can train their people to use and reap the promised rewards, without having to change the organization.

Implementing TQM isn't proving to be that easy. There have been numerous articles and books written about the failures of TQM. E. Deevy[7] states that 75 percent of TQM and business process reengineering efforts fail to deliver on their promises. He doesn't provide a source for his statistics, but there is clear evidence that in many cases TQM hasn't met management expectations.

Several contemporary authors, such as Peter Senge,[8] Tompkins,[9] and Deevy, suggest a reason for why TQM fails. Each says it differently, but a common thread is that management has typically had a mechanistic approach to TQM implementation.

1. Hire a consultant to train upper management.

2. Organize and train teams.

3. Support team efforts.

A mechanistic approach—a force-fit on the organization—will not work or work effectively and is the cause of many failures.

Tompkins uses the term "genesis enterprise" to describe what an organization has to become to survive and prosper. It is an organization that continually reaches for higher performance levels by creating a culture that continuously improves relationships with its employees and outside partners (suppliers and customers). Reaching this position requires several basic changes in how organizations operate (these are further discussed in following chapters). The genesis enterprise requires

- Changing from managing to leading
- Shifting organization relationships from individuals to teams
- Changing the relationships between customers and suppliers to partnerships
- Changing the framework of recognition and rewards so they become motivators

Deevy's model for the new enterprise constitutes a new social contract between the people who run the business and the people who work for them. He refers to it as "the resilient organization." It emphasizes rapid response, and its achievement is based on two ideas

1. Shifting from control to commitment and removing bureaucratic constraints.

2. Developing the ability to cope with the unexpected. This is valued over order and predictability. The need for this ability is why a mechanistic approach to improvement won't work. Also, the organization should respond to the environment and operate accordingly, rather than depend on a bureaucracy. Organizations have to be living, adapting, and resilient.

Deevy's three core conditions for converting from a traditional organization to a resilient, self-organizing enterprise that will learn are as follows:

1. Allow each person to know what's going on. All members must have free access to the business data of the organization. They need to know how the business works and is performing.

2. Be totally customer oriented and proactive. Remove the bureaucracy of functional elements. Reduce function specialization. Emphasize organization, process, and simplification.

3. Motivate people by giving them a stake in the outcome. Avoid the illusion of participation. People have to believe that they have a real stake in the organization's success if they are to respond to needed changes. Compensation should be tied to business strategy. Broaden job descriptions.

Senge believes that the organizations that will truly excel will be those that discover how to tap people's commitment and capacity to learn, at all organization levels, faster than their competitors. This kind of learning requires organizations, and their members, to expect and adapt to change. They are continually enhancing their capability to create the future. A basis for this is a shared vision; that is, when a team member sees the connection between his or her task and the organization's vision. Other elements to this thesis are explored in Senge's writings.

The ideas of these thinkers are presented in this discussion of TQM because they describe the initial understanding that must be reached, first by management, of how radical the changes must be before initiating TQM. If TQM is considered from a mechanistic point of view it will not be effective and will likely fail.

A Different Operating Policy

Another radical difference between traditional management and managing for the future is the adoption of a philosophy and policy of continuous improvement (CI). CI applies to every aspect of organization activity and is a cornerstone of TQM. CI means, literally, that improvement can never stop. Every objective met becomes the starting place for the next objective. Status quo means atrophy; the new status quo is that there is no status quo. For example, many businesses used to talk a lot about achieving a market share. Certainly every business wants as big a piece as it can capture. But businesses can't settle for a market share because the markets are changing too rapidly. Some managers first encountering the TQM approach say, "I thought the main business objective was profit and to satisfy the stockholders." That is still the objective. But instead of trying to manage or push the enterprise to success, the nature of markets and competition today is such that businesses also require leadership, with management and employees acting as a knowledgeable, flexible team dedicated to higher performance and focused on the customer. Profits and return on investment are the result of successfully exploiting those factors.

Kinds of Improvement

Performance improvements can be incremental (steadily, step by step, each problem solved in order) or breakthroughs (big jumps). Juran identifies them in his trilogy:[10] quality planning, quality control, and then quality improvement where a major breakthrough advance is made. Both approaches to improvement are needed. Also, if the improvement activities are going to become the theme of the organization on a long-term basis, they also must include improved relationships between managers and employees, and the organization and its customers and suppliers.

TQM represents a change from systems and procedures-based to process-based management. This refers to the traditional management method of establishing systems and procedures for functional organizations to do the work. It all seems very orderly, but work actually gets done by flowing from department to department, across the vertically structured functions. TQM recognizes and is applied to managing those processes by which work really gets done. That requires a different, more comprehensive way to manage. It involves a knowledge of the principles and techniques of the behavioral sciences, quantitative and nonquantitative analysis, economics, and system analysis to continuously improve the quality of all activities and relationships.

One way to look at the relationship between the important activities in a TQ organization is shown in Figure 1.1. Organization functions are integrated differently than in a traditional organization and with different objectives.

Objective	Philosophy	System elements	Element description
Customer satisfaction	Continuous quality improvements. Reduce variation	Management commitment	• Strategic quality planning • Business quality plan • Quality deployment • Management audit
		Total participation	• Companywide involvement • Multifunction improvement teams • Supplier participation
		Internal/ external customer	• Every task is a process • Next process is our customer • Customer feedback • Measure of customer satisfaction
		Internal/ external suppliers	• Align objectives and policies with suppliers • Select suppliers using process management • Systematic exchange between customers and suppliers
		Systematic analysis	• Common methods • Analyze bad, good, and best • Resources on prevention • Minimize variation • Statistical tools and techniques • Decisions based on facts and data • External benchmarks

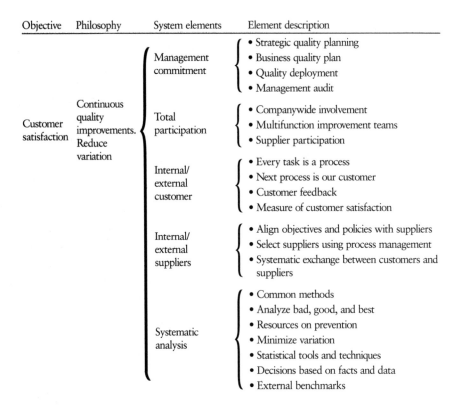

Figure 1.1. Total quality management model.

Terminology

The following are some terms frequently encountered in TQ language and references that warrant defining at the outset. More are included in the glossary at the end of the book.

Process—Any series of connected work tasks or activities. Each has an input and an output. Each has a customer and a supplier. They can be internal, or connected to an outside customer or supplier.

Variables—The factors in the operation of a process that can be measured to determine performance. A more explicit definition is used in the discussion of control charts in Chapter 5.

Variation—The changes in process variables over a period of time.

Process capability—A statistical measure of how well a process meets requirements; that is, how well a process produces within specification requirements and whether or not the capability is acceptable. This measure is only applicable to processes that have measurable variables.

Quality function—This term has both a broad and a narrow application. In its broad use it identifies those activities that contribute to meeting the quality objectives of the overall organization. In its narrow use it refers to the more specialized quality organization within the overall organization.

Big Q and little Q—A terminology resulting from the change in the quality function from a manufacturing orientation (little Q) to its inclusion of all organization activities, products, and services (big Q).

What's Involved: An Overview

The philosophy and fundamentals of TQM are a way of thinking about how to structure and run an organization. It is a holistic approach, a philosophy that affects or forms the basis of all decisions. TQM is not a set of tools, a formula, or a set of rules imposed upon other departments.

Every organization must find the methods that work in its organization. Some TQM failures have been caused by not finding the methods that fit the unique needs of the organization and then blaming the philosophy. The methods described in this book must be used to pursue the philosophy. Some organizations give up and say TQM doesn't work, when what most likely happened is that they didn't find the right combination of teams, managers, data, and methods. Getting an effective combination takes flexibility, tenacity, and patience.

As mentioned previously, success requires management leadership and commitment. It is critical because introducing this way of managing means introducing significant and continual change. Change is unsettling to employees, and it will be resisted unless top management can demonstrate, by its words and actions, that the change is necessary. Therefore, to be successful, organization members must perceive an honest commitment by upper management to a vision of where the organization must go, and a consistency in the efforts. Only then will employees trust management enough to take the risk and support change and accept some of the strain that will result. The nature of the changes is so fundamentally different from past practices that they can't be mandated. The first requirement is leadership from the top by involvement and participation so that the leaders are affected by change themselves.

Before adopting this management philosophy, it must be understood that success will require a steady investment of resources and that significant results will take time. Fundamental change cannot be scheduled to fit within a fiscal year. Failures have occurred when these realities were not recognized, but the value of the TQM approach has been demonstrated by many organizations worldwide and identified in the business press. In a report published in the spring of 1996, the National Institute for Standards and Technology, in analyzing the performance of the companies who won the Baldrige Award, reported that the winners outperformed the Standards & Poor's Stock Index by a factor of 4-to-1.

1.B. Theory of Variation (Common and Special Causes)

Everything in the universe varies: the Earth's diameter hour by hour, a human's blood pressure and temperature minute by minute, the number of errors made in a paperwork process, the performance of individuals, the thickness of a conductor on a microchip substrate cut by an X-ray beam.

In industry, engineers have recognized that variation exists in product size and performance parameters. In the past they allowed for acceptable design variation by putting tolerances on dimensions. and manufacturing did the best with what it had. When a specified tolerance couldn't be held, those parts out of tolerance would end up scrapped, reworked, or in the nonconforming review cycle. Engineering would then often change the drawing tolerance to what the shop could actually manufacture. This was not a very scientific approach, and an expensive way to operate.

Missing was the knowledge of the actual variation of the production process, a measured capability to produce to specification. Few managers were aware that production variation could be measured, or of the value of fairly simple statistical methods to measure and aid in its control.

The same lack of understanding about variation and process control has existed in so-called "soft" processes, such as the service industry. Here, variation has been more difficult to analyze because the work systems were not defined as a process. But they are in fact processes and can be measured and improved. Many of the improvement tools discussed in Chapter 5, as well as team management, are applicable to nonmanufacturing processes.

Variation Basics

There are two basic concepts about variation for industrial or service processes.

1. All variation is caused.

2. There are four main types of causes.

    a. Common causes—Random shifts in performance due to the nature of the process. They are always present.

    b. Special causes—Factors that sporadically cause variation, over and above the common causes. They can be identified.

    c. Structural variation—Systematic changes in output caused by such things as seasonal factors or long-term trends (for example, slow equipment wear).

    d. Tampering—Unnecessary adjustments made to a process in an attempt to compensate for common causes. They drive a process out of control and out of random variation.

It is critical to correctly identify the types of causes present in a process because the appropriate response is different for each. The wrong action may increase variation.

The alternative to identifying and correcting variation is usually corrective actions that have no relationship to the actual cause. They are the traditional reaction of management to *do something* when there is a problem. The root cause can be difficult to identify without data or an in-depth understanding and consideration of the process and its natural (that is, random) variation. When only the symptoms are treated, the true cause of variation surfaces elsewhere as another symptom, resulting in an endless game of hide-and-seek.

The basic approach to measuring and controlling variation, in simplified form, is to

- Define the process.
- Analyze and simplify it.
- Establish measures of performance.
- Collect performance data over a time period.
- Construct the appropriate control chart.
- Identify the special causes and remove them.

The resulting process is then in statistical control and will continue to operate within the calculated control limits until a special cause is introduced. If the process variation is not adequate to meet requirements, or if it would be valuable to further improve it, the proper techniques would have to be applied to reduce common causes.

Benefits from reducing variation depend on the nature of the process, but some general benefits include

- Reduced variation in delivered products or services, which means fewer errors/defectives and higher reliability, and a more satisfied customer
- Lower product costs due to less scrap and rework
- Lower capital costs because more capacity is available
- Lower costs from better competitive position
- A more productive work force, less frustration, and higher morale

1.C. Continuous Process Improvement (CPI)

Most managers, if asked, could identify and describe various improvements they have initiated or in which they have participated. Such activities would likely be methods improvement, procedure clarification, suggestion writing, or special training. Most efforts probably had some positive effect; they saved time, for a while at least. But the dynamic events of the workplace kept these managers busy reacting to problems, fighting fires. The different functional organizations did their own thing: Operations satisfied its own needs; quality engineering documented the inspection procedures, records, and reports; and finance decided what cost data it would collect and report.

The common element in these activities is that each functional organization operated for its own interests. The boundaries of these interests were pretty much the boundaries of the organization structure. There was no continuous, systematic approach.

Work gets done through a process (good or bad) crossing organization boundaries. If work is a continuous or sustained process, improvements not based on that reality wouldn't have much effect. Functional boundaries and self-interests would inhibit any changes.

CPI is not just an activity, it is a management philosophy and methodology fundamentally different from the traditional practice of managing specialized functional organizations. It is the core operating principle for a TQ organization.

Managers have always been interested in and receptive to ideas on how to improve. But there have been some unstated, and critical, constraints as to what they would allow. They maintained complete control; they tried changing some things like various organization responsibilities, but the power base, operating methods, and policies didn't change in any significant way. This is one of the reasons the adoption of CPI often does not meet management's expectations. Too often managers have embraced the idea of constantly improving and, while they could see the advantages to team problem solving, were reluctant to give up control. The thought of change can be unnerving but, like the need for major surgery, the alternative is more serious.

What often happens is that a CPI activity is added to the existing organization. This approach can provide some improvements, but it will not lead to the most valuable changes because it is soon limited by existing management and organization barriers. More important, it doesn't lead to a change in management's thinking about what kind of an organization is required for tomorrow's marketplace. CPI can't be considered just another organization activity. It should be considered a means of providing one methodology in the evolution toward becoming the way organizations operate.

The Concept

CPI is a management operating policy as well as an objective. It says that the organization will seek never-ending improvements in the important (if not all) organization activities. The primary focus is on improving the internal processes and those externally connected to the suppliers and customers.

One way to conceptualize CPI is to analyze a picture of it from initiation to reaching tough improvement objectives. A process is a sequence of steps, tasks, or activities that converts an input into something else as an output. A useful process adds value to the input. The sequence of steps can be the activity of one person or the linking of tasks to define a more complex process. A valuable concept is to treat every process activity, as well as the entire process, as having a supplier and a customer. In actual operation, each producer has the responsibility to add value and strive to improve the supplier-customer relationship, forever.

The process depicted in Figure 1.2 is for a process in which *variables* measures can be taken; that is, numerical characteristic measurements such as number of meters, cycle time, and cost. This figure represents the

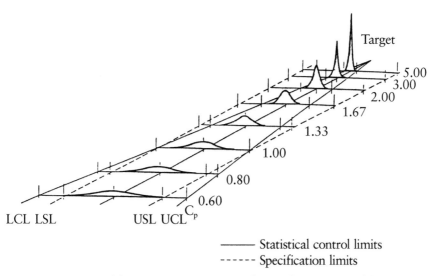

——— Statistical control limits
- - - - - Specification limits

Continuous measurable improvement means reducing the variation of the process with respect to requirements (specification limits.) The calculated indicator of improvement is the capability index (C_p).

Figure 1.2. Continuous measurable improvement.

concept of time-based improvement, or variation reduction. For other processes involving *attributes* measures, such as good/bad or number of errors, improvements can be pictured using a trend chart that shows the process functioning over time. Improvement efforts would reduce variation, and, as typically plotted, the chart would show a downward trend.

Process Description

The *macro* process of the total organization is the sequence of tasks performed from order entry to delivery; for example, from when a patient is admitted to a hospital to when he or she exits the hospital after satisfactory treatment. The *micro* processes are each of the linked tasks required to complete the macro process, such as registering of the patient, completing forms, and so on.

A generic process module would look like the one in Figure 1.3. This module can represent the macro or micro level. This module idea represents a tool for a systems approach to improvement. The system is the

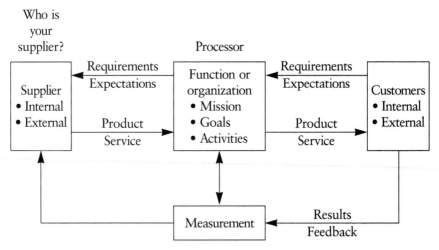

Organization relationships that form a process. Every function or activity plays all three roles at one time or another in its operation.

Figure 1.3. Systems approach to improvement.

linkage of modules. Individual tasks or an entire process can be described and then analyzed. The central element of a process module is the processor or producer. The module illustrates the concept of every producer or processor having a supplier (input) and a customer (output) and shows that the role of each can vary at different times.

- The producer provides requirements to its suppliers and goods and services to its customers.

- Suppliers can be internal (other connected modules) or external (another organization or end user).

- Customers can act as processors or producers in that they provide requirements to their suppliers and are receivers of a product or service from their suppliers.

The module approach can be useful in CPI because modules represent processes that improvement teams can describe, measure, and improve. It can be a useful concept tool used in conjunction with its extension, process mapping (see Chapter 5). This kind of modeling also supports one of the fundamental ideas in TQ, that work should be managed as it really gets done: as a process.

Process improvement results in the following:

- Reducing or eliminating errors and defects

- Reducing cycle time to shorten the development-to-delivery time or any process sequence

- Reducing overall resources needed for a given output

Additional continuous improvement techniques are discussed in Chapter 5.

1.D. Cycle Time Reduction

Cycle time is a valuable measure of organization and process performance and a powerful competitive factor. It is also important in satisfying the needs and expectations of external and internal customers. It directly affects the time it takes to recover development costs and reach the break-even point in sales. Using cycle time as a key performance metric can often produce some of the quickest and most sizable improvements.

Definition. A cycle is the time to complete a task or series of tasks, measured from the time of input to the task or process to the time of its successful completion.

Application. There are many different cycles in an organization's operations. Some of the most important are the time from product concept to first delivery and the time from order entry to delivery. Having the shortest times in these two activities provides a significant competitive advantage. Other important cycles (these will vary with the organization type) include the following:

- Product marketing concept to product definition
- Order entry to production release
- Laboratory order to receipt of results
- Internal service request or order to completion
- Engineering development to manufacturing release
- Purchase order release to supplier delivery

A focus on cycle time reduction requires continuous process improvement. A reduction in time generally lowers costs, and process improvements generally improve quality. Response to customers, both internal and external, is quicker, and there are fewer opportunities for errors when there are fewer steps. Cycle time is a valuable measurement because

- It is an easily grasped concept and measure. It appeals to managers who like hard, simple measures. It directly equates to cost savings.
- It is a good comparative measure of the competitive health of an organization.
- Total cycle time is a factual baseline for objective decisions and monitoring progress.
- It indicates, by comparison with competitors or other organizations with similar processes (that is, benchmarking), where the organization should be.
- The cycle times of important internal processes suggest priorities for applying resources for improvement.

- It is an ongoing indicator of the effectiveness of process improvements.
- Short cycle times facilitate organization learning.

Methodology. The approach to reducing cycle time depends on where the organization is in implementing TQ. If process improvement teams exist they can adopt cycle time as one of their quality measures. The basic steps for introducing the use of cycle time in process improvement are as follows:

1. Organize and train a management team, with all functions present, to flowchart the highest-level organization processes. The process elements would not go below the functional level (each functional representative would be the leader in step 3).

2. Identify a cycle time for each process. Good approximations are sufficient. This step is usually quite enlightening since management frequently doesn't know what each process entails.

3. Organize a team of key people from each functional organization and train the members in process mapping methodology (see Chapter 5E). Have each team map its process element from the upper-level flowchart. Begin with only a few key processes.

4. Measure the cycle times for those processes.

5. Have these teams begin the process analysis and process simplification activity. If product improvement teams do not exist, the cycle time improvements will not continue. The greatest cycle time improvements will come from the long-range work of such teams.

6. Measure cycle times as any process changes are made.

7. Publish a cycle time status report and distribute to all functions within the organization. Include the effective changes used for improvement.

1.E. Supplier Quality Management

Buying Policies

It has been a common practice for most organizations (industry, services, and government), to seek the lowest price for what they buy. Lowest price has been a firm policy in most cases and a legal requirement for most government agencies.

In many organizations, whether business or service, the quality of purchases is critical to the buyer's success in achieving quality improvement objectives. What is purchased is a part of what is delivered. Materials can be those that are consumed in the process, those made a part of the end product, equipment used in the process that effects process variation, or those shipped directly to a customer as part of the purchase. Purchased services can be training programs or manuals, quality auditing, laboratory analysis, or customer repair service.

Organizations have often used procurement activities to make their own prices more competitive, passing on some of the savings in the form of lower market price for their products. This philosophy is based on several beliefs and attitudes.

- Tough competition between potential suppliers will drive the price down.

- Suppliers are essentially interchangeable for like products or services.

- Making suppliers compete against each other creates buying leverage.

- One must keep a tight leash on suppliers and control all information to and from them.

Of course low material or service process costs will help the buyer control its costs, but following these policies maintains distrust between the two parties and is a short-term view of a buyer-seller relationship.

One consequence of making competitive advantage dependent on supplier pricing alone is that internal inefficiencies are never corrected and improvements are never made. Deming[11] considered this issue of such importance that it became one of his 14 points for management: End the practice of awarding business on the basis of price tag alone.

Deming's view was that a more important measure for supplier selection is the total cost of a purchase. Total cost includes the cost of incoming inspection, the cost of managing defective material, and the cost of material of unknown variability entering the buyer's processes and products. Material variation can be a critical issue for a buyer that uses statistical process control and continuous process improvement methodologies.

The approach currently being used in forward-looking, leading organizations is to create a strategic alliance, a partnership with important suppliers (this is discussed further in Chapter 5). Effective supplier management is a significant factor in the Baldrige Award assessment. Jim La Torre, leader of the high-tech team at Coopers and Lybrand management consultants, says, "I don't have a single technology-driven company in my portfolio that isn't looking for a strategic partner. Investment bankers won't look at you unless you have two elements: a visible product and a strategic partner."[12] A partnership is strategic when two organizations find that in examining their core competencies and future paths, they identify a source of synergy and areas of complementary strength.

Considerations for a TQ Approach
The following should be taken into account when entering a supplier partnership.

1. The suppliers of purchased products or services that affect the satisfaction of the buyer's customer are an extension of the buyer's processes and should be subject to the same management consideration as internal processes.

2. A buyer implementing a CPI program cannot risk accepting products or services from supplier processes of unknown variation. This could introduce special causes of variation in the buyer's processes, and the buyer could not control its own variation, cycle time, or quality costs.

   Therefore, any buying organization implementing TQ will generally require that suppliers of important material implement a CPI activity and/or generate rigorous incoming material specifications. If this is a requirement it should be included in the purchasing agreement and include authority for buyer audits.

3. The number of suppliers used should be minimized based on an analysis of risk, supplier history in meeting requirements, their capability based on the buyer's quality audit or survey, and their willingness to implement a CPI program, or at a minimum, effective process control. This will reduce product variation and internal management costs.

4. Supplier selection shifts to evaluation of total cost, not just price. Total cost to the buyer includes historical or estimated costs of poor quality of supplies. These are costs such as inspection and test, rework, reinspection and test, delays, packaging and shipping, and contact time. For this reason, important suppliers should be approached as partners, or strategic allies, with a long-term commitment between buyer and supplier.

5. A mutual objective of the buyer and supplier is to achieve a level of certification in which the buyer would have a very low risk of accepting supplier material or services without acceptance inspection. Certification plans and procedures and requirements must be mutually agreed to in the buying process and be a part of the contract. An effective certification program reduces failure and inspection costs and cycle time. It financially encourages the supplier to engage in CPI, especially if the benefit is a long-term contract.

   The basic supplier certification steps are as follows:

   a. Document the requirements and procedures for a certification program. Invite discussion and proposals from prospective supplier candidates.

   b. Define the procedures to be applied.

   c. Select a key supplier and negotiate a certification agreement. This first application is to refine the procedures.

   d. Audit supplier compliance. The audit should include process control plans and implementation as well as all other requirements.

   e. The first material received should be inspected, using tight sampling or screening as needed.

   f. Certify suppliers when requirements have been satisfied.

   g. Conduct periodic supplier audits and random inspection of received material.

   h. Take corrective action according to contract agreement.

6. Buying complex products or services should be managed by a purchasing-led team of people who will be involved with the use of the items. Purchasing leadership is necessary to manage the contractual aspects of procurement. Such a team might be composed of representatives of all or some of the following organizations, depending on what is purchased.

   - Sales (representing the customer)
   - Research, technical staff, engineering, software development
   - Internal operations or production
   - Finance
   - Facilities
   - Quality/process engineering
   - Customer service

   These teams should also be involved, as appropriate, in the selection of important suppliers.

7. Buying organizations should publish, for both internal and supplier use, the quality policies and procedures that will follow. The policies should reflect an organizationally integrated approach. These may include such elements as the following:

   - Assignment of prime responsibilities
   - Chain of communication
   - Methods of supplier evaluation and selection
   - Methods of initial and ongoing surveillance
   - Procedures for design control
   - Procedures to settle disputes
   - Maintenance of privacy and information control
   - Methods and procedures for product or service acceptance
   - Supplier quality certification.
   - Support, including training of suppliers

1.F. Customer Service

The idea of satisfying the customer as a prime objective is commonly mentioned in regard to the focus of TQ, remaining competitive and gaining a leading market share position. One important factor in satisfying the customer is customer service. For several years there have been companies that focused on customer service and satisfaction. T. Peters and R. Waterman, in their popular book, *In Search of Excellence,* analyzed some of these companies and concluded that a dedication to the customer was a major factor in their success.

One definition of customer service is the activity concerning an organization after a product has been delivered or a service completed for a customer. A simpler one is everything an organization does to enhance and assure customer satisfaction.

This is not an easy objective in light of rising customer expectations. What was new and interesting today will be taken for granted tomorrow. Narrowing the subject to objective product quality requirements doesn't simplify the equation because customers' quality expectations vary widely and are affected by price and features.

The first step in managing customer satisfaction is to listen to the customer. This means developing broad lines of communication to all kinds of customers. It means attuning organization members to also become listeners.

It is a difficult task to devise the means to improve customer service that goes beyond just responding to customer complaints. That is passive; what is needed is a proactive attitude. Many customers don't complain; they change suppliers and the supplier never knows what happened. The method most frequently used to improve service is conducting customer surveys. Great care must be used, however, in designing the survey and in interpreting results. This is discussed further in Chapter 4. It is also discussed in some detail by P. J. Danaher and R. T. Rust.[13] They point out that there is a basic difference between internal industrial quality (process variation, cycle time, and cost reduction), where quality is measured against standards, and service quality, which is focused on revenue expansion and nonstandard quality, and on flexibility and the differences in required quality. They argue that this customer-centered view is an important way of viewing quality for all organizations, but especially in situations where customers can choose a competitor. Their study concludes that improving service quality can increase revenues through

- Higher customer retention rates
- Attracting more customers through word-of-mouth
- Increasing the frequency of usage by existing customers

The customer service activity is not a totally independent function or activity. It should be tied to several organization functions that must be integrated into a system.

Principles

- Identification of customer needs and expectations
- Collection analysis and reaction to information based on customer experience in fitness for use
- Education of the customer in the proper use of the product or service
- Rapid satisfaction of customer needs after delivery of product or service

To ensure customer satisfaction, quality planning should consider all of the factors in product or service development, production, packaging, delivery, and customer acceptance and use. The use of planning tools such as quality function deployment will support planning that maintains customer focus.

Internal-External

A TQ organization manages to satisfy both the internal and external customers. Therefore, the principles of customer service discussed here apply to internal customers as well. The idea of internal customer service must become a part of the working culture in every process; it is an element in the CPI objectives.

1.G. Quality Awards/Standards Criteria (Baldrige, ISO 9000, GMP)

Quality Awards

Quality awards are a ceremonial recognition of achieving quality improvement objectives. They can be an effective motivational tool, and action taken in their pursuit can lead to valuable improvements. Awards can be internal or external. Many quality improvement programs include monetary incentives to reach quality goals. Others are entirely ceremonial with recognition as the reward.

External awards can be earned from customers, trade or professional associations, and government agencies. Internal awards are valuable because they provide some satisfaction of the human need for work to have value other than pay. Combined with the use of teams in TQ, pursuing quality awards fosters group efforts and a feeling of participating and contributing to the goals of the organization.

Some of the most prestigious external quality awards include

- *The Deming Prize.* Awarded by Japan to companies achieving high and challenging quality improvements by applying companywide quality concepts, particularly statistical techniques. It uses 10 criteria, all with equal scoring weights. Open to international applicants, it was won by an American company, Florida Power and Light, in 1991.

- *The Malcolm Baldrige National Quality Award (MBNQA).* This award was established in 1987 by the U.S. Congress to encourage organizations to commit to TQ, raise productivity, and improve competitiveness. It is intended to recognize significant, sustained performance improvement. The criteria no longer include the word "quality," but it is still a significant measure of success in the examination. The criteria evaluate the way companies manage in the current world marketplace. Some aspects of the design of the award are listed in Figure 1.4.

  A board of examiners reviews the written applications and conducts site reviews. Reviewers use the criteria shown in Figure 1.5. Each of the categories is divided into 24 examination items. The criteria have continued to evolve over the years.

P.L. 100-107 sets a number of key requirements for the U.S. National Quality Award, but nevertheless affords considerable latitude in Award criteria and processes.

To ensure a broad base of input to the design of the Award, many quality leaders—manufacturing, service, academic, consultants, and retired—were contacted regarding characteristics that should be incorporated into the award. In addition to stressing total quality, quality improvement, CEO-level quality leadership, statistical process control, and human resource utilization, several other features were mentioned repeatedly as highly desirable for inclusion in the Award. Those features most frequently mentioned were:

1. **Performance.** The Award should be heavily performance based. That is, it should give considerable weight to quality improvement results, in preference to specific techniques or processes for achieving results.

2. **Innovation.** Award application should permit firms to highlight and get credit for unique approaches to achieving higher quality.

3. **"Measurables."** Award criteria and application evaluation should focus on quantitative results and positive trends, rather than on narrative descriptions of processes an anecdotal information. To be in a position to respond convincingly, firms would have to have in place a good quality measurement system, along with associated analytical capabilities.

4. **Customer Satisfaction.** Award consideration should consider not only customers' view of products and services, but also the entire functioning of the customer interface in planning products and services.

5. **World-class Quality.** Award evaluations should, where appropriate, explore the degree to which firms recognize the quality requirements of international markets, their systems for assessing where they stand, and their plans for establishing a leadership position.

6. **Quality Early in the Process.** Award criteria should reflect the need to address quality early in the design phase, both to reduce delays in bringing products to market and to enter markets with higher-quality products.

7. **External Leadership.** Award evaluations should give some weight to applicants' efforts to lead and support national and local activities in support of quality and its related infrastructure. This includes assisting suppliers, supporting quality standards, creating community councils, etc.

Figure 1.4. Design of the Baldrige Award program.

1997 Categories/Items	Point Values
1 Leadership	**110**
1.1 Leadership System	80
1.2 Company Responsible and Citizenship	30
2 Strategic Planning	**80**
2.1 Strategy Development Process	40
2.2 Company Strategy	40
3 Customer and Market Focus	**80**
3.1 Customer and Market Knowledge	40
3.2 Customer Satisfaction and Relationship Enhancement	40
4 Information and Analysis	**80**
4.1 Selection and Use of Information and Data	25
4.2 Selection and Use of Comparative Information and Data	15
4.3 Analysis and Review of Company Performance	40
5 Human Resource Development and Management	**100**
5.1 Work Systems	40
5.2 Employee Education, Training, and Development	30
5.3 Employee Well-Being and Satisfaction	30
6 Process Management	**100**
6.1 Management of Product and Service Processes	60
6.2 Management of Support Processes	20
6.3 Management of Supplier and Partnering Processes	20
7 Business Results	**450**
7.1 Customer Satisfaction Results	130
7.2 Financial and Market Results	130
7.3 Human Resource Results	35
7.4 Supplier and Partner Results	25
7.5 Company-Specific Results	130
Total Points	**1000**

Copies of the detailed criteria are available from MBNQA Office, National Institute of Standards and Technology, Gaithersburg, MD 20899-0001; Phone 301-975-2036.

Figure 1.5. 1997 Baldrige Award criteria—item listing.

Two awards can be given each year in each category: manufacturing, service, or small business. The award is presented annually by the president or the secretary of commerce. Organizations winning the award are permitted to use their achievement as a bragging point in their advertising.

Organizations applying for or winning the award have reported that the most valuable aspect of their resource investment was the significant improvement in all operations and in customer satisfaction. The award has been motivational in that respect.

Every year a Quest for Excellence conference is held to provide a forum for the previous year's award winners to discuss their experiences and lessons learned. The conference gives attending business leaders the opportunity to listen and question the winning companies' management teams. Audiotapes of past conferences are available.

- *U.S. Senate Award.* The U.S. Senate provides an annual award to organizations in each state that have demonstrated to an examining board that they have achieved significant quality improvement. Each state has developed its own criteria, and winners are chosen by the state's senators.

- The European Economic Community (EEC) has established a European Quality Award.

- *Quality Digest* magazine publishes a yearly listing of U.S. states that administer quality awards.

Quality Standards

International Organization for Standardization (ISO). ISO 9000 is a set of international standards designed to give buyers assurance that suppliers are using recognized effective management methods to control the quality of their products. They are used to certify that an organization meets the minimum criteria for a quality system as defined by the standards. Registration is not, however, a certification of product quality. Companies are allowed to advertise their achievement but may not stamp their product with the ISO 9000 registration logo.

The standards require that a manufacturer document and maintain a system for ensuring the quality of a process output. They also require that a company control its nonmanufacturing functions, such as engineering, purchasing, and service. The management system as a whole is reviewed, and ISO registration is granted. Recertification is required every three years for many certification bodies, with semiannual visits to review corrective actions. If a company has multiple sites, certification is achieved separately by each facility. The three standards and their supporting documents are as follows:

1. ANSI/ISO/ASQC Q9000-1-1994, *Quality Management and Quality Assurance Standards—Guidelines for Selection and Use.*

2. ANSI/ISO/ASQC Q9002-1994, *Quality Systems—Model for Quality Assurance in Production, Installation, and Servicing.*

3. ANSI/ISO/ASQC Q9003-1994, *Quality Systems—Model for Quality Assurance in Final Inspection and Test.*

Supporting documents include the following:

ISO 9000-2:1993, *Quality management and quality assurance standards—Part 2: Generic Guidelines for the application of ISO 9001, ISO 9002 and ISO 9003.*

ISO 9000-3:1993, *Quality management and quality assurance standards—Part 3: Guidelines for the application of ISO 9001 to the development, supply and maintenance of software.*

ISO 9000-4:1993, *Quality management and quality assurance standards—Part 4: Guide to dependability programme management.*

ISO 9004-2:1991, *Quality management and quality system elements—Part 2: Guidelines for services.*

ISO 9004-3:1993, *Quality management and quality system elements—Part 3: Guidelines for processed materials.*

ISO 9004-4:1993, *Quality management and quality system elements—Part 4: Guidelines for quality improvement.*

ANSI/ISO/ASQC Q10011-1-1994, *Guidelines for Auditing Quality Systems—Auditing.*

ANSI/ISO/ASQC Q10011-2-1994, *Guidelines for Auditing Quality Systems—Qualification Criteria for Quality Systems Auditors.*

ANSI/ISO/ASQC Q10011-3-1994, *Guidelines for Auditing Quality Systems—Management of Audit Programs.*

ISO 10012-1:1992, *Quality assurance requirements for measuring equipment—Part I: Metrological confirmation system for measuring equipment.*

ISO 10013:1995, *Guidelines for developing quality manuals.*

ISO Handbook 3:1989, *Statistical methods.*

The requirements of ISO-9000 are depicted in Figure 1.6, and an overview of the ISO standards is shown in Figure 1.7. Copies of the standards can be purchased from ASQC.

DuPont Corporation prepared a step-by-step road map for its ISO 9000 registration preparation (see Figure 1.8). Thorough planning of this kind is needed if registration is to be achieved and resources minimized. Becoming ISO registered is a minimum business requirement to do business in some countries, but registration alone will not result in becoming a continuous improvement, TQ organization and all that it implies.

Good Manufacturing Practices (GMP)

The U.S. Food and Drug Administration is authorized to regulate the medical device industry. The device GMP[14] regulation is designed to prevent the manufacture of poor-quality medical devices. It requires all device manufacturers to design, implement, and continually monitor a comprehensive quality assurance program. The program includes the application of good quality assurance principles. Special provisions are

- Preproduction design validation to assess device performance
- Recall authority without notice or hearing for probability of death, serious injury, or illness

Comparisons

There are some basic differences between the criteria and objectives of the standards and awards. Standards are requirements that must be met. to

ISO 9001	ISO 9002	ISO 9003
1. Management responsibility	■	●
2. Quality system	■	●
3. Contract review	■	■
4. Design control	▲	▲
5. Document control	■	■
6. Purchasing	■	▲
7. Purchaser-supplied product	■	■
8. Product identification and traceability	■	●
9. Process control	■	▲
10. Inspection and testing	■	■
11. Inspection, measuring, and test equipment	■	■
12. Inspection and test status	■	●
13. Control of nonconforming product	■	●
14. Corrective action	■	●
15. Handling, storage, packaging, and delivery	■	■
16. Quality records	■	●
17. Internal quality audits	■	●
18. Training	■	●
19. Servicing	■	▲
20. Statistical techniques	■	●
■ Full requirement ● Minimal ▲ Not required		

Figure 1.6. Requirements of ISO 9000.

maintain registration. Awards are a recognition of achievement in meeting award criteria. Both undergo continuous revision.

- Deming Prize. Requires organizationwide involvement and improvement. The wide application of statistical methods is emphasized. Methods and results are evaluated.

- Baldrige Award. Similar to the Deming Prize, with emphasis on improvements over time and objective evidence of customer satisfaction. Applies to industry, service, and small business.

The Standards at a Glance

The standards explosion started with ISO 9000, and now there is ISO 14000, QS-9000, and TE-9000. With the number of standards that continue to be developed, there might be some confusion regarding their content. So, before another one is introduced, here are brief descriptions of the existing major standards.

ISO 9000

ISO 9000 is a series of three informational standards and supplementary guidelines on quality management and quality assurance, which were first published in 1987 and revised in 1994. The standards are not specific to any particular products and can be used by both manufacturing and service industries. These standards are nonprescriptive; they do not specify how a firm's quality assurance processes must occur, but they do mandate that a company define appropriate quality standards, document its processes, and prove that it consistently adheres to both. The standards require that a basic quality system be in place to ensure that the company has the capabilities and systems to provide its customers with quality products and services.

The ISO 9000 series includes:

- ISO 9000. A set of guidelines that helps users select and use the appropriate (ISO 9001, ISO 9002, or ISO 9003) standard.

- ISO 9001. The most comprehensive standard, covering design, manufacturing, installation, and servicing systems.

- ISO 9002. A standard that covers production and installation.

- ISO 9003. A standard that covers final product inspection and testing.

- ISO 9004. A set of guidelines for internal use by a producer developing its own quality system to meet business needs and take advantage of competitive opportunities.

To become registered to ISO 9001, ISO 9002, or ISO 9003, a company must have an accredited, independent third party conduct an on-site audit of the company's operations to verify that it is in compliance with the requirements of the appropriate standard.

ISO 14000

The ISO 14000 series of generic environmental management standards, which are currently under development by the International Organization for Standardization, will provide structure and systems for managing environmental compliance with legislative and regulatory requirements and will affect every aspect of a company's environmental operations.

(continues)

Figure 1.7. Overview of ISO 9000.

The components of ISO 14000 include the general categories of environmental management systems, environmental auditing, environmental labeling, environmental performance evaluation, and life-cycle assessments.

These universal standards, which can be used by all countries and organizations, don't require a start-up performance test or audit, a final performance goal, or a single manual for documentation. They also don't have a prescribed performance improvement rate or mandated governmental or organizational policy.

The foreseen benefits of the ISO 14000 standards are that they will provide a worldwide focus on environmental management; promote a voluntary consensus standards approach; harmonize national rules, labels, and methods by minimizing trade barriers and complications and by promoting predictability and consistency; and demonstrate commitment to maintaining and moving beyond regulatory environmental performance compliance.

ISO 14001 is the standard that will be used for third-party registration. Registration to the ISO 14000 standards will require evidence of implementation of an environment management system, procedures that maintain compliance to applicable laws, commitment to continuous improvement, and commitment to pollution prevention (e.g., recycling, process changes, energy efficiency, and materials substitution).

"The ISO 14000 standards will be released in 1996," said Joel Charm, director of occupational health and safety for Allied Signal Corp. in Morristown, NJ, and chairman of the U.S. Technical Advisory Group (TAG) for Subcommittee 1, which is charged with creating environmental management systems and environmental auditing. "It is anticipated that the standards will be completed by the end of May and published by the end of July."

With the precedent that has been established with the ISO 9000 series, it is likely that soon after the ISO 14000 series is published, companies will need to be certified to those standards to compete globally—especially in Europe.

QS-9000

QS-9000 was developed in September 1994 by the Big Three's—Chrysler, Ford, and General Motors (GM)—Supplier Quality Requirements Task Force to define their fundamental quality system expectations, those of several heavy truck manufacturers, and other subscribing companies for internal and external suppliers of production and service parts and materials.

According to Tripp Martin, director of quality at Peterson Spring, QS-9000 applies to all internal and external suppliers that provide production materials, production or service parts, or heat treating and other finishing

(continues)

Figure 1.7. *Continued.*

services directly to the Big Three or other original equipment manufacturers subscribing to QS-9000.

Martin explained that QS-9000 uses the ISO 9001 standard as its foundation. "QS-9000 is not a standard, but it contains the ISO 9001 standard; its requirements are much broader than ISO 9001."

While some say that QS-9000 doesn't really go beyond the ISO 9001 requirements, a comparison of the two shows that QS-9000 requirements are much more rigorous, Martin said, "There are 137 'shalls' [requirements] in the ISO 9001 document and 300 'shalls' in the QS-9000 document."

QS-9000 is divided into three sections:

- Common requirements, which include the exact text of ISO 9001 with the addition of automotive/heavy trucking requirements

- Additional requirements, which include requirements beyond the scope of ISO 9001 that are common to all three manufacturers

- Customer-specific sections, which contain requirements unique to Ford, GM, or Chrysler

Martin said, "The Big Three are serious about the completion dates. QS-9000 audits will begin in the first quarter of 1996, and there are no plans to back down on the registration dates."

GM will require third-party registration of current suppliers by Dec. 13, 1997, and new suppliers by Jan. 1, 1996; Chrysler will require third-party registration of current and new suppliers by July 31, 1997. Ford has not yet announced dates for third-party registration of suppliers.

TE-9000

TE-9000 is expected to be released as a supplement to the Big Three's QS-9000 requirement. As many as 50,000 tooling and equipment suppliers of nonproduction parts (items that are used in making parts for cars or trucks, such as tools, production equipment, dies, and molds) and even suppliers of some production items such as coolants could be affected by TE-9000.

TE-9000 is expected to include ISO 9001 in its entirety, along with additional industry-specific requirements. Since the Big Three are requiring third-party registration from approved ISO 9000 registrars, TE-9000 will probably be treated in a similar fashion.

According to Martin, TE-9000 is still being revised and the final draft has not yet been completed. His advice for companies that are waiting for the draft is to pursue ISO 9001 and follow the automotive industry's *Reliability and Maintainability Guideline for Manufacturing Machinery* until the requirement is published.

Figure 1.7. *Continued.*

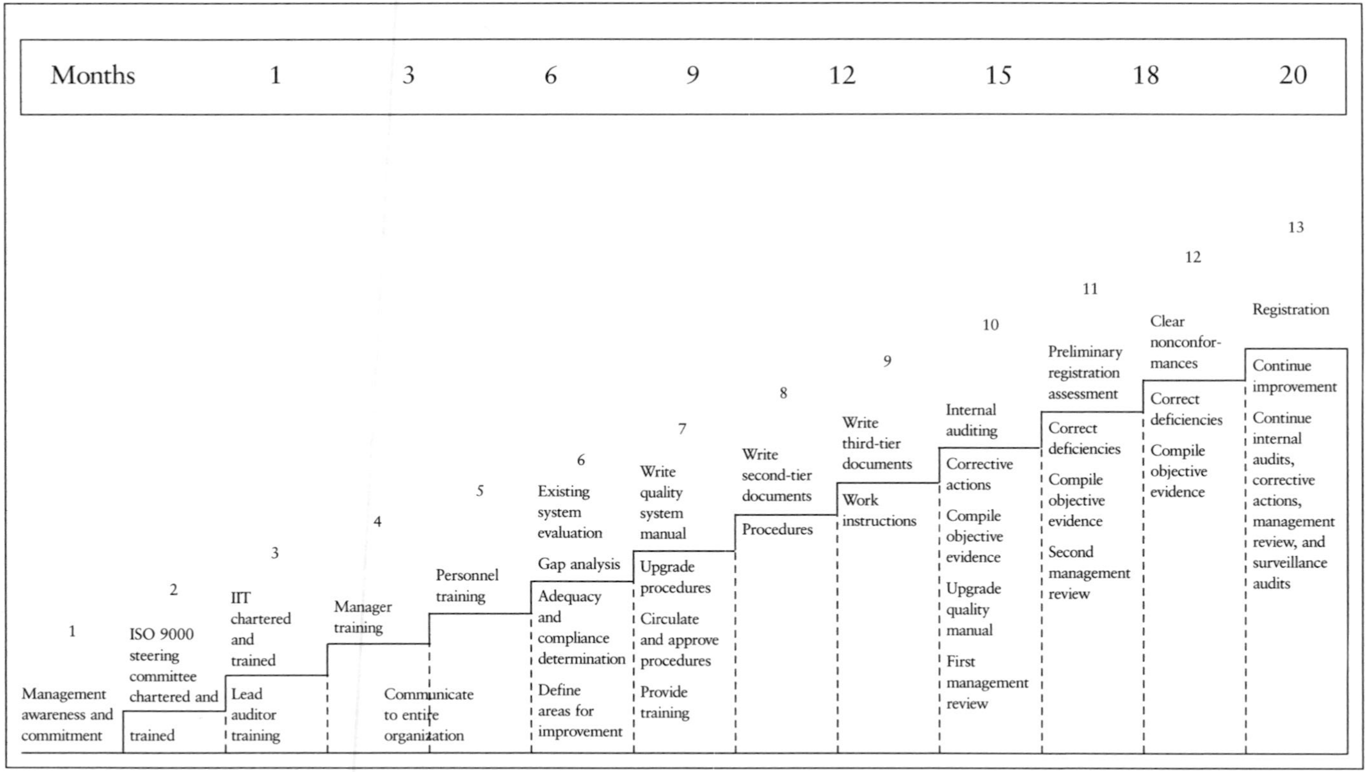

Figure 1.8. DuPont's road map to ISO 9000 registration.

- Senate Awards. Most are similar to the Baldrige Award.

- ISO 9000. Requires systems and procedures to plan, implement, and improve quality. It is currently not performance oriented.

Key Ideas—Chapter 1

1. Managing for quality has evolved from an evaluation of end product or service performance to a holistic philosophy of managing the process and organization using the tools and techniques of the quality profession.

2. Before you can improve or change a process, you must understand (measure) it.

3. Continuous improvement is more than a policy; it is a key to staying competitive.

4. Managing the process inputs, internal or external, is a key to controlling process variation and costs.

5. Satisfying the customer is more than saying thank you or providing on-time delivery. Keeping the customer as the focus is the first priority, rather than an afterthought.

References

1. Shewhart, W. A. 1939. *Statistical Method From the Viewpoint of Quality Control.* Milwaukee, Wis.: ASQC Quality Press.

2. Feigenbaum, A. V. 1991. *Total Quality Control,* 3d ed. New York, N.Y.: McGraw-Hill.

3. Deming, W. E. 1986. *Out of the Crisis.* Cambridge, Mass.: Massachusetts Institute of Technology, Center for Advanced Engineering Study.

4. Juran, J. M., and F. M. Gryna, 1988. *Juran's Quality Control Handbook,* 4th ed. New York, N.Y.: McGraw-Hill.

5. Kinni, T. B. 1996. *America's Best: Industry Week's Guide to World-Class Manufacturing Plants.* Boston, Mass.: John Wiley & Sons.

6. Drucker, P. R. 1992. *Managing for the Future.* New York, N.Y.: Truman Talley Books/Dutton.

7. Deevy, E. 1995. *Creating the Resilient Organization: A Rapid Response Management Program.* Upper Saddle River, N.J.: Prentice Hall.

8. Senge, P. 1990. *The Fifth Discipline: The Art and Practice of the Learning Organization.* New York, N.Y.: Doubleday.

9. Tompkins, J. 1995. *The Genesis Enterprise: Creating Peak-to-Peak Performance.* New York, N.Y.: McGraw-Hill.

10. Juran and Gryna. *Juran's Quality Control Handbook.*

11. Deming, *Out of the Crisis.*

12. Maynard, R. 1996. "Striking the Right Match." *Nations Business* (May).

13. Danaher, P. J., and R. T. Rust. 1996. "Indirect Financial Benefits From Service Quality." *Quality Management Journal* 3, No. 2.

14. Trautman, K. A. 1996. *The FDA and Worldwide Quality System Requirements Guidebook for Medical Practices.* Milwaukee, Wis.: ASQC Quality Press.

Related References

Bemowski, K., and B. Stratton. 1995. "How Do People Use the Baldrige Award Criteria?" *Quality Progress* (May).

Benson, R. S., and R. W. Sherman. 1995. "ISO 9000: A Practical, Step-By-Step Approach." *Quality Progress* (October).

Bossert, J. L. 1994. *Supplier Management Handbook.* Milwaukee, Wis.: ASQC Quality Press.

Cartin, T. J. 1993. *Principles and Practices of TQM.* Milwaukee, Wis.: ASQC Quality Press.

Deming, W. E. 1994. *The New Economics for Industry, Government, Education,* 2nd ed. Cambridge, Mass.: MIT Center for Advanced Engineering Study.

———. 1986. *Out of the Crisis.* Cambridge, Mass.: MIT Center for Advanced Engineering Study.

Dettmer, H. W. 1997. *Goldratt's Theory of Constraints: A Systems Approach to Continuous Improvement.* Milwaukee, Wis.: ASQC Quality Press.

Dobbins, R. D. 1995. "A Failure of Methods, Not Philosophy." *Quality Progress* (July).

Flynn, M. F. 1990. "All Answers Are Approximate—and Temporary: Statistical Thinking and TQM." *Annual Quality Congress Transactions.* Milwaukee, Wis.: ASQC.

Hare, L., R. W. Hoerl, J. D. Hromi, and R. D. Snee. 1995. "The Role of Statistical Thinking in Management." *Quality Progress* (February).

Harrington, H. J. 1991. *Business Process Improvement.* San Francisco: Ernst & Young, L.L.P.

Hayes, B. E. 1991. *Measuring Customer Satisfaction.* Milwaukee, Wis.: ASQC Quality Press.

Hohner, G. 1993. "Integrating Product and Process Designs." *Quality Progress* (May).

Joiner, B. L. 1994. *Fourth Generation Management.* Madison, Wis.: Joiner Associates.

Joiner, B. L., and M. A. Gaudard. 1990. "Variation Management and W. Edwards Deming." *Quality Progress* (December).

Juran, J. M., and F. M. Gryna. 1988. *Juran's Quality Control Handbook,* 4th ed. New York, N.Y.: McGraw-Hill.

Knowlton, J., and R. Keppinger. 1993. "The Experimentation Process." *Quality Progress* (February).

LoSardo, M. M., and N. M. Rossi. 1993. *At the Service Quality Frontier.* Milwaukee, Wis.: ASQC Quality Press.

Memory Jogger 9000. 1996. Methuen, Mass.: GOAL/QPC.

Micklethwait, J., and A. Wooldrige. 1996. *The Witch Doctors: Making Sense of the Management Gurus.* New York, N.Y.: Time Books/ Random House.

Nakhai, B., and J. J. Never. 1994. "The Deming, Baldrige, and European Quality Awards." *Quality Progress* (April).

Nolan, T. W., and L. P. Provost. 1990. "Understanding Variation." *Quality Progress* (December).

Peters, T., and R. Waterman. 1982. *In Search of Excellence*. New York, N.Y.: Harper and Row.

Rackham, N., L. Friedman, and R. Ruff. 1995. *Getting Partnership Right: How Market Leaders Are Creating Long-Term Competitive Advantage*. New York, N.Y.: McGraw-Hill.

Struebing, L. 1996. "9000 Standards." *Quality Progress* (January).

Thomas, P. R. 1990. *Competitiveness Through Cycle Time*. New York, N.Y.: McGraw-Hill.

Tompkins, J. 1995. *The Genesis Enterprise: Creating Peak-to-Peak Performance*. New York, N.Y.: McGraw-Hill.

Trischler, W. E. 1996. *Understanding and Applying Value-Added Assessment*. Milwaukee, Wis.: ASQC Quality Press.

Voehl, F., P. Johnson, and D. Aston, 1995. *ISO: An Implementation Guide for Small to Mid-Sized Businesses*. Delray Beach, Fla.: St. Lucie Press.

Windham, J. 1995. "Implementing Deming's Fourth Point." *Quality Progress* (December).

Chapter 2
Organizations and Their Functions

This chapter discusses the key elements involved in how organizations function, their responsibilities and structure, how they are evaluated and communicated, and the role of management style in their performance.

In keeping with the current emphasis on change, the important role of change agents is discussed. Particular attention is paid to quality factors involved. These issues have been the subjects of considerable research over the past few decades under rather slow-changing conditions, but in recent years the rapid changes in markets and competition had made them even more critical. They must be reexamined to determine their applicability today.

Terminology. The word *function* has several usages. It is commonly used to identify a special activity in the total organization, such as engineering, production, or quality control. The quality function, however, can be the specialized quality organization performing activities such as audit, inspection, and quality engineering, or it can be, as Juran identifies it, all the activities in the overall organization required to produce a quality product or service. With the growing emphasis on the management of organization processes resulting in the integration of organization elements, the term *quality function* needs a reference when it is used. This book identifies which usage is intended.

2.A. Organization Assessment

Historically, quality management organizations have been more involved in quality audits and surveys than in assessments, as the term is currently used. Traditionally audits were, and still are, conducted primarily to determine how an organization is complying with its own policies, procedures, standards, requirements, regulations, and, sometimes, customer requirements.

The other most common quality evaluation activity has been surveys by which an organization evaluates the quality systems or capability of potential or active suppliers. The usual objective is to determine whether the auditee has the system elements required and is using them. Some businesses have found it valuable to combine audits and surveys into one activity.

The assessment activity has grown in the quality function primarily as a result of the establishment of the Baldrige Award. The term *assessment* does not appear in Feigenbaum's *Total Quality Control,* written in the early 1980s. Juran, in his *Quality Control Handbook,* prefers the term *survey,* but his description is closer to what is now commonly meant by an assessment. The Japanese use the term *survey* for companies competing for the Deming Prize. But their process is closer to what those in the United States now call assessment. Juran suggests that a comprehensive view of quality assurance should provide management with nonspecific quality factors like those related to the marketplace, self-analysis, and customer and employee perceptions on quality. He identifies this approach as a quality assessment or comprehensive audit.

ISO standards are not much clearer. ISO 8402, paragraph 4.6, treats assessment as follows: quality evaluation is sometimes called "quality assessment," "quality appraisal," or "quality survey" in specific circumstances.

This discussion is presented to illustrate that there is no consistency in the application of the three terms and a specific content can't be assumed. It does seem clear that organization assessment has come to mean a comprehensive evaluation, and this is what the following discussion covers.

Definition

Assessment is the evaluation at any level of an organization to determine compliance and effectiveness. *Compliance* refers to whether procedures are followed, or government regulations or special contract requirements are being met; that is, whether the organization is doing things right. *Effectiveness* includes an evaluation of whether policies are followed and objectives achieved—whether the organization is doing the right things. An assessment is broader than a typical audit. A comprehensive assessment includes all the elements that might normally be used in audits and surveys, but more subjective issues as well. These would include whether policies reflect current market needs and customer, employee, and supplier perceptions of quality.

In a TQ organization an assessment would be made to determine whether the objectives of policies and practices, such as continuous process improvement, customer satisfaction, and team management, were being achieved and to identify roadblocks to meeting objectives.

An assessment can be made by an agent external to the organization, or it can be a self-examination. A self-assessment can be conducted by the organization itself or by another internal function, such as quality auditing. Using both approaches may reveal more useful and comprehensive information. An important factor in the selection of an assessor is his or her independence from the assessee and its management.

As previously discussed, success in developing a TQ organization requires a change in culture.[1] In order to change something, its current status must be determined or assessed. One method of achieving culture change is to begin with a technique called *culture gap analysis*, which can be adapted to the development of a desired quality culture. The six steps in this method are as follows:[2]

1. Identify quality competitors and their attributes. Determine whether the organization is primarily competing on

   • Tangible product quality attributes

   • After-sales service and support

   • Customer interface

   • All of the above

2. Identify necessary organization quality values to suit the competitive environment.

3. Identify target groups that must have the desired values listed in step 2.

4. Identify the current quality values of the target groups and compare them to the desired quality values.

5. Decide formal and informal mechanisms to introduce the desired quality values in the targeted groups.

6. Review each target group's quality performance and repeat appropriate steps.

The Baldrige Award process is an assessment of an applicant by an outside agency. The examination team bases its evaluation on data that demonstrate the achievement of any professed improvements. Many organizations are tailoring the Baldrige Award criteria and process to conduct an organizationwide self-assessment. The Baldrige Award criteria are listed in Chapter 1G, Figure 1.5, and reflect the holistic nature of the assessment.

This section discusses the factors involved in the assessment process.

The Assessment Process

Self-Assessment. An effective self-assessment can only be conducted if there is a climate of trust. An accurate self-assessment is a form of self-revelation. Flaws in people and processes are revealed, as well as their strengths and weaknesses. Without a climate of trust, exposing weaknesses can create fear and cover-up.

Trust of management is developed starting at the top by assuring lower management and employees that flaws will not be punished but will be treated as opportunities for improvement. One basis for developing trust and making decisions that are effective is to make decisions based on data, not opinions.

One example of a corporation that has successfully used the self-assessment process is AT&T. It used self-assessment as a way to achieve two major goals.

1. Aligning its business management systems more closely with customer needs

2. Integrating quality principles into every business practice

To achieve these goals, an assessment process was introduced. A Chairman's Quality Award was established at an early step, with a process modeled after the Baldrige Award (see Chapter 1G). Business units assessed their performance against published, objective criteria and shared their successes. This assessment also identified areas for improvement. The assessment guidelines are shown in Figure 2.1.

Within three years the eight business units involved scored improvements of 50 percent against the seven Baldrige-related criteria. Two of the units later became Baldrige Award winners. Small organizations lacking the labor or expertise can use outside specialists in conducting or facilitating an assessment.

Assessment Structure. The approach in designing an assessment procedure is to consider not only adequacy and compliance issues, but to identify the broader issues affecting organization success now and for the future, such as culture, communication, evaluation of human resources, strengths and weaknesses, and technology. The example shown in Figure 2.2 includes questions that would elicit the kind of information needed for

---

**1993 Chairman Quality Award Process Examination
Team Design Guidelines**

Objective: Create diverse self-managed teams that offer a broad knowledge base.

Criteria/attributes:

- Have five to six examiners on each team.

- Include one experienced senior examiner and one assistant senior examiner on each team.

- Includes two examiners with site-visit experience.

- Match senior examiner's background to applicant's type (manufacturing, service, corporate, etc.).

- Do not include examiner from applicant's organization.

- Do not include examiner who evaluated applicant during previous year.

Diversity factors:

- Business unit and division representation

- Functional representation (manufacturing, development, finance, etc.)

- Business perspective

- Quality system perspective

- Job levels

Figure 2.1. AT&T examination guidelines.

As an example of a broad survey, a consultant was engaged to evaluate the operations of one division of a large processing company. The objectives of the survey were stated in broad terms:

Objectives
1. To discover where the company wants to be with respect to quality
2. To discover where the company is now with respect to quality
3. To recommend plans and policies which can economically move the company closer to its objectives

Operations were studied in six different plants, various data were reviewed and discussions were conducted with plant personnel and with personnel in manufacturing and nonmanufacturing functions at the division level. The consultant reached five conclusions.

Possible Conclusions
1. The division was generally well equipped to do a good quality job in terms of adequate processes, modern technology, capable personnel, a a favorable organizational climate.
2. Personnel were doing a good job on meeting the quality policies as interpreted by them.
3. Personnel interpretation of policy, however, did not match that of most division executives.
4. A considerable amount of money was being wasted as quality losses, without anyone having a clear idea how much this was or how much of it was readily avoidable.
5. There was a good chance for worthwhile cost reduction, while at the same time improving outgoing quality.

The consultant then presented 14 specific recommendations in areas such as quality policy, losses due to poor quality, machine capability studies, responsibility for deciding when the machines may run, supplier relations plans, measuring ongoing quality, evaluation of the usefulness of process control charts, and evaluation of the effectiveness of lot acceptance plans.

In a different type of survey, a consultant was asked to define specific responsibilities in the quality program for all major departments of a health care company. The consultant used five questions to interview the department managers.

Organization Questions
1. What tasks in your department affect quality?
2. Should any additional quality-related tasks be performed in your department?
3. Should any additional quality-related tasks be performed anywhere else in the company?
4. What quality-related tasks have unclear responsibility?
5. What quality-related tasks currently done in your department require more definitive written procedures?

Source: J. M. Juran and Frank M. Gryna, eds., *Juran's Quality Control Handbook* (New York: McGraw-Hill, 1988). Reproduced with permission of The McGraw-Hill Companies.

Figure 2.2. Creating a self-assessment survey.

management to evaluate its strategic position and decide what improvements should be made in objectives or operating methods.

Additional issues in an assessment include

- Basic questions on quality practices and results, common to all organization elements. They should cover quality planning, adequacy of training, management perspectives at every level, and effectiveness of improvement activities in support of continuous improvement by management.

- Special questions to be asked of all functional organization members, such as their participation in the quality function, customer relations (internal and external), their awareness of competitor quality, what they perceive are the top quality problems, supplier relationships and problems, whether process yields are adequate or improving, problems with management, and whether they understand the quality responsibilities of their organization.

- Other such factors such as culture, communication, learning from mistakes, career paths, and personal growth.

Criteria. The Baldrige Award criteria, tailored to the organization, are an excellent basis for conducting self-assessments. This is a good place to begin.

Audits. A comprehensive audit should be conducted as a part of the overall assessment in accordance with published procedures. Audits are conducted for compliance with policies, procedures, regulations, and customer requirements. Audits should be planned and conducted based on reference material such as that shown in Figure 2.2.

Reporting. Audit results should be reported to the functional organizations affected. After discussion and corrective actions, reports to higher levels should be made in accordance with published procedures.

Personnel. Those performing audits should be highly knowledgeable of the organization and processes involved. They should have good people skills and the ability to remain objective. (Audit knowledge and skills can be demonstrated through the ASQC Certified Quality Auditor program.)

2.B. Organization Structures (Matrix, Hierarchical)

The rapid changes in competition, driven by technology and customer demands, have forced change in organization structures. Organizations are formed to have people get work done. Organizing involves defining the work to be done and a structure to identify who is responsible and accountable for doing it. The overall structure selected is most successful when determined by the effective activity in satisfying the customer. Internal organization structures are then designed to manage important processes that support the end goal.

Organization Trends. With the identification of a quality function as a responsibility of the total organization, the responsibility for quality work elements has shifted from a special quality organization to the organizations doing the work. Tasks that affect quality objectives are the responsibility of those performing the work. These changes have affected organization structure.

- Tasks such as inspection and test are performed by production. The groups doing the work are responsible for the quality of their output.

- Many quality specialists operate primarily on process improvement teams as direct improvement participants, or to provide special knowledge to teams, such as statistical tools or training in problem solving or traditional quality techniques.

- The quality function organization is focused primarily on system, process, and product audits; surveys; supplier quality management; quality measurement; and reporting and maintenance of measurement standards.

None of these arrangements are universal; various combinations are dependent on the TQ growth and management history of the organization.

Another structure change frequently made after adopting TQ is broadening the span of control and eliminating layers of management.[3] This is often done because the implementation of TQ leads to more self-directed work groups that manage their own processes. The groups do some of the work that was previously the responsibility of the first-line manager. Having both first- and second-line management is then redundant.

The groups still need a manager but in a different role. The manager becomes a facilitator as well as a representative of upper management and still must ensure that company policies and objectives are met. A new part of the manager's job is to assist his or her group in dealing with other groups, to acquire resources and training needed for improvement, and to be the communication vehicle up and down the organization. Eliminating management layers helps in this communication process. The remaining managers are given more work groups to replace their previous activity of day-to-day work direction. Achieving this simpler structure requires an evolutionary approach. (Note that in spite of all the reported downsizing and flattening, economist D. M. Morgan[4] reports that in industry the ratio of supervisors to subordinates has risen, not fallen.) Accepting and understanding this different way of managing requires an attitude change and management training, first and foremost by senior management.

As organizations grow larger or include more diverse specialties and functions, a strict hierarchical structure is less effective. The structure most used for this situation is a matrix. Hybrid structures are also used that reflect management's decision on how to make the organization functions work best. (The old idea of a pyramid structure is no longer automatically accepted.) A major consideration is now given to organizing on a basis that will best serve the customer, both internal and external, and how to meet quality improvement and other organizational objectives.

Types of Structures

Hierarchical. These structures are typically organized by function; for example, marketing, engineering, finance, manufacturing, quality, and human resources. Authority is delegated from top to bottom. It is usually represented by a pyramid, with authority at the top.

Matrix. These organizations exist in many forms. They resemble the functional organization, with project or program management operating at the same level as a function but directing work across functional lines. This can be considered an informal team structure, with the project manager acting as team leader. The purpose is to direct the functional work to satisfy a specific customer or product needs.

Projects are often structured with functional members assigned to take direction from the project leader. When tasks are completed the functional members return to their home function for reassignment. In another variation, projects are also assigned dedicated production resources. Project management is discussed in Chapter 8.

Program management can sometimes differ in that it assigns tasks and budget to functions then tracks and reports their performance. The functional members take direction from their own organization managers. It is the function's responsibility to satisfy the program requirements.

Team. These matrix organizations are hybrids, combinations of a hierarchical structure and some form of project overlay. In organizations that are advanced in their use of change agents and teams (see Chapter 2E), there is often a loose form of matrix in which the team leaders (the innovators and change agents) act like project managers. The projects are improvements the teams devise. They begin when a project is approved and end when it is fully proven and implemented. They do not usually appear on an organization chart. In fact, mature team organizations that function well in their environment don't rely much on charts. Communication and dialogue are frequent and an important self-management vehicle for getting work done.

Structures—Positives and Negatives

Every organization structure is a compromise. There are many variables to be balanced, such as business type, size, market, regulations, technology, and skills.

Structures are rarely static because the importance of each variable changes. Some of the most significant changes are a result of the emphasis on quality and customer satisfaction. Such organizations tend to use the informal organization to operate rather than the one shown on the organization chart. But there are always factors to consider when designing or evaluating organization structure.

Hierarchical. A structure divided into functions (specialties) and levels.

Advantages:

- Comfortable for managers; they are the decision makers and are in charge.
- Good top-down communication.
- Reflects the value of tradition.

- More controllable in the short term.
- Good use of employee skills.
- Continuity in functional disciplines.
- Good control of personnel. Employee has one boss.

Disadvantages:

- Lack of clear accountability for total work or projects.
- Generally slow response to customer or market changes.
- Weak customer focus.
- Creates barriers to communication between the functions; information is compartmentalized.
- Vertical relationships dominate; little horizontal interaction.
- Members only work by direction from above. Upper levels expected to know all. Members are limited to what they are permitted to do rather than what they can contribute.
- Tends to give function goals priority; overall goals are not the prime interest. There is a tendency for some functions to dominate.
- Poor structure for solving system problems.
- Each function is expected to solve its own problems.
- Functions can easily develop jealousy toward other functions.

Matrix (Traditional). A form of decentralization. A collaborative form of managing.

Advantages:

- Provides a mechanism for managing and integrating several projects or products sharing the same resources.
- Responsive to special customer requirements or changes.
- Limits the number of permanent organization elements.
- Provides project managers with control through budget.
- Specific project policies and procedures can be implemented.
- More visible, measurable accountability for the product or project.

Disadvantages: Most of the hierarchical disadvantages, plus

- Less accountability for the corporate system as a whole.
- Too many bosses; weak decision making.
- Requires complex tracking activities.
- Needs considerable experience to manage.
- Complicates communication.
- Complicates operating procedures. Each group tends to develop unique procedures and policies.
- Limits innovation.
- Precipitates conflict over resources.
- Requires people to multitask, creating inefficiencies in all activities.
- Typically higher administration costs.
- Greater potential conflict over priorities.
- Creates barriers to communication between groups. Learning is not shared.

Matrix (Teams). A looser structure. More informal.

Advantages:

- Provides an environment for accepting innovation.
- Taps full capabilities of members. Encourages contribution.
- Faster communications.
- Faster response to changing conditions.

Disadvantages:

- Loss of technical edge if specialties become increasingly responsible for more general activities.
- Hard for outsiders to enter. Community develops its own leaders.
- Takes a long time and continuous management nurturing to develop.
- Core, systemic issues can be left unattended by senior management in the activity of managing interaction between communities.

Smaller Companies. Small and medium-sized companies have been very successful in managing internal projects using departmental project management, especially when only a few functional groups must interface. Line managers might wear multiple hats as project managers.

2.C. Quality Functions Within the Organization

As a result of the world trend in recognizing quality as a critical objective for all types of organizations, both organization structures and their quality functions are changing. The quality function, which used to be viewed as the responsibility of a separate special organization, like quality control or quality assurance, is now evolving to an identifiable responsibility of all organization elements.

The quality functions within organizations are

- Those activities necessary to meet the overall organization quality objectives, both short term and strategic

- Those quality improvement projects and objectives selected by any organization function for self-improvement

The specific kinds of quality activities vary widely based on such factors as

- Type and size of organization

- Nature and source of regulatory or special customer requirements, such as ISO 9000 or GMP (see Chapter 1G)

- Management philosophy

- Degree of commitment to TQ principles

- Organization structure

Traditional Organization Functions. Traditional industrial organizations, regardless of structure but dependent on the size and nature of the business, have had separate quality functions. The quality functions had the responsibility to manage the work elements listed in Table 2.1.

If working on defense contracts, such organizations tended to have the most comprehensive quality activities and organizations because they were required to do so by military specifications, particularly MIL-Q-9858 (this specification can be replaced by the ISO 9001, 9002, or 9003).

Table 2.1. Work elements.

Reliability engineering working elements
    Establish reliability goals
    Reliability apportionment
    Stress analysis
    Identify critical parts
    Failure mode, effects, and criticality analysis (FMECA)
    Reliability prediction
    * Design review
    * Supplier selection—certification
    * Control of reliability during manufacturing
    Reliability testing
    Failure reporting and corrective action system

QC engineering work elements
    Process capability analysis
    Quality planning
    * Establish quality standards
    Test equipment and gage design
    * Quality troubleshooting
    * Analyze rejected or returned material
    * Special studies (measurement error, etc.), DOE
    * Software QA

Quality assurance work elements
    * Write quality procedures
    * Maintain quality manual
    * Perform quality audits—system, products, services
    * Quality information systems
    * Quality certification—in-house
    * Training
    Quality cost systems

Inspection and test work elements
    In-process inspection and test
    * Final product inspection and test
    * Receiving inspection
    * Maintain inspection records
    * Gage calibration
    * Supplier quality control—process audits
    * Pre-award surveys
    * Supplier quality information systems
    * Supplier surveillance
    * Source inspection
    Supplier certification

*In TQM, prime responsibility of quality organization

Source: J. M. Juran and Frank M. Gryna, eds., *Juran's Quality Control Handbook* (New York: McGraw-Hill, 1988). Reproduced with permission of The McGraw-Hill Companies.

Organizations using a project or matrix management structure usually had a quality functional organization that operated like the other functional units. The project or program office included a quality representative to ensure that the project quality requirements were met, operating through the quality functional unit.

TQ Organization Functions (Team Managed). The transition from traditional to TQ team-managed organizations has resulted in a significant change in the nature and accountability of quality functions.

Table 2.1 also identifies the quality functions typically shifted to all organization units in a TQ organization. Only a general guide can be presented since the responsibility for quality functions and work elements varies so widely and is often in a state of transition. The important point is that responsibility for quality and improvement is being shifted from quality specialists to the people doing the work. The fundamentals in each organization are that quality work elements are needed, identified, and that some person or unit is responsible and accountable for their effectiveness and improvement.

Service Organizations. These organizations do not have a tradition of identifying and assigning responsibility for quality activities. This situation has changed with the growth of the service industry and the recognition of changes in competition and the marketplace. Many have adapted a version of TQ that fits their operations. Again, depending on size, they may have a designated quality leader responsible for coordinating and facilitating the process improvement activities.

2.D. Communication Within the Organization

Organization communication is frequently not analyzed, systematized, and integrated, but is taken for granted even though it is necessary for organization success and critical in a TQ organization. Most people are not good communicators. Therefore, management must make a continuous effort to improve its communication skills, set the example, and provide the climate, systems, and information for all organization elements to communicate effectively.

A major component of leadership is effective two-way communication. Managing the modern organization, creating meaningful change, and keeping the work force motivated at continuous improvement depends on effective communication. It is the means to transmit the organization vision, objectives, plans, status, progress, and methodologies.

Management frequently announces such things as goals and objectives but fails to communicate how the organization will achieve them. Announcements, like slogans, are not a demonstration of leadership or good communications. They are simply autocratic actions. There is a place for them, but not when they require an organization response, such as working toward specific goals. Communicating to motivate is not like a marketing campaign. In communicating the need for change, a critical action in adopting and managing TQ, leaders must identify what new behavior is required, why, and what the priorities are. The new requirements should be based on assessment data and the results of listening to organization members and customers. Employees are also always looking for consistency between management's actions and communications. If management calls for a focus on quality improvement and then acts to satisfy cost and schedule over quality issues, organization members will recognize the hypocrisy. They will remain cynical and nothing will change.

Communication plays a key role in becoming a responsive, agile organization. Information systems support employee empowerment. They override the communication barriers between people and organization functions. Effective communication networks provide workers and teams with the information they need to support continuous improvement in processes, products, and services.

Organization computer networks (intranets) are changing the way organizations and their members exchange information. According to Cognitive Communications, a consulting firm, 85 percent of large companies either have intranets or are developing them. A result is the breakup of the previous information systems departments. Their members are going to work in the network user organizations, serving them directly and maintaining some control over the network development.[5]

The Communication Model
The essence of successful communications can be described as *the transfer of information from the sender to the receiver, with the information being understood by the receiver, to effect desired change.*

With ever-improving systems to speed up communications the three elements in this definition become more important. The three elements are

- Sender
- Message transfer
- Receiver

Communication is a process represented in Figure 2.3.

This simple process becomes more difficult as organizations become larger and more specialized. The noise factor, which creates distortions and sometimes blockage, exists in every organization and requires careful consideration in the design and the operation of communication systems. Managers and team leaders are key players in both the formal and informal communications system and therefore must be considered key sending and receiving points.

Traditional Quality Communications. Quality activities in industry are quite varied and often complex. They deal with a multiplicity of problems involving many people and organizations, internal and external. In traditionally organized companies the quality organization serves a key role in communicating, horizontally and vertically, indicators of overall organization quality status. Product defect rates, quality costs, and quality problem status are prime examples of such indicators. This information has not

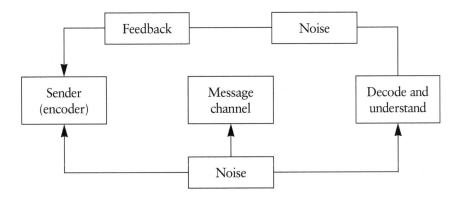

Figure 2.3. The communication process.

always been welcome because it appears to blame a specific function for quality problems. It is hard to respond to because quality problems are mostly caused by unknown system and process problems. The most common result is fighting symptoms rather than the true cause. With the process orientation of a TQ organization, however, quality information can be tied to each process and used for process quality improvement.

Quality Communications in Project Management. With the increasing use of project management, good communication becomes more complex. In a traditional organization, quality information is communicated primarily to functional managers. Adding project management adds another active communication station. Project managers need complete, regular quality information so they can determine the impact on their projects of quality problems. Project management's response is to seek improvement from the responsible functional manager, or even the quality manager. Quality data can be a source of conflict because the work process concept is missing, which makes problem identification and correction more difficult. Frequently, a functional manager takes some corrective action to resolve the conflict, which removes the symptom, not the cause.

In improving an organization, communications—formal, informal, written, or verbal—should be identified as a process to be managed and improved. Unfortunately, the subject is often considered too elementary for management attention. But unless someone is accountable for communication management, it will not reach the level of effectiveness needed. As more organizations are in transition to meet modern demands, formal and informal communication chains are broken and many errors may occur before new links are formed. Clear communication of goals, strategy, and results is a management and quality management responsibility.

Team Communications. A key objective in establishing teams is to produce a flexible, fast-responding, self-learning, and correcting organization, one that can respond quickly to changing market and customer needs. One of the elements needed to make this possible is fast and accurate communications between people and organizations responsible for responding. By its nature, team communications will be mostly direct and informal. Overly formal and complex communication requirements will defeat efforts to improve responsiveness.

Effective, informal team communications takes time to develop. Team members have to learn each other's strengths and weaknesses. Communications between members and with other organizations is an integral part of team development and is emphasized in team training. It must be a major interest of the team leader throughout the team's life. It easily fits the category of something that requires continuous improvement, but it is difficult to measure progress if communication is primarily verbal or informal.

A valuable mechanism for developing team communications is the principle of identifying process customers and suppliers, both internal and external. Effective communications can be developed by determining, by direct contact with customers and suppliers, their needs and expectations. Each contact should improve communications, establishing the important senders and receivers. Important processes have many customers and suppliers. Within each process communication links are established directly across organization boundaries.

The Value of Communications in an Organization. Communication operates to integrate the management functions. It is needed to

- Disseminate the policies and goals of the organization.
- Form the vehicle for developing organization plans.
- Organize human and other resources in the most effective manner.
- Provide for the evaluation of organization members.
- Provide a vehicle to lead, direct, and motivate people to achieve organization goals with satisfaction.
- Allow for the control of performance.
- Provide upward information to all management levels.
- Provide members with the information necessary to satisfy customers and the external communities.

Effectiveness. The following are fundamentals of communication system design.

- Information must be timely.
- It must go to the right person and organization.

- It must be accurate and in a useful form.
- The system must provide feedback paths for rapid, accurate response.
- Information must cross organization boundaries without distortion.
- The system must be flexible enough to accept unplanned inputs and outputs.
- Information must be periodically validated to ensure its accurate transmission to recipients.

External communications are also of critical importance in meeting strategic goals and objectives. They are discussed in Chapter 4G.

2.E. Change Agents and Their Effect on Organizations

Change agents are those people in organizations who are adept at the art of anticipating the need for, and of leading, productivity change. They are the ones with the ideas that move beyond established practice, ideas they convert into visions and then into realities. Change agents are the people who can exploit their environment, build coalitions and teams, implement the visions, and reach or exceed objectives.

As the rate of change increases in the business environment, companies must rely even more on their people to make decisions for which there is no routine response. Creative answers are needed. For this to happen, the circumstances for idea contribution must be created and the empowerment provided to enact these ideas. It does not happen in the normal course of business or under the traditional hierarchical organization. In recent history, the companies that followed progressive human resource practices have been among the most successful, profitable, and expanding: Xerox, General Electric, Hewlett-Packard, Motorola, and other Baldrige Award winners.

Innovation. Establishing a climate that encourages innovation results in a growth of new ideas, with innovation piggybacking innovation. Problems are solved in new and unique ways.

Innovation, if it is to occur, requires an openness to new ideas and a willingness to try them. True innovation is always testing the limits. The past cannot be allowed to control the future; successful innovation requires a look forward. Organizations or functions cannot dominate actions. Innovation requires the integration of knowledge and ideas. Traditional organizations limit integration and control actions and events.

Management's problem is how to create conditions that stimulate creativity, how to achieve a problem-solving culture that helps generate novel solutions. Part of the problem lies in organization structure. Compartmentalizing activities limits interchange, resulting in solutions to only selected parts of a problem because there is no mechanism to integrate the parts and achieve a new and superior solution for the whole.

In traditional organizations the members see only local manifestations of a problem and therefore only local solutions are sought. There is little incentive to try to solve system or other functional group problems because it only means more work and little reward. These organizations limit members' thinking to their own realm of responsibility. A compartmentalized view of the problem affects the accuracy in assessing the problem and the speed and effectiveness of the answer.

All these factors in traditional organizations limit their ability to cope with major external changes occurring in the global economy. The traditional organization becomes a victim of its past.

Managing Change. Organizations that need to change or are in the process of changing must have a change agent leader at the top. Jack Welch of General Electric is such an agent. He has been given much of the credit for GE's change in the way it operates and for its success. When such a leader agent exists, similar change agents in the rest of the organization will make themselves evident. Once they recognize that upper management wants to change the culture and direction, their true nature will appear. Management has to look for such people and give them open support. That is how the change message is effectively transported down through the organization.

Organizations that are change oriented have an open and integrated approach to problem solving with several mechanisms to do so. People are empowered to act on information, which is freely exchanged. New problems are considered opportunities to improve. People feel that they work in a community, not a function. The result is freedom of expression and cooperative teamwork across the organization chart. These organizations also invest quickly in new solutions, not after long justification procedures. Incentives for innovation are opportunities to take on larger projects.

Executives often talk about wanting change and innovation, but the message lower-level members get is that they are not really supposed to do anything outside of their assigned job responsibilities. It's as if there were a set of rules operating to stifle innovation. Rules for management might read like this:[6]

1. Regard any new idea from below with suspicion—because it's new, and because it's from below.

2. Insist that people who need your approval to act first go through several other levels of management to get their signatures.

3. Ask departments or individuals to challenge and criticize each other's proposals. (That saves you the job of deciding; you just pick the survivor.)

4. Express your criticisms freely, and withhold your praise. (That keeps people on their toes.) Let them know they can be fired at any time.

5. Treat identification of problems as signs of failure, to discourage people from letting you know when something in their area isn't working.

6. Control everything carefully. Make sure people count anything that can be counted, frequently.

7. Make decisions to reorganize or change policies in secret, and spring them on people unexpectedly. (That laso keeps people on their toes.)

8. Make sure that requests for information are fully justified, and make sure that it is not given out to managers freely. (You don't want data to fall into the wrong hands.)

9. Assign to lower-level managers, in the name of delegation and participation, responsibility for figuring out how to cut back, lay off, move people around, or otherwise implement threatening decisions you have made. And get them to do it quickly.

10. And above all, never forget that you, the higher-ups, already know everything important about this business.

These rules reflect some traditional organizations in action. If this is the environment perceived by employees, there will be little significant improvement and no innovation. All the declarations by management about wanting to be a TQM organization won't change anything.

Creating Innovation. Creating a forward-looking organization would involve the following:

- Everyone in the organization working toward the same overall objectives, the same strategic plans. A quality focus must be deployed.

- The creation of an environment of trust, particularly in the areas of uncertainty, where the future outcomes are not clear.

- The use of participative mechanisms, like teams, to support an attitude of respect for the individual. Teams can provide the stimulus for individual contributions. They can give people a broader outlook and more knowledge and skills to contribute new ideas.

These elements also reflect the basics of the Baldrige Award criteria.

Conditions for Successful Managerial Innovation. There isn't a simple prescription for organizations to follow to become innovative, but innovative organizations share the integrative form just described, with common characteristics that foster improvement.

1. A culture of pride and climate of success as demonstrated by

- Freedom and responsibility for managers to act, to do the right thing.

- Extensive dialogue and interpersonal relationships.

- Emphasis on teamwork and teams.
- Innovation is main-stream, not counterculture.
- Integrative, participative management approach.
- Managers can handle uncertainty.
- Job charters are broad; assignments are ambiguous, nonroutine, and change oriented; areas of responsibility intersect.
- Local autonomy is strong but there is mutual dependence between groups.
- There is complexity in middle-management operations: more relationships, more information, a variety of inputs on problems, more ways to get human resources involved, more freedom to investigate.

2. Entrepreneurial, innovative managers have the power they need to negotiate for necessary resources and support for an innovative action.

- Information: open communication systems across the organization.
- Support from other organizations through networking devices.
    —Mobility; circulation of people through other jobs.
    —Employment security through long-term relationships.
    —Use of teams at middle and upper levels, with horizontal and multifunctional representation.
    —Complex ties horizontally and vertically; access anywhere.
- Decentralization of resources; local access to loosely committed funds.

Types of Change. The following changes are required to create the kind of organization needed to operate for continuous improvement with a focus on customer satisfaction.

- Policy: describing the vision and direction for the overall organization and the role of its elements.
- Strategy: how the new policies will be followed; how the new objectives, products, and markets will be obtained.

- Structure: a definition and plan for the structure that will be most effective.

- People: what the new organization and personnel development needs will be to support and facilitate the climate and working relationships.

2.F. Management Styles (By Facts and Data, Coaching, Other Leadership Styles)

The traditional responsibilities of management remain the same in a TQ organization. They include planning, organizing, controlling, delegating, and directing to economically produce products and services for the customer. (Nonprofit organizations must also produce revenue income above costs—a "profit"—to spend on growth and improvement. Such profits are not distributed to owners.) The result is meeting the business objectives. In the period before approximately 1985, the typical management focus was on maximizing profits and the return on stockholder investment, usually for the short term. This is still a business objective, but now there is a growing recognition that to remain competitive and reach those same objectives, and long-term objectives, the focus has to be on satisfying the customer. The result of satisfying the customer is meeting the business objectives.

Reduced budgets and new competition are also driving improvements in service quality, such as medical services, education, and government agencies reducing costs and improving service quality to meet customer expectations. These changes in focus require a different but definable style of management and managers. The new component is leadership, not just managing. This means getting an organization to change, to motivate members to follow the leader. Leadership in applying TQ principles is also a new way to manage by changing the focus of the goal. A brief summary of the contributions in the field of motivation theory will illustrate the predominance of the psychological factors involved in management. In management studies these are frequently referred to as human factors.

The identification of management as a separate discipline began with Frederick Taylor[7] in the early part of the 20th century. He called it *scientific management*. He described how industrial work processes could be accurately repeated and could be learned. He added the idea of measuring human performance and setting performance standards; his emphasis was on efficiency. Taylor also formed the basis for the development of what has become work measurement in industrial engineering. His approach is now considered the ideal model of authoritative management.

Abraham Maslow's[8] contribution in 1954 was the identification of a pyramid known as the Hierarchy of Needs (see Figure 2.3). Human needs ascend from the most basic, or *physiological,* needs to what he termed *self-actualization.*

Maslow's stages imply an order of importance. If management wants employees to perform at the highest level, it must recognize that the lower stages have to be reasonably satisfied first (as determined by the employee assessment).

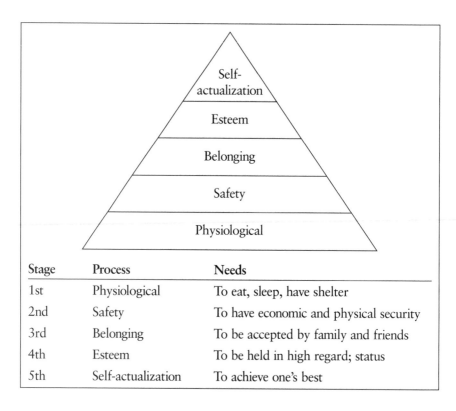

Stage	Process	Needs
1st	Physiological	To eat, sleep, have shelter
2nd	Safety	To have economic and physical security
3rd	Belonging	To be accepted by family and friends
4th	Esteem	To be held in high regard; status
5th	Self-actualization	To achieve one's best

Figure 2.3. Maslow's Hierarchy of Needs.

In 1971, Herzberg[9] identified *hygienic factors* in work, such as wages, working conditions, challenging work, growth and learning, group identity and participation in work planning. These provide job satisfaction but will not stimulate superior performance and can create dissatisfaction if inadequate.

Douglas McGregor's[10] contribution was to analyze the components and spectrum of management styles. The result was his representative Theory X and the Theory Y.

Theory X managers act on the belief that workers are lazy, unmotivated, and have to be told what to do. These managers are dictatorial and believe that fear is a motivator; they need to control.

Theory Y managers believe that people want to do a good job and, if management provides the right climate, they will become self-motivated to do their best. Identifying managers as X or Y types is an overly simplistic exercise but these concepts are of value. All managers should analyze their beliefs and style to understand where they are in the spectrum and how they are probably perceived and to identify how well they match their organization and its goals.

In studying the management aspects of TQ it is clear that autocratic, Theory X managers would have great difficulty in honestly accepting its basic tenets, such as allowing employees to reach a level of self-management in teams, empowerment, and trust. Other researchers have carried these seminal works further; they can be found in the literature on management styles and motivation. A more expansive discussion is in M. Silverman's *The Technical Manager's Handbook*.[11]

Basic Management Styles

There are several identifiable styles of management, as any management text would describe. They reflect McGregor's classifications.

Autocrat (The Boss). Concerned primarily with developing an efficient operation with little concern for people. One who commands and expects compliance. Looks to him- or herself as the pacesetter. Thinks this behavior is leadership.

Participative. Concerned primarily with people, but trying to balance with the concerns of the business of the organization.

Team Manager. Dedicated to people and the business of the organization. Can integrate the needs of the organization with the needs of the people. Frequently acts more like a facilitator and coach, giving subordinates a high degree of freedom of action. Encourages ideas and uses them. Develops trust. Communicates effectively up and down the organization. Demonstrates leadership, resulting in subordinates who will follow and accept change.

Management styles are a continuum. A successful manager adopts elements of all styles in various circumstances, but one of the three is always dominant.

Effect of Management Styles

Autocratic. Direction and objectives are set by management. There is little ownership or participation by nonmanagement. Goals are short term and arbitrary and not always within organization capability. Missed goals are considered a management failure. Employees feel no satisfaction in their jobs, show little initiative, don't think management cares, have low motivation, and have high absenteeism and turnover. Typically, there are lower-quality products and less-satisfied customers. In a highly competitive market the autocratically managed organization will find difficulty in competing, long term, with other organizations that have a high level of employee participation in quality and productivity improvement. Employee's contributions make a significant difference.

Participative. Input is solicited from all organization levels on goals, objectives, and how to operate. With a lack of leadership the organization can drift unsteered and fail to set or meet important objectives. Lack of direction and satisfaction is frustrating and demoralizing. There is little initiative on employees' part because there are few satisfactory results. It is not a very effective style for businesses that require strong coordination between functions.

Team Manager. Management is art superimposed on logic. This style can be learned through practice if it is based on solid research theory and the successful experience of others.[12] The autocrat follows the military model, which makes sense for military operations where qualified replacements are needed immediately to take over when the leader is lost.

In this model the boss makes the decisions and the subordinates obey. But this model no longer serves organizations that need to compete in a highly competitive, fast-changing marketplace and where satisfying the customer is the prime objective. In this environment, a team-based model is proving to be the most effective.

The management of team-based organizations is still evolving in both theory and practice, but it clearly requires its own management style. The autocratic component plays only a small part because it runs counter to the idea of having employee teams manage work with a minimum of management direction. Team management is mostly team leadership. Upper management must consider itself the leader of teams, not the manager of functions (even though functions may be retained as the repository of function specialists).

The key functions of team managers and which describe the style, are

- Openness to different ideas and behavior
- Flexibility to learn and use the ideas of others
- Confidence in letting others make decisions
- Goal setting using the needs and data of others, including the customer
- Leadership, to motivate others to follow and work toward common goals

Team management is an amalgam of the participative style and leadership. The effects of the team management style are demonstrated by today's top-performing, world-class organizations. It best fits the needs of today's marketplace and the customer demands for high quality and fast reaction, combined with the need to apply leading-edge knowledge of the pertinent technologies. Internally it results in more motivated employees, who are willing to learn, change, and commit to organization objectives.

One manifestation of the team management style is *management by walking around*. It means frequent personal observations of the work activities and locations of all organization elements. The managers become visible and approachable; they listen, observe, and question to learn and draw conclusions about morale, attitudes, cohesiveness, effectiveness, and what needs improvement, all through firsthand observation.

In an effectively managed team, organization members accept and work on the principle of continuous internal and external customer satisfaction. Good communication and information provides motivation and a feeling of useful participation in all employees. Teams will often reach or exceed goals and provide innovative ideas that can result in breakthrough improvements.

Decision Making

Autocratic managers are practiced in making decisions based on data, but usually only data, about cost, schedule, and financial forecasts.

As they say, "It's the bottom line that counts." In business that is obviously a fact. The autocrat, however, uses the threat of making changes if performance numbers don't improve. This is the prime motivation, whether expressed or not. The lower managers and workers don't really know what to do to change the numbers and didn't participate in setting them. In fact, the autocratic manager doesn't know how to get them consistently, either. There is little systematic thinking and little concept of managing variation. The performance objectives may be what the organization needs to compete, but their achievement is delegated to the lower echelons to figure out.

For example, management looks at a monthly report for a product line. It concludes that the inspection and testing reject rates are too high. Its response is

1. Who is responsible for that line?

2. What is the manager doing about it? Have him/her submit an improvement plan of action in a week.

3. What is the quality department doing about it? Are the inspectors being too critical? (Of course, when a customer experiences poor quality the question becomes, "Why didn't quality catch it?" Management looks for someone to blame.)

4. Does our competitor have a lower reject rate? (Looking for justification and a comfort zone.)

5. The boss has a meeting with all the managers involved to motivate them. They had better get the message: He wants action! What is going to happen next month? No one knows, and it's unknowable.

A team style manager would solicit ideas about processes, variation and process improvement activities, and possible results. The concentration would be on preventive actions that would result in improvement.

One of Deming's rules for managing is to make decisions based on data, on facts, and on the analysis of data. The analysis is to obtain the meaning of the data so that the right decisions can be made on how to improve. Reactions purely based on numerical data, such as " too high" or " looks good enough," are meaningless and may be the completely wrong response. Data from operating activities contain information on whether a process is operating satisfactorily, but only by applying the proper statistical tools can management find out what is really happening, why a process is behaving as the data show.

The kind of data needed are performance measurements that indicate how a process is operating. The data should come from across as well as up and down the organization. These are not just data compiled monthly and published in thick computer printouts. The data should be those taken by the people (teams) operating the process.

Until processes are defined and understood, and key process data are taken, management doesn't know how the organization is doing, whether it is doing the right things, or what it is capable of doing. If the sum of all the processes is not satisfactory, the bottom line can best be achieved by process improvement.

This is where the autocratic style and making decisions often come in conflict. Adopting a process improvement policy (strategy) requires management at all levels to modify some of its basic ideas about management and people. Managers have to relinquish some control and decision making to the people doing the work. This is usually a difficult transition. These organizations have spent years selecting and training managers in the image of top autocratic management. The work force will also require time and training to change. It has been conditioned to be told, not asked.

In reality, such decision making is often difficult. Managers rarely have all the data they would like before making a decision. This creates uncertainty as to what response is most likely to succeed. But decisions have to be made and we often have to make them on data that are (a) inadequate, (b) inaccurate, and even (c) nonexistent . . . . We routinely make many life decisions with such data. We minimize this problem by creating information or extrapolate from experience. If the data were available beforehand a computer could replace managers.[13]

Coaching

Coaching is an element of management style that is very valuable to an organization, primarily because it motivates people to think about their work rather than wait for direction. Unless people are thinking seriously about what they are doing they will not be able to contribute to any significant improvement. Coaching is most frequently in a manager's discomfort zone. Managers frequently don't understand coaching because they themselves didn't experience it and were not taught how to do it. It is of more importance today because it is an element in the job of manager in an effective TQ concept organization. This kind of organization has been discussed in other chapters; it includes a motivated, self-directed work force that manages its own work and processes, with an overlay of innovative improvement teams. It is important for managers to be able to coach, rather than try to direct, improvement teams and members.

There is a lot of similarity in coaching athletic teams and improvement teams. Successful coaching depends on the skills of the coach and the receptivity of the team. The receptivity of the team can be improved by providing important basic information of interest to team members, such as job expectations and the basis of standards and criteria for success. A coach monitors team operation and identifies success; that is, what works. Coaching encourages open communication and learning from others and asks leading questions to help understand the thought process in the analysis of problems.

Coaching Fundamentals

1. Coaching can only take place if there is some level of trust and rapport.

2. Problems must be clearly identified and similarly understood by both parties.

3. The people being coached must describe assumptions they hold about actions they take.

4. These people must have a clear understanding of what is expected.

5. The coach must primarily use a questioning approach to help people think things through.

6. The coach may offer ideas on how problems can be approached and solved.

7. Expected outcomes should be established for each coaching session.

8. Coaching involves listening and not judging.

9. The coach should have frequent work contact with those being coached to observe progress.

Coaching requires experience, maturity, patience and a sincere interest in assisting people to reach their full potential.

2.G. Business Functions

Every business includes a variety of functions external and internal to its operations which have an important role in viability and success.

1. External

Business Climate. With the rapidly, unpredictably changing competitive climate every business must keep itself informed of world events that could change and shape the marketplace or the work environment.

Some of these are slow moving, like cultural changes resulting from immigration and strong religious differences. (The political stability of strategically important countries is another.) World environmental issues can also affect a business. These and other global issues can become important at the local level. For example, environmental regulations, increasing worldwide, are affecting the costs and competitive position of a broad spectrum of businesses.

Inattention to the seriousness of the improvement in Japanese automotive quality decades ago still affects U.S. automakers.

Some traditional sources of information to monitor these issues are trade and professional organization publications, as well as business journals and newspapers.

Safety. In addition to the importance of operating a business that causes no injury to employees, safety issues can involve government agencies such as the Occupational Safety and Health Administration (OSHA) and the Environmental Protection Agency (EPA), insurance rates, and legal requirements. Management must assign clear authority for, and ensure, effective compliance with all safety requirements.

Legal and Regulatory. An effective quality control system plays an important role in many legal and governmental regulatory issues. Product liability has become increasingly important for any business producing a product for the industrial, drug, food, or retail markets. A business is generally held responsible for injuries caused by its product. Product liability insurance is costly, and some product liability lawsuits in recent years have resulted in settlements in the billions of dollars. A producer must have complete records supporting research and design decisions, development results, manufacturing process management, tooling, training, and testing results if it is to adequately defend itself. This requires a good information and quality control system to ensure that complete records are retained and retrievable.

The present judicial and legislative trend is toward adoption of a doctrine of strict liability of a manufacturer for product defects and even misuse, usually for as long as the product exists. To limit liability and maintain customer satisfaction or goodwill the producer must take rapid corrective action, such as a recall, when defects are disclosed. Accurate and timely communication by management again becomes critical.

Regulatory agencies of the federal, state, and local governments are ubiquitous and their regulations often comprehensive. Their impact on business operations can be costly, directly for compliance and indirectly for noncompliance. Management must stay informed on the requirements of such agencies as the Food and Drug Administration (FDA), the EPA, and consumer protection agencies. An international case in point is the ISO 14000 environmental management system.

Warranties. These are a legal, competitive, and customer satisfaction issue. They must clearly state the extent of the warranty, conditions covered, and the options to the user for corrective action. The judicial trend is to assume a product warranty (implied) whether or not it is published.

Technology. Technology-driven changes taking place in processes and products are occurring rapidly. This factor alone makes it difficult for an organization to achieve and sustain a competitive position. Customers routinely expect newer, higher quality, lower cost products. To stay competitive, management establishes some form of activity that tracks technological developments to assess their potential applications, impact, and how they can affect customer needs. Trade and professional associations, publications, and benchmarking are important information sources. An effective, capable quality system can play an important role in assessing the impact of technology changes on process or product cost and quality. Important quality tools to reach adequate assurance levels are quality function deployment (QFD) and concurrent engineering.

Environmental. Environmental factors are an important consideration in establishing and operating almost every business. There are a variety of laws and regulations issued by federal, state, and local governments that must be understood and followed. In addition, community considerations, such as being a good citizen, can justify environmental controls beyond those required by law.

Environmental regulations can have a serious impact not only on operating a business but on the cost of expansion—modifications, additions or new facilities. Work environment and safety issues frequently overlap. Manufacturing process changes and improvements can also be affected by regulations.

2. Internal

Business functions, in addition to quality control, vary in scope depending on the organization type and size. But all businesses have some of these.

Human Resources functions exist in every business. Typical activities in a large business are

- Personnel selection(hiring, recruiting)
- Discharge
- Performance review management
- Compensation management
- Benefits management
- Training and development

The human resource function is covered in detail in Chapter 7.

Engineering functions include product and software design, manufacturing process and tool design, quality technology, and field service. Each contains technological specialists educated and skilled in the technical needs of the different organizations.

Sales and Marketing functions exist to some degree in every business. They are the prime contact for customers to buy products or services. Sales usually refers to advertising and seeking and taking orders. The marketing function also does product and marketing research and market development.

Finance, in a small business, can be a single bookkeeper or, in a large organization, can include personnel responsible for cost accounting, budgeting, analysis, billing, taxes, investments, and external finance. It has these internal responsibilities but also those that are external, to assure compliance with legal and regulatory requirements.

Research and Development varies considerably in size, nature, and organization position. Large organizations have large budgets for basic or applied research for products or process development. In many businesses, research and development (R&D) is part of the science or engineering function. There are businesses that only do R&D and sell their results, frequently on a royalty basis.

Purchasing is a basic activity in every business and a major participant in quality improvement. It can vary from buying ordinary supplies to a complex organization that selects supplies and subcontractors and negotiates price and conditions.

The modern team concept places purchasing as the leader of multifunctional teams to achieve a long-term relationship with qualified suppliers. As Deming said, total cost, not simply price, should be considered when purchasing.

Safety. Management must ensure occupational health and safety for its employees. This concern is motivated by a regard for human life, legal status, and cost avoidance. Insurance rates are usually determined by the number of safety-related incidents as a percentage of the employee population and hours worked. Safety can be a factor in making process improvements.

Key Ideas—Chapter 2

1. Organizational assessment is the evaluation of achieving business goals and objectives using quality auditing tools. There are two levels in this type of assessment: compliance (doing things right) and effectiveness (doing the right things).

2. Organizational structure will vary based on how to best manage processes and which structure is most effective to meet the overall goal.

3. Management *style* is a reflection of personal philosophy. Management *methods* will vary dependent on a combination of style, training, organizational structure, and corporate culture and expectations.

4. A traditional organizational structure is often treated as static, but the business environment is constantly changing.

5. The need to survive in a constantly evolving environment will drive change. Effective, successful change is deliberately planned using data from accurate, thorough, and timely organizational assessments.

References

1. Cound, D. 1988. "What Corporate Executives Think About Quality." *Quality Progress* (February).

2. Saraph, J. V., and R. J. Sebastian. 1993. "Developing a Quality Culture." *Quality Progress* (September).

3. Morgan, D. M. 1996. *Fat and Mean: The Corporate Squeeze of Working Americans and the Myth of Managerial Downsizing.* New York, N.Y.: Martin Kessler Books/The Free Press.

4. Morgan. *Fat and Mean: The Corporate Squeeze of Working Americans and the Myth of Managerial Downsizing.*

5. Koprowski, G. 1996. *Forbes ASAP.* 7 October.

6. Kanter, R. M. 1983. *The Change Masters.* New York, N.Y.: Simon & Shuster.

7. Taylor, F. W. 1911. *The Principles of Scientific Management*. New York, N.Y.: Harper & Row.

8. Maslow, A. H. 1960. *Motivation and Personality*. New York, N.Y.: McGraw-Hill.

9. Herzberg, F., B. Mausman, and B. Snuderman. 1959. *The Motivation to Work*, 2d ed. New York, N.Y.: John Wiley & Sons.

10. McGregor, D. 1960. *The Human Side of Enterprise*. New York, N.Y.: McGraw-Hill.

11. Silverman, M. 1996. *The Technical Managers Handbook: A Survival Guide*. New York, N.Y.: Chapman & Hall.

12. Ibid.

13. Ibid.

Related References

Brown, G. B., Hitchcock, D. E., and M. L. Willard. 1996. *Rx for Business: a Troubleshooting Guide for Building a High-Performance Organization*. Milwaukee, Wis.: ASQC Quality Press.

Cummings, T. C. 1980. *Systems Theory for Organization Development*. New York, N.Y.: John Wiley & Sons.

Drucker, P. F. 1988 "The Coming of the New Organization. *Harvard Business Review* (January/February).

Howe, R., D. Gaeddert, and M. Howe. 1992. *A Failure to Communicate: Quality on Trial*. New York, N.Y.: West Publishing Co.

Hutton, D. W. 1994. *The Change Agents Handbook: A Survival Guide for Quality Improvement Champions*. Milwaukee, Wis.: ASQC Quality Press.

Juran, J. M., and F. M. Gryna. 1988. *Juran 's Quality Control Handbook* 4th ed. New York, N.Y.: McGraw-Hill.

Kerzner, H. 1995. *Project Management*. New York, N. Y.: Van Nostrand Reinhold.

Kotter, J. P. 1996. *Leading Change*. Boston, Mass.: Harvard Business School Press.

Locke, E. A. 1991. *The Essence of Leadership: The Four Keys to Leading Successfully.* New York, N.Y.: Lexington Books.

Pyzdek, T., and R. W. Berger. 1992. *Quality Engineering Handbook.* New York, N.Y.: Marcel Dekker, and Milwaukee, Wis.: ASQC Quality Press.

Rice, C. M. 1994. "How to Conduct an Internal Audit and Still Have Friends." *Quality Progress* (June).

Russell, J. P. 1995. *Quality Management Benchmark Assessment,* 2d ed. Milwaukee, Wis.: ASQC Quality Press.

Wickman, R. F., and R. S. Doyle. 1993. *Breakthrough Quality Improvement for Leaders Who Want Results,* Milwaukee, Wis.: ASQC Quality Press.

Zaremba, A. J. 1989. *Management in a New Key: Communication in the Modern Organization.* Norcross, Ga.: Institute of Industrial Engineers.

Chapter 3
Quality Needs and Overall Strategic Plans

General

The goal of planning is to make an organization better than its competitors. This could be market competitors, or in the case of a nonprofit, competition for a budget. Planning is also a continuous process since the competitive environment is dynamic. Competitors often copy each other's successes, so new and innovative competitive strategies are needed to achieve or maintain a leading position.

Strategy, mission, vision, and objectives are interrelated, but their development is not a three-step process of mission and vision, strategy, and then objectives. Planning is a difficult and complex task, an iterative process. Competitors are also strategizing, which may very well result in everyone having to change. This is why strategic or tactical planning should not be scheduled as a one-time activity, completed and issued to everyone to follow. The information input into the strategic planning process is largely the result of the insights into the external competitive world, as well as the nature and capability of the organization (particularly its creative capability). The variables involved can change rapidly and in a way that raises questions about previous decisions.

Without effective, continuous planning an organization has no guide to achieving goals and is unprepared for changes in outside factors that can threaten its future. This is particularly true of the present, when operating environments are changing rapidly and unpredictably.

Planning is identified by type and time scale. *Strategic* is planning for the future and is usually based on a three- to five-year projection. *Tactical* planning is short term, usually a year. It commonly coincides with the financial or budget year, but it should be flexible. Rapid changes in tactics may become necessary to meet a new challenge.

The two types of planning are used by the overall organization as well as the internal functional units (marketing, quality, facilities). Planning is the road map of how an organization is going to continue to operate and grow. The following lists some general reasons why planning is required.

- Change in the scope and type of competition
- Increase in deregulation, privatization, and changing markets
- Changing customer expectations toward higher quality
- Globalization of economic and financial factors
- Changes in world government policies and trade agreements
- Rapid change in technology and information systems
- Change in workplace skills
- Widespread downsizing in all types of organizations
- The mobility of work and jobs

In light of the dynamic nature of all these factors, upper management must frequently ask

- What business are we in/want to be in, in the next 5 to 10 years? What plans do we need?
- What do we do in response to the answers to those questions?
- How is the market changing? How will that affect us? How do we prepare for it? How do we organize for it? How do we lead the organization toward the new objectives?
- What are the organization's strengths and weaknesses?
- What will the opportunities be, and what will the threats be?
- Who and what will the competition be?
- What are the probable timing factors?

Strategic Planning. According to Mintzberg,[1] a strategy is the embodiment of an organization's vision. For example, a vision statement could be, "to become a leader in the field of health care delivery." This reflects the strategy of the organization management, from which it will devise the actions to achieve it. Some of the elements of these strategic actions may include becoming a systems thinking organization or a learning organization, or developing a management methodology using self-directed process improvement teams.

Strategic planning is the tool to manage the achievement of strategies. It is not the strategy itself. It should be integrated with internal goal setting. In autocratic organizations, planning is done by upper management and dictated to the lower levels. TQ organizations operate to encourage individual and team ideas. Planning activities involve the solicitation and discussion of the strategic and other quality objectives submitted by every level. Each level of the organization is expected to meet its goals. An open management style will allow members to contribute. This kind of activity is rare in autocratic organizations because upper management doesn't think in terms of employee participation but rather that planning and goal setting is management's job.

A part of the ongoing strategic planning process is to fully define whether previous plans were met and, if not, why not. In a TQ organization this is not to assess blame but to learn whether the planning process is flawed and needs improvement, whether objectives were unrealistic, or if any organization weaknesses were a factor. One way to evaluate the planning process is to benchmark the processes of other similar and successful organizations. The strategic and other internal quality planning processes are the foundation of a successful TQ organization. Strategic planning, development, and deployment is a category item in the Baldrige Award criteria. These processes lead to the development of an organization that can handle change.

One of the critical issues in strategic planning is the subject of quality. What will be its role in being competitive and satisfying future customers? What must be done internally to ensure that quality goals are met? An approach to answer these questions is described in the next section.

3.A. Linkage Between Quality Function Needs and Overall Strategic Planning

The overall strategic plan identifies future changes in technology, products, services, processes, quality goals, skill requirements, finances, and how the organization will respond. All the internal functional organizations must identify their needs to meet those changes. There must be a free flow of information and discussion between functions to ensure that all facets of the needs are explored.

The linkage between quality function needs and the strategic plan is that the quality function (all organization elements) must evaluate the strategic plan and assess the impact of change on the following, and develop the necessary plans to respond.

1. Market

   • What new markets will be entered?

   • What new regulations or quality standards will apply?

   • What new language skills will be needed?

   • What will customer needs be?

   • What is the competition doing?

2. Product or service

   • What modifications will be made to existing products or services?

   • What new products are expected?

   • What new materials will be used?

   • What design standards will apply?

   • What reliability levels will be required?

   • How will quality proofing be managed?

3. Processes

   • How will present processes change?

   • What new processes will be needed?

   • What new process equipment will be needed?

   • How will new processes be evaluated and controlled?

   • Will tolerance requirements change?

- What new inspection and testing equipment will be needed?
- Will new calibration standards be needed?
- What new skills will be required? How will they be obtained?
- What will the training requirements be?
- What new standards or regulations must be introduced?
- Will there be installation and customer use testing?

4. Packaging and transportation
   - What will new climactic limits be?
   - How will new packaging be evaluated? New test equipment?

5. Suppliers
   - What new suppliers or subcontractors will be needed? What new specialties?
   - Where in the world will they be located?
   - How will suppliers be managed for quality?

6. Administration
   - How will changes impact organization structure, size, and location?
   - What will information systems requirements be?
   - What language skills will be needed?
   - Will present quality policies satisfy future customers?
   - What will total facilities requirements be?
   - What will the investment needs be?

The needs identified from this comprehensive evaluation, with the improvements driven by the strategic plan, are the quality plans for the overall quality function.

3.B. Linkage Between Strategic Plan and Quality Plan

The objective in linking quality planning with the total strategic plan is to fully integrate quality and operational planning with the business plan (the business plan is how to meet all objectives). The primary objective of the quality plan is to meet the needs of the customer. The overall organization quality plan is usually prepared annually, after the strategic plan. It may contain one-, three- or five-year steps, reflecting the overall strategic plan structure. This quality plan includes what each organization element does to meet the immediate and long-term quality objectives.

Quality Objectives

In a total quality organization, quality objectives could include such goals as

- Reduce process variation by 5 percent and cycle time by 20 percent. (Key processes would be identified as well as the metric.)

- Benchmark three (named) processes for breakthrough improvement.

- Reduce new product development-to-market time by 10 percent per year. (This could also be a strategic plan item.)

- Introduce quality function deployment planning on one new product or service this year.

Satisfying quality objectives of this nature will reduce variation and, thereby, cost and cycle time and provide better products and services to customers.

The Quality Functional Organization Needs

With respect to the overall strategic planning, quality functional organization needs are a result of an analysis similar to that required of every organization element, as described in the previous paragraphs. The needs are dependent on the targeted quality organization's type, size, structure, assigned responsibilities, types of processes, and specializations.

Planning. The quality organization needs are identified during the overall organization planning process. The quality manager or specialist is normally a part of the strategic planning activity, providing input information such as the state of key business processes (determined by audits), quality organization skills, product or service quality levels, and customer complaint levels and trends.

As a participant in the overall planning activity the quality manager must know what the overall strategic plans are to be able to evaluate their impact on the quality organization. For example, if the enterprise is going to launch or expand a continuous quality improvement program the quality manager should be able to provide guidance to upper management on such things as

- Requirements for success and likely problems
- Type and amount of training needed
- Effort required for team operation
- Probable time scale
- New skills needed
- New requirements for supplier management
- Role of the quality organization

If the strategic plan is to apply for a Baldrige Award, the quality manager should be able to apprise management of the elements in the award criteria and in the role and impact on the overall organization and quality organizations. If the plan is to become certified to ISO 9000, the quality manager will need to plan what the system requirements are and the steps to achieve them.

Organizing for Quality

A common and successful approach to quality planning is to establish a quality council or quality steering committee. This is a top-level group, with representatives from every functional organization. Occasionally key suppliers or customers are invited to participate.

The function of the council is to plan the activities and establish responsibilities required to satisfy the strategic quality objectives of the overall organization and the quality plans for each functional organization. (Establishing quality policies is a requirement of ISO-9000 certification.) It deploys the quality policies and objectives down through the organization.

The council uses a tracking and reporting system to monitor progress. Another common function of the council is to issue or update a quality policy for the enterprise. The policy typically states the enterprise's intent toward quality. Sometimes this policy is called, or is part of, the mission statement. It may identify the important objectives of the enterprise as such, wanting to have product or service leadership or establishing a continuous process improvement approach in operations. It may also include a policy of establishing top-level quality audits.

The Planning Process

Beginning with organization objectives, a quality plan must include all the necessary operational details as to what the different functions do, how joint functions are conducted, the kinds of resources required, and the time sequence for achievement.

Preparing the quality plan should be conducted using the appropriate quality tools and techniques since they are the most effective and efficient way to manage any group requiring

- Situation and system analysis. Applicable tools are flowcharts, Pareto analysis, fishbone diagrams, trend analysis, and quality function deployment.

- Solutions. Flowcharts, Pareto analysis, fishbone diagrams, run charts, design of experiments, benchmarking

Therefore, effective quality planning is based on progressively using the results of analysis techniques to answer the following questions[2] (these questions also fit well in the preparation of the production section in QFD).

1. What specific quality work needs to be done?

2. When, during the product-development, production, and service cycle, does each work activity need to be done?

3. How is it to be done? By what method, procedure, or device?

4. Who does it? What position in what organizational component?

5. Where is it to be done? At what location in the office, plant, on the assembly line, in the laboratory, by the supplier, or in the field?

6. What tools or equipment are to be used?

7. What are the inputs to the work? What is needed in the way of information and material inputs to get the work accomplished?

8. What are the outputs? Do any decisions have to be made? What are they, and what criteria should be used for making them?

9. Is any record of the action to be made? If so, what is the form of the data? What kind of analysis is required? To whom is it sent? What form of feedback is to be used?

10. Are there alternative courses of action to be taken, depending on certain differences in the quality encountered?

The final output of the planning process is a set of detailed instructions necessary for all organizations of the quality function to carry out the prescribed action plan to meet the objectives of the strategic plan and satisfy established quality policies.

3.C. Quality Function Mission

In a TQ organization, the quality function is the activity of all organization elements in meeting planned quality objectives to produce products and services that satisfy customer needs and expectations.

Organization elements have their assigned responsibilities for their specialized and normal activities but are also assigned their share of the quality function. This is somewhat analogous to their responsibility for fulfilling other organizationwide objectives, like finance and human resources.

Top-level leadership is necessary to develop and manage the quality mission. This is frequently provided using some form of management group, such as a quality council.

Quality Council

The organization designated as quality control or quality assurance and upper management serve an oversight and leadership function, respectively. The functional quality organization operates to ensure that the other specialized organizations fulfill their obligation to meet quality objectives and customer requirements, measure and report quality status, maintain standards, and measure customer satisfaction. The scope of the quality organization's responsibilities varies widely with different kinds of companies and agencies.

For an enterprise with a specialized quality organization it is useful to have a mission statement to describe to everyone what its purpose and objectives are. Such a statement gives the quality organization legitimacy and authority to do its job. This requires crossing all organization boundaries to gather (quality audit) and analyze data from all the important organization systems and to conduct any product or service evaluation and publish the results.

The mission statement can vary widely from platitudes to specific responsibilities for the quality organization. The statement should be forward looking. It should not be mixed with specific objectives, which belong in the quality plan.

The quality organization statement is primarily for the enterprise's internal use, but it should be made available to outside reviewing agencies. The statement should identify the role the quality organization plays in achieving strategic goals as well as its participation in meeting the tactical quality plan. It is useful to also note the principal quality functions it performs.

The mission of all organizations, to satisfy their quality improvement responsibilities, is related to the fact that the collective efforts of all organization elements produce customer satisfaction. One well-known methodology is the Juran Trilogy.[3]

The Quality Trilogy

Managing for quality is done by using the common managerial processes of *planning, control,* and *improvement.*

Planning. This is the activity of developing the products and processes to meet customer needs. It includes identifying and describing the following:

- The customers

- Customer needs

- Product or service features to satisfy customers

- The processes, in detail, to produce those features consistently

- The performance of the processes as affected by planning

- The status of completion of the outstanding quality plans

- The demonstrated capability of the organization in the quality function

- The improvements suggested by improvement teams

- Upper management selection of the overall quality objectives

- The resources required to meet objectives
- The internal organization's plans to meet overall objectives
- The related plans to be used by the process operators

Control. This is the activity used to collect, evaluate, and report on actual performance.

- Evaluate ongoing operating process performance.
- Compare actual performance to goals.
- Ensure action to eliminate differences.

Improvement. One theme and strategy of modern management is continuous process improvement. It applies to every process that might affect the product or service received by the customer. It involves the concept of measurable objectives and the use of feedback loops.

Improvements are then tracked against the objectives in the strategic quality plan. Typical process improvement teams will provide a steady stream of incremental improvements. This will not usually provide products and services that will result in the organization becoming a leader in its field. Imagination and innovation are required to provide breakthrough improvements—improvements in leaps, on top of incremental improvement. This will result in a market leadership.

The following is the basic Juran Trilogy sequence for achieving a breakthrough rather than incremental improvement.

- Proof of need. Loss of market share, lower costs, shorter cycle time, competitive advantage.
- Project identification. An important problem selected for solution. An important process needing significant improvement.
- Organization to guide projects. Multifunction innovative project team (see Chapter 2F).
- Organization for diagnosis. Make project team responsible for diagnosis.
- Diagnosis. Identify and analyze symptoms and causes.
- Development of remedies. Choose a remedy for dominant causes and recommend corrective action.

- Proof of the remedies. Prove remedy effectiveness under operating conditions.

- Dealing with cultural resistance. Evaluate social impact of change. Determine how change will be introduced.

- Control at new level. Make gains permanent as the basis for next improvement, breakthrough or incremental.

- Use benchmarking to find stretch goals.

3.D. Priority of Quality Function Within the Organization

Factors in the business world today, such as global competition, mergers, technological change and obsolescence, unexpected competition, world government regulatory requirements, and the growth in information availability, are well known. They are the cause of turmoil in organizations and their employees. This trend is expected to continue. The result is radical change in the way business and other agencies operate.

One of the most common responses is to give priority to customer satisfaction by continually delivering a higher quality product or service. It is one of the most significant changes in management practice since Taylor's division of labor principles in the early part of this century, which led to so-called scientific management. It is a change from a primary emphasis on costs and functional management to process management (improvement). The quality function within the organization plays a major role. In the 1990s it is evolving into a different activity in industrial organizations and being established in some form in many service organizations. Quality is being given priority because higher quality is a competitive imperative and it takes the efforts of an entire organization to achieve it.

Quality Organization Functions

The most common activities of a traditional (pre-TQ) industrial quality function are

Quality Control. The activities required to ensure that product design requirements are met at manufacturing time (inspection).

Quality Assurance (QA). The systematic actions required to provide confidence that the requirements of the quality function are being fulfilled in the overall organization. Quality goals, objectives, and requirements are set by elements of the total organization. The QA function acts to ensure that the proper activities are instituted to result in meeting objectives, goals, and requirements, and to measure their performance (prevention).

Inspection. The activity of physically inspecting the products, drawings, and so on, to determine their conformance to requirements.

Quality Engineering. The quality system planning activity. Also, the activity performing process measurement and evaluation, as well as management of the corrective action system.

Quality Audit. An organizationwide evaluation of all organization elements' conformance to quality policies, procedures, and requirements.

Supplier Quality Management. Establishing supplier quality requirements, approving supplier quality capability, evaluating delivered supplies or services, and, when it exists, managing the supplier quality certification program.

Metrology. Maintains measurement standards and manages the measuring instrument calibration and repair system. It also evaluates new product or technical measurement requirements.

Reliability. A function to determine the probability that a product will perform its intended function for a specified time interval under stated conditions. Most frequently this function is in the design engineering organization and is called *reliability engineering.* The responsibilities may also be split, with reliability engineering supplying designers with special design data, and reliability assurance providing activities that ensure, through product test and evaluation and failure analysis, that the reliability levels predicted are being achieved. This latter function could be in the quality organization.

As discussed in Chapter 2C, the implementation of TQ has transferred the emphasis and responsibilities for quality conformance from a specialized quality organization to the organizations doing the work. The emphasis is then on preventive methods like process control and capability improvement. The quality organization is then responsible for working with the process improvement teams, with the quality specialist providing them with statistical tools, and conducting product and system quality audits, metrology, and supplier quality management. But even in the last item, procurement is now held responsible for supplier quality performance, and the quality specialist provides special skills as a member of the procurement team.

3.E. Metrics and Goals That Drive Organization Performance

Goals. A quality goal, or objective, is the target on which resources are expended, to be reached by a specified time. Targets are the metrics (measurement) selected to indicate achievement.

Goals can be long term (strategic) or short term (tactical or operating). Goal setting is a part of the planning process. A strategic goal for the overall organization could be, for example, reducing key process variation by 50 percent in five years.

Operating goals would then be established by the responsible organizations by making detailed plans to achieve their part of the strategic goal. A quality council would evaluate the compatibility of the plans.

A primary factor in setting goals is to improve customer satisfaction. Therefore it is of critical importance that quality goals remain in alignment with that ultimate objective, and be deployed from the top down. This will ensure that resources will be expended most effectively. Any organization element's internal goals are only as important as their contribution to the higher goals.

Criteria. Goal-setting criteria should be

Measurable. Objectives which are stated in numbers can be communicated with precision.

Optimal as to overall results. Objectives which "suboptimize" performance of various activities can easily damage overall performance.

All-inclusive. Activities for which objectives have been set tend to have high priority but at the expense of the remaining activities.

Maintainable. Objectives should be designed in modular fashion so that elements can be revised without extensive teardown.

Economics. The value of meeting the objectives should be clearly greater than the cost of setting and administering them.

No less important is the list of criteria as perceived by those who are faced with meeting the objectives. To these operating forces, objectives should be:

Legitimate. Objectives should have undoubted official status.

Understandable. They should be stated in clear, simple language—ideally in the language of those who are faced with meeting the objectives.

Applicable. The objectives should fit the conditions of use or should include the flexibility to adapt to conditions of use.

Worthwhile. Meeting the objective should be regarded as benefiting those who do the added work as well as benefiting the organization which established the objective.

Attainable. It should be possible for "ordinary" people to meet the objectives by applying reasonable effort.

Equitable. Since performance against objectives is frequently used for merit rating of individuals, the objectives should be reasonably alike as to difficulty of attainment.

Goals related to customer satisfaction should be in terms of exceeding the competition in such factors as

- *Reliability.* Having a product work for as long a time as economically attainable.

- *Service.* A no-questions-asked replacement policy. Convenient, rapid service available.

- *Safety.* Products must be safe, not only to satisfy the customer but because of the high cost of liability lawsuits.

- *Style.* The style of the design is a critical factor in many products. It is the emotional quality factor that can be the reason for a customer selection.

As an example of a goal, the Institute of Electrical and Electronics Engineers' *Spectrum* magazine, October 1995, reported a landmark agreement between Boeing and a major customer, United Airlines, for the purchase of the Boeing 777 airplane, prior to its design. At the time it was the largest and most advanced commercial two-engine jet ever produced. The agreement was not a stack of specifications but a note simply stating that from day one, the plane would have

- The best dispatch reliability in the industry.
- The greatest customer appeal in the industry.
- Be user friendly with everything working.

The Boeing approach was to launch an airplane, on time, that would exceed the expectations of flight crews, cabin crews, maintenance and support teams, and, ultimately the passengers and shippers. Boeing has met those objectives. (At the time, the program was also the biggest successful demonstration of computer-aided design and concurrent engineering.)

Goal Setting. Quality goal setting should be based on what management believes is necessary to improve and grow. Employees, managers, and teams are motivated by goals that are clearly important and in which they can identify their role in achieving. Periodic status reporting, up and down the organization, is necessary to maintain motivation as well as to keep activities on track.

Goal Basis. Goals have often been based on historical performance. Marketing made the sales forecast, engineering and manufacturing equated it into effort, and budgets were set. Any improvement objective was supplementary. A number was selected based on what organization managers thought could be done. Very often the number was negotiated with higher management. There wasn't a clear picture of how it would be accomplished. The concept of work processes or the tools for improving variation were unknown or only vaguely recognized. The term *process* was pretty much assigned to how manufacturing made things.

Modern improvement goals are based on what is required to satisfy the customer and become more productive and competitive. In a TQ organization, where process status and capabilities are known, goals can be set more rationally and realistically.

Goal Types. The two general types of goals are incremental and breakthrough. Both are necessary to maximize improvement.

Incremental refers to the small continuous process improvements contributed mostly by team actions. Breakthrough goals are set to provide a significant process improvement, beyond what the incremental trend would indicate. They both can be achieved by methodology or equipment changes and the reduction of common causes of variation (see Figure 3.1). Breakthrough goals are large increases in performance in a short period of time.

Goals resulting from benchmarking can be among the most significant, challenging, and breakthrough. These stretch goals are more acceptable to organization members' when management establishes them because someone else has demonstrated that they can be achieved. This overcomes any attitude that they are too tough. Benchmarking is discussed further in Chapter 8.

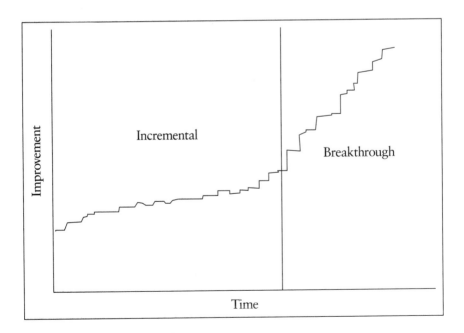

Figure 3.1. Relationship between incremental and breakthrough goals.

Metric (Measurement). Process measurement is necessary to know how a process is performing—how far it is from the improvement goal—and to indicate status as improvements are made. The primary purpose of measurement is to support continuous process improvement.

Metric Fundamentals. The system or process to be measured must be completely defined, and the boundaries of the measurement must be established. Measurement is not an end in itself. Selected measures should only be those vital factors related to performance. Vital factors are those that affect the goal of satisfying the customers and providing comparison to competitors. Internal and external goals should include customer input. Examples of vital measures and metrics are

- Cycle time (see Chapter 1)
- Process variation: errors per unit, process, supplier
- Value added (nonvalue-added reduction)
- Cost: per task, unit, hour, rework
- On-time: tasks or items

The idea of critical or vital measurement points is illustrated in Figure 3.2.

Other temporary measurements can be devised and tracked by process improvement teams to evaluate the effect of their incremental changes.

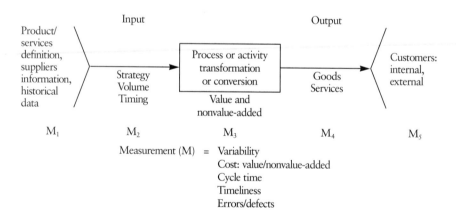

Figure 3.2. Process quality measurement points.

Frequently, measurements with great accuracy are difficult and expensive to obtain. In such cases, good estimates, established by consensus, may be all that is necessary since the most common application of process measurement is for comparison from baseline to when improvements are made. The information system should be designed to collect and report the quality function metrics.

3.F. Formulation of Quality Principles and Policies

Quality policies are the strategic direction to the organization on quality matters.

- They set the course of action for the overall organization.
- They represent a statement as to what the overall organization stands for, its principles, and what it wants to be to insiders and outsiders.
- They are the foundation for the formulation of objectives at all levels.
- They can identify the quality leadership the organization wants to take.
- They are as important as other organization factors.
- They are the basis for all quality procedures.
- They must go beyond platitudes and generalities to the important specifics.
- They should be widely circulated internally and to customers.

Formulation. Quality policies vary with the size and nature of the organization, but there is a basic commonality. Frequently included subjects are

- The importance of quality to the organization.
- Quality with respect to completion.
- Customer satisfaction, internal and external.
- Employee involvement/empowerment.
- Continuous improvement.
- Policy toward suppliers: Partnerships, fairness.

- Guarantees: Types.

- Audits: Types, scope.

Large organizations, business or other, usually have subdivisions. Each should have its own published policies tied to the higher-level policies but tailored to its own activities and customers. They would tend to be more detailed. For example,

- They may set a policy for process improvement teams.

- They may identify the independence of the special quality assurance organization.

- They may require quality function planning annually.

- They may require that system quality audits be conducted.

- They may state that adequate training will be furnished.

- They may specify what regulatory requirements will be met.

Policy Content. The quality policies should address the following:

- Definition of quality. This should be stated in terms of quality parameters such as safety, performance, reliability, and conformance.

- Linkage to business goals and the strategic goals of the overall organization.

- Nonquantified goals such as described previously.

- Commitment to employee involvement in customer satisfaction through continuous improvement.

- Management commitment and leadership in meeting goals.

3.G. Resource Requirements to Manage the Quality Function

Managing any function, whether pre- or post-TQ, requires resources: money, labor, equipment, and facilities to successfully satisfy policies, strategies, and planning objectives. Resources for the quality function are the differently skilled employees, measurement and test equipment, laboratories and offices, and operating budgets needed to meet the objectives of the quality function.

These resources are dependent on the type or status of the quality organization.

- *Pre-TQ.* Still doing inspection and repair. A special quality organization exists for all the quality tasks.

- *Post-TQ.* Overall organization quality function. A quality organization exists to perform special quality tasks.

Pre-TQ

Large industrial organizations have had the most comprehensive quality organizations. Their scope was discussed in Section D of this chapter. In these organizations, staffing requirements are the biggest quality budget item.

Staffing. In pre-TQ, typically, inspectors are a part of the quality organization, assigned to inspect purchased material and in-house production. When product testing is required, the same policy applies, although sometimes quality just verifies that production performed the test. Sometimes inspection costs are carried in overhead, sometimes in direct product costs.

The size of the inspection staff varies with the nature of the product and process. It can also be affected by the requirements of outside regulating agencies or customers. Measurement and testing equipment used and calibrated by inspection personnel also adds to staffing and skill requirements.

Quality engineering or quality assurance staffing also varies with the nature of the work. It is most concerned with the following:

- Quality systems
- Audits
- Process evaluation and control
- Corrective action
- Supplier evaluation and oversight
- Inspection procedures
- Design drawing reviews

The qualifications for these personnel should be at least equal to those for the ASQC Certified Quality Engineer or Certified Quality Auditor.

Technicians. There are many different technician skills in quality organizations They should have education credentials in their technical specialty and ASQC Quality Technician certification.

Management. Managers in the quality organization should be knowledgeable of the work in the area of assignment and basic management principles, as well as a thorough understanding of quality systems and quality statistical fundamentals. The quality manager and key professional direct reports should fully understand the subject matter in the body of knowledge for the ASQC Certified Quality Manager. Quality staffing issues are discussed further in Chapter 6B.

Training. Training programs should be adequately planned and budgeted. The plan should identify who should be trained, the subject, schedule, instructor, and cost. ISO 9001 requires that personnel training records be maintained. The Baldrige Award also evaluates the extent and effectiveness of personnel training and development.

Some training should be conducted for the users of quality procedures and work instructions. Specialized training and certification may be required in some industries, such as that given for inspection using nondestructive test techniques by the American Society for Nondestructive Testing (ASNT). The categories include magnetic particle, liquid penetrant, radiography, eddy current, ultrasonic, leak testing, neutron radiography, acoustic emission, thermal infrared, and vision testing.

Certification by the American Society of Mechanical Engineers (ASME) is required for welders in the production of pressure vessels. Certification of weld inspectors is often required for compliance to weld design criteria of the American Welding Society (AWS), a recognized standard of international reciprocity agreements. (Training issues are discussed further in Chapter 7.)

Reliability. Those industries involved in product reliability studies and testing should have reliability engineers with the appropriate technical education and the ASQC Reliability Engineer certification.

Post-TQ

The functions and responsibilities of most quality organizations change when the TQ concept is adopted. In the TQ approach, primary responsibility for quality and process improvement is placed with the organizations doing the work. Those responsibilities also extend to all organizations and all processes.

In this context, a specialized quality organization is reduced in size and scope. In a fully functioning TQ industrial form it is responsible for quality systems and product audits, metrology, some sampling inspection of purchased material, supplier quality management, support to process improvement teams, statistical consultation, and team membership in concurrent engineering projects.

Outside Resources. Many organizations are depending on buying special quality skills and services on an as-needed basis rather than retaining their own staff. This also corresponds to a trend to outsource special organization needs. Some common outsourcing is for

- Quality training and education
- Quality system audits
- Statistical expertise
- Testing laboratories
- Metrology
- Off-site inspection (at suppliers)

Key Ideas—Chapter 3

1. Mission and vision will determine the goals. Strategic planning is the road map to achieving the goals.

2. A critical and often forgotten factor in effective strategic planning is evaluating the success or failure of past plans and how to improve the accuracy of the planning process itself.

3. The overall strategic plan will define the needs of the support functions. These support functions will, in turn, create strategic plans based on the core plan.

4. Planning, control, improvement (the Juran Quality Trilogy) all involve the use of metrics in recognizing and achieving goals. Goals may be incremental or breakthrough.

References

1. Mintzberg, H. I 994. *The Rise and Fall of Strategic Planning.* Upper Saddle River, N.J.: Prentice Hall.

2. Feigenbaum, A. V. 1989. *Total Quality Control.* New York, N.Y.: McGraw-Hill. Reproduced with permission of The McGraw-Hill Companies.

3. Juran, J. M., and F. M. Gryna. 1988. *Juran's Quality Control Handbook,* 4th ed. New York, N.Y.: McGraw-Hill. Reproduced with permission of The McGraw-Hill Companies.

Related References

Hart, C. W. L. 1993. *Extraordinary Guarantees.* New York, N.Y.: AMA-COM.

Morgan, M. W. 1996. Measuring Performance With Customer-Defined Metrics." *Quality Progress* (December).

Sheridan, B. M. 1993. *Policy Deployment: The TQM Approach to Long-Range Planning.* Milwaukee, Wis.: ASQC Quality Press.

Struebing, L. 1996. "Measuring for Excellence." *Quality Progress* (December).

Chapter 4
Customer Satisfaction and Focus

The most significant change in managing quality in recent years is the focus on customer satisfaction as the prime organization objective. Satisfying customer needs and expectations has become the driving force for quality improvement. It is interesting to note that customer satisfaction and focus is given major weight in the Baldrige Award evaluation. It is the highest priority of quality management.

Shifting the focus of the typical organization, away from satisfying self-interests to a dedication to the needs and expectations of the customer (internal and external), requires an understanding of what is involved. This chapter discusses important factors of management leadership required to become customer focused.

Whiteley[1] identifies several fundamental requirements that are quite often not found in business today but can develop an organization into a highly motivated competitor. The requirements to be embraced are summarized as follows:

- Create a *customer-retention* vision within everyone in the organization.

- Include *the voice of the customer* in every organization decision. Become close and communicative with the customers.

- Study, adopt, and/or adapt the methods of leaders from every kind of organization in products or services. Benchmark the winning organizations.

- Make your employees believe that the customer is their number one job. Managers must demonstrate this in all their activities and lead by example.

- Break down barriers between and within organizations that inhibit serving the customer. This should happen through the adoption of the policies and proper application of the continuous process improvement methodologies.

- Develop and use performance and effectiveness measures. They must be tied to customer satisfaction measurements. Other organizations can be benchmarked to identify useful measures.

4.A Types of Customers (Internal, External, Intermediate, End-User)

In its most general usage, the term *customer* is anyone who buys a product or service. It is a reference used mostly in business; professional service sellers commonly use the term *client* or *subscriber.* In TQ usage all of these are external customers, and TQ also adds the concept of internal customers. In relation to actual business market structure it is useful to add another category, the intermediate customer.

- *Internal customers* are the people, or processes, in an organization who receive work from another person or process, work on it, and deliver it to the next step, either another internal or external customer. For example, an internal customer could be manufacturing, which receives the output of the engineering process: the product design package. Another example is a patient care process that receives the output of a blood test evaluation process.

- Businesses often have a customer between them and the ultimate end user. This is their *intermediate customer,* such as a distributor. The intermediate customer is actually a forward extension of the producer's processes, a stop on the way to the end user.

- The third type of customer is the *end-user.* This is the one that receives and uses the final product or service. This is the appropriate focus of customer satisfaction for continued success.

This concept of internal and external customers creates a more holistic view of the process within a traditional or functional organization. It assists change because priorities have changed, and the view of improvements is less territorial or divisive.

4.B. Elements of Customer-Driven Organizations

The External Customer

Organizations with a strong commitment and dedication to customer satisfaction exhibit some distinctive characteristics in the way they are managed and operate that don't exist to the same degree in noncustomer-driven organizations. The key elements usually present are the following:

1. Total customer satisfaction is an all-consuming objective of all members.

2. The relationship between customers and suppliers is based on practices reflecting a partnership. Improvement decisions are made with supplier-customer input.

3. The operating policy and practice is structured for continuous improvement in process and product quality.

4. Comprehensive strategic and tactical planning, containing quality objectives for processes and products, is given equal weight with schedule and profit.

5. Human resource development is ongoing to meet quality objectives.

6. Products and services are competitive.

Whiteley recognizes customer-driven organizations by their

- Reliability—dependably delivering what was promised.

- Assurance—the employees' ability to convey trust and confidence.

- Tangibles—attention to detail and appearance of the facilities, equipment, and personnel.

- Empathy—the interest in and attention provided to customers.

- Responsiveness—willing and attentive service to customers (a sense of urgency).

Management Factors

In further detail, the continuous activities in managing a customer in a market-driven organization are

1. Internal support—Organization development, to develop the right structure, management, and employee skills for growth and marketplace changes.

2. Use of knowledge—Application of market research and analysis tools. Getting customer feedback and assessing changing customer expectations and needs.

3. Use of metrics—Establishment of market-based process performance measures that result in improvements that are tied to the customer rather than the interests of an internal function.

4. Communications—Publication and reporting within the organization of progress toward meeting customer needs.

The Internal Customer

The dedication to satisfying the external customer is enhanced by maintaining a similar internal focus; that is, by using the internal supplier-customer relationship. If external customer needs and requirements are reflected in strategic and tactical quality planning, and planning objectives are deployed throughout the organization and translated into related process improvement objectives, they will be become the needs of the internal process customers. Internal improvements will then be connected to the external customer. The entire organization will then be customer driven.

4.C. Customer Expectations, Priorities, Needs, and Voice

Determining customer expectations, needs, and priorities is a demanding and never-ending task. It is not a single objective but a moving target; expectations and needs are never fully satisfied. Expectations measured at one point in time, when satisfied, become the new standard taken for granted. The customer then develops new expectations. But anticipating and satisfying them is critical to remaining competitive.

Expectations, priorities, and needs are also interrelated. This complicates the job. For example, people buying a car now expect, need, and give a high priority to reliability and style, within various price ranges. An expectation met creates a new norm and further demand, and the benchmark continues to rise. Reliability has improved dramatically in recent years. According to the J.D. Power quality survey of new car owners, there is still a gap between Japanese and American cars. The Japanese have steadily improved. The United States has not caught up, but is progressing.

A manufacturer, before committing any model to production, must decide (years ahead) what combination of attributes the buyers of the future will prefer. It's a very difficult and risky task. There are many variables to satisfy, not the least of which is assessing future competition and trends. A few years ago Chrysler started a new trend when it marketed the minivan. Other manufacturers scrambled to enter that market. Chrysler had anticipated and defined a need and market and held a competitive advantage for several years As markets become more global, customer needs, expectations, and priorities become even more complex to identify and satisfy. For example, the Ford Taurus was not well accepted in Europe but was subsequently a big success in the United States.

To complicate matters further, buyers often don't have a clear idea of what their expectations are, combining needs and expectations in their thinking. A business must continually search for customer information that will provide a basis for making decisions. That is the function of market research.

The needs of business customers are usually more definitive, but there is still a need to communicate with them regularly. Their needs and expectations can change or be changed by a competitor. Suppliers using continuous process improvement, and all that it entails, should be able to keep customers satisfied by raising quality and lowering cycle time.

Being driven to satisfy internal customers, knowing their expectations, needs, and priorities, is key to satisfying external customers. It hasn't been common practice to sit down with internal customers, the receivers of work or process output, and determine exactly what they expect and need, in what form and in what order. When satisfying the internal customer becomes an organization practice, there is a chain reaction in overall organization effectiveness, out to the external customer. It becomes a way of thinking and acting.

Basic Approach

A growth company needs an organized way to challenge its thinking. It can begin by answering these five questions.

1. What are the customer needs and expectations, and which matter most to them?

2. How well are we meeting those needs and expectations?

3. For external customers, how well are our competitors meeting them? What are they doing?

4. How can we go beyond the minimum and truly delight them?

5. For internal customers, do we routinely determine and satisfy their needs and expectations?

Methodologies

An approach to defining customer needs and expectations is to focus on answering these questions.

1. Do we have a practice of doing effective market analysis: what's new, who is buying what, where, at what price?

2. Do we get data from customers and others, analyze them, and act on results?

3. Do we do an analysis of competitors' products, services, and practices?

4. Do we benchmark our processes to find the best?

The voice of the customer is a term used to identify the existence of customer requirements as the main objective of all processes. If this voice is lost (if requirements are changed or diluted), customer and market needs will less likely be met. A powerful tool used to keep the voice of the customer in the process, from initial to final organization activity (delivery), is quality function deployment (QFD). It is a planning tool that begins with a complete identification of customer requirements and translates those requirements, throughout the work processes, into the basis for each process design. QFD is finding application in all types of organizations and activities. It is discussed in more detail in Chapter 5A as one of the quality management tools.

4.D. Customer Relationship Management and Commitment (Complaints, Feedback, Guarantees, Corrective Action)

Satisfactory customer relationships require management and the commitment of the entire work force. An examination of the practices of leading companies of all kinds will indicate this focus on customer relationships. The Baldrige Award gives this activity a significant weight.

Key factors in managing customer relations are the use of effective systems to gather information, take corrective action, and adequately train the employees who deal with any facet of customer relations. The subjects in this section were partially discussed in Chapter 1, Customer Service, as the topics overlap. Many of these concepts also apply to both external and internal customers. It is intuitively obvious that organization success rests on satisfying customers. The question TQ raises is how far to go and what to do to ensure that success. It goes beyond just delivering a good product or service.

This section deals with the activities involved in customer relationship management following delivery, the period of customer use. These factors could be classified as both assurance factors and information gathering opportunities. They are used to ensure that the customer is satisfied and, if not, to gather information to take corrective action. The data from these ongoing activities are also a source of information for continuing organization improvements.

Complaints from either an external or internal source should be the hot-button for an organization reaction. Complaints mean a dissatisfied customer. Proactive customer-oriented suppliers solicit feedback. They seek information on any kind of product or service deficiency, as well as customer likes and dislikes as a rich source of ideas for improvement.

Complaint solicitation can take several forms: service or information desks, delivery follow-up with customers, surveys, or sales representative reports. The intelligence from this feedback should be sought aggressively and continuously. In addition to providing useful improvement information it can contain important early warning information about customer concerns and market changes. Analysis of these data and resulting conclusions as well as market sales data can indicate switches by customers to competing products or services. Dissatisfied customers often resort to this because they don't like to complain, they don't think it does any good, or they think a response won't help them in a timely manner. Switching to a competitors' products becomes the path of least resistance.

Success in this aspect of customer interface requires effective solicitation, collection, and analysis followed by corrective action. It takes management leadership to overcome the inertia of organizations that prevents their thinking beyond their own activities.

Achieving the improvements necessary requires education and training in the customer relations process, particularly for those who interface with the customer. Some product suppliers have a practice of visiting the sales sites to assess how their products are marketed and how their customers are treated. They sometimes interview customers immediately after a purchase to determine why they made their choices. An increasing number of organizations are also, after the proper training, empowering employees who interface with the customer to make on-the-spot decisions in a broad range of situations to solve a problem immediately and keep the customer satisfied.

Sales and product return policies play a significant role in customer satisfaction. One major policy change at the retail level in recent years has been the "no questions asked, money back" product return. This has been the policy for high-price, high-quality stores for many years, and its growth in the 1980s is attributed to use by Nordstrom and others. Warranties and product services are other important elements in customer relations management. The use of warranties or guarantees to satisfy the customer has grown in scope and application to the point where widespread customer expectation is the norm. Guaranteed satisfaction takes its most common form in the no-questions-asked policy, but there are variations, such as free years of repair service. Automakers use various mileage-time service warranties to attract customers.

A relatively new development in guarantees to delight the customer is described in C. W. L. Hart's book, *Extraordinary Guarantees*.[2] This type of guarantee promises uncompromised quality and satisfaction and backs the promise with a payout intended to fully capture the customer's goodwill, with few strings attached. One fundamental difference between this and traditional guarantees is that it forces an organization to deliver excellence and to fight for, win, and retain customer loyalty. Several large companies have introduced this policy with outstanding results, in both external and internal operations. If every supplier pledged to guarantee customer satisfaction, improvements would have to be made. With that pledge in mind, an organization that guaranteed its work would be announcing that it knows what it is doing and that its processes are in control.

4.E. Customer Identification and Segmentation

Customer identification and segmentation are essential in developing a business strategy. Market segmentation is the process of analysis leading to the identification of distinct subgroupings of customers, in terms of how they respond to product offerings and communications. (Two additional interrelated marketing activities are *targeting* and *positioning*. Targeting is the selection of segments for focused marketing effort. Positioning is the process of identifying the important dimensions that customers use to evaluate competitive product offerings and communicating the company's product offerings on those dimensions relative to the competition.)[3]

Most markets have many segments. The analytical process involves segmenting the market into distinct groupings that are different from each other but within which the customers share a large degree of similarity, and then matching needs with products.

One consumer product example of segmentation is athletic shoes, which are mostly purchased for reasons of fashion. They vary widely in shape, sizes, materials, and style. Each is intended for a different market segment, based on price, gender, activity, and so on. The objective is to match customer needs and wants to each product. This analysis is classified under market research.

Businesses spend large sums on market research, in segmentation, targeting, positioning, market/customer surveys, test marketing, and evaluating the competition. The results are a market database with comprehensive information on such things as profiles of products, customers, potential customers, and competitors' customers, with detailed demographic information on each. The data contain such information as region, occupation, income, age, race, sex, preferences, buying habits, wants, and definition of value.

Industrial marketers typically segment their market demographics in terms of location, size, and industry and use variables related to the nature of the buying process for more detailed segmentation analysis.[4] Consumer marketers tend to use population demographics and psychological factors (psychographics), such as life style, self-concept, and attitudes.

The segmentation process is only complete when observable and measurable customer characteristics can be found that are closely related to the definition of value and buying habits. For example, an analysis may show in an industrial market that the three segments identified have the buying behavior shown in Table 4.1.[5]

Quality Aspects of Segmentation

In the business-to-business market, customer requirements include such variables as

- Effective process control

- A continuous improvement policy

- Certification to the appropriate ISO standards

Table 4.1. The segmentation process for industrial products.

Technology sensitive	Technology-sensitive demographics	Technology-sensitive buying behavior
Price sensitive Want lowest price	Large companies Steel, brick, and glass industries	Use closed bidding Purchasing managers dominate process Very knowledgeable abut market prices
Service sensitive Easy ordering, quick delivery	Small- to medium-size companies Nonurban areas Service companies	Marketing and operations managers heavily involved Buy on annual purchase contract, negotiate price
Technology sensitive Want latest	Large- to medium-size manufacturing companies High-tech industries Small start-ups	R&D and operations managers most involved, along with purchasing Negotiate cost-plus contracts

In the consumer market, with products and services becoming more and more alike, dependable service and high quality have become more important to differentiate brand names. These factors have become a customer expectation.

4.F. Partnerships and Alliances Between Customers and Suppliers

External Partnerships

In the traditional (non-TQ) relationship between corporate customers and suppliers the customer has dominated the relationship. The buyer selected a supplier based on its own criteria. If the supplier wanted the order it accepted the buyer's requirements and then tried to meet them. Suppliers were rarely asked for ideas, or how the item might be changed to improve quality or lower the price. Buyers had little loyalty for any one supplier and usually didn't care if an order was profitable to the supplier. The contract was based on the understanding that either party had recourse to the law if terms weren't met.

Quality Improvement Trend

An important element of the TQ movement has been a new approach to supplier-customer relationships. The trend in the 1990s has been for the customer to select a few key suppliers based on their interest and ability to become long-term business partners. The benefit to both can be higher quality, lower costs, and more dependable deliveries. The supplier and customer are bound to each other's future.

As a part of the partnership agreement the supplier must agree to process quality control and continuous improvement. Sometimes the supplier has to dedicate production capacity to the customer. The customer, with a multifunctional buying team, will work with supplier to establish both design and customer quality criteria compatible with the supplier capability, and will often help the supplier establish process controls to improve process capability (in both the technical and general sense). Price is negotiated based on maintaining an economically stable source of supply, recognizing the savings from costs expended to establish new sources. The supplier is treated as an extension of the customer's process. The supplier usually will become quality certified by the customer and ship directly to customer stock without inspection. Note, however, that this kind of partnership arrangement is usually not practicable for purchases of short-run or infrequently purchased material.

Benefits—Buyer Perspective. In a customer-supplier partnership, the buyer gets a more dependable quality supplier, and the long-term costs to both parties will be lower. There is a strong mutual interest in continuing the relationship. Some partnerships also extend into joint planning activities for new product development. In some cases the buyer (customer) gains some access to technical expertise that it doesn't have to develop itself.

Suppliers gain by having a more predictable business future. Smaller suppliers benefit by obtaining the usually greater technical expertise of their larger customers and better information on the world marketplace requirements.

This approach puts greater importance on supplier selection. Some important selection criteria include the following:

1. The supplier must be economically viable.

2. Its strengths and weaknesses must be accurately determined, and needed improvements targeted.

3. It must have appropriate facilities and equipment.

4. It must have related, current experience with similar products and processes.

5. It must have related appropriate work force skills and a willingness to continue training.

6. Its management must be committed to continuous improvement.

7. It must be willing to meet customer (or MBNQA) criteria.

8. It must be willing to develop or share quality history to evaluate trends.

Benefits—Supplier Perspective. The purpose of the marketing research effort is to create and satisfy customers. A strategic resource is the customer base and the related marketing data. Continuing customer relationships have become the preferred way of doing business. Relationship marketing has been most common in business-to-business transactions but is becoming more common in consumer marketing because of the application of information technology, which allows interactive communication and data-based management. Catalog sales and financial service companies are examples.

Strategic Alliances

A strategic alliance is a cooperative effort by two businesses in pursuit of their separate strategic objectives.[6] Alliances have become more common in business-to-business relationships. An alliance involves the commitment and sharing of resources. Sometimes an alliance creates a joint venture, creating a new entity. The alliance also takes the form of a just-in-time (JIT) agreement, usually as a sole source. This effectively makes the supplier a true extension of the buyer's internal processes.

Strategic alliances can be a valuable competitive tool. They have to be carefully negotiated and closley managed by both parties. Complacency could allow the product, price, or delivery to become noncompetitive.

Internal Partnerships

The partnership idea can be used effectively in internal customer-supplier relationships. In this application it is related to the policy of employee participation or empowerment. Just as external business-supplier partnerships provide for the exchange of improvement information and greater loyalty, they can provide the same benefits internally. Partnership will aid in the development of trust between individuals and organizations and lead to improved morale when employees believe that they are working together toward a common goal. One way to begin this internal partnership is to identify and survey the process customers. An example is given in the following section.

4.G. Communication Techniques (Surveys, Focus Groups, Satisfaction/Complaint Cards)

Surveys are the most common method of collecting customer information and ideas useful in making product and service improvements. Survey questionnaire design is critical. The questions must be crafted to give a high probability of reliability and validity with respect to the information sought. These two factors are discussed in Chapter 6E.

The objectives of surveys are to

- Establish/define the actual and perceived quality.
- Disclose competitive information.
- Indicate useful quality measures.
- Uncover information to provide competitive advantage.
- Identify problems or defects requiring improvement or even immediate corrective action.

The effectiveness of surveys varies widely. Some factors influencing results include

- Length and complexity of questionnaire.
- Customers' interest in the subject.
- Poor correlation between question answers and information needed.
- Overlooking some useful information.
- Improperly trained surveyors in face-to-face surveys.

The following are some common information collection methods.

Surveys. Obtaining data from many sources using sampling, direct, or written.

Focus Groups. Small groups of product or service users assembled to address quality issues.

Customer Councils. Groups of people that meet regularly to advise management. This gives management the opportunity to ask questions directly of the customer. Sessions can be videotaped and shown to employee groups to devise ways to improve.

Satisfaction/Complaint Cards. Consumer question cards delivered with the product or service or sent after a short period of consumer use.

Other Data Sources. Obtaining reasons for returns, refunds, or replacements; cause of service calls; employee and management visits to customer or product outlet sites; testing of new products or services by employees; limited test marketing before general release.

Internal quality communications can be improved using the same techniques. For example, the Northrop Grumman Corporation group in Maryland has a defined process for evaluating the internal customer-supplier relationship by survey. Each supplier determines its internal customer requirements, perceptions, and values. The survey is a guide for discussion between the two groups. The resulting information provides ideas for improvement, with an internal customer satisfaction and value index that can be included in quality planning. Figure 4.1 depicts Northrop Grumman's survey process. The program includes training in how to develop and conduct the survey as well as a budget number to which customers charge their time for survey completion and follow-up discussions.

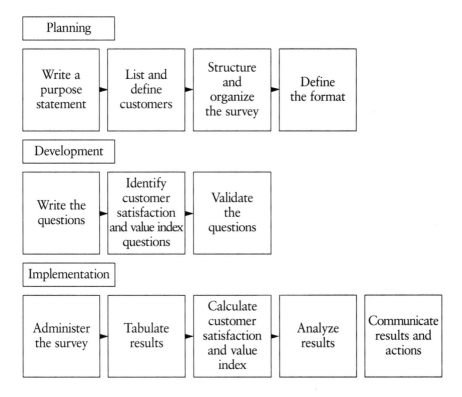

Figure 4.1. Northrop Grumman's internal customer survey process.

4.H. Multiple-Customer Management and Conflict Resolution

Customers define a business by placing a set of demands on it. The company must be careful to select those customers it has the capability of satisfying and serving properly.[7] The company must then be tailored to most efficiently satisfy those customers' requirements. Every organization has limited skills and resources, so they must be carefully committed.

Multiple-Customer Management

Multiple-customer management involves managing the customer base. It starts with market research and the creation of a database that includes the following:

1. Learning who the customers are and categorizing them: most frequent, most profitable, least profitable, infrequent, infrequent but profitable; cost of doing business with each type; infrequent, geographic concentrations; returns and complaint information.

2. Correlation of customers with products and services they use.

3. Defining and examining the processes used to satisfy customer orders, to improve the processes. Usually done by sales volume and product category.

4. Evaluating the risks of dependency on a few large customers, if that situation exists.

5. Identifying the expected trends: customer order size, product or service, distribution methodologies, government regulations, potential customers, profit opportunities, best method of communication.

6. Developing ways to reward the best customers for their loyalty (for example, special warranties).

7. Assuring correlation of results with strategic plans.

Conflicts

When an organization has a strong focus on customer satisfaction, conflict avoidance and resolution are critically important. Disagreements and problems will always occur, but it's how they are handled that counts.

Sources of Customer Conflicts

- Product or service failure
- Failure to meet customer expectations
- Late or damaged deliveries
- Billing errors, late payments
- Customer interface with organization members
- Misunderstandings, mistakes, warranties, guarantees, advertising
- Bad-faith customers
- Legal actions
- News stories
- Product recalls
- Lack of candor on the part of management

Conflict Resolution

Basic to conflict resolution and avoidance of further conflict are organization policies and management commitment to actively avoid or correct every customer conflict. These two factors largely control the effectiveness of correction systems, employee's attitudes, and customer-directed communication systems.

Methodologies

1. An effective, closed-loop reaction system, with responsibilities identified, to handle the communication from customers, representatives, or contact employees related to any customer concern or difference of opinion. A basic precept in a TQ organization is to move decision making down to people in the operating processes, but customer-related issues must be given upper management leadership, with frequent checks to see that the system is effective.

2. An avoidance system based on policies, system design, and training of employees, any intermediate customers, and final customer transaction personnel. This involves attention to all forms of customer communication, ensuring it is unambiguous, accurate, and consistent with policies.

3. Respect for the customer. Enforce the old saying "the customer is always right," except when there is suspicion of illegalities. Even then, management should handle the problem. A business can be damaged by clumsy handling of even illegal customer behavior.

4. Integrity. Make sure that every promise is kept, regardless of who in the organization makes the promise (unless it's an obvious human error or illegal).

5. Offer compensation for mistakes or dissatisfaction.

4.I. Customer Retention and Loyalty

Customer retention is related to market segmentation and targeting. If a poor job is done in the segmentation process there can be mismatches between the organization capabilities and its customer needs and expectations. This can lead to conflict and loss of customers, even good ones, because the organization has misused its limited resources and not adequately satisfied anyone.

Customer loyalty is a valuable strategic resource. The purpose of an effective marketing activity is to create customers, not just make sales. Loyal customers are more valuable than new ones. They provide the opportunity for repeat sales at a lower cost than that required to attract new customers. Automobile leasing is a popular method to create loyal customers who will more likely lease or buy again. A satisfied customer is more likely with leasing because there is a lower probability of problems with cars in their early years.

Customers are best retained when a product or service meets their needs, requirements, and expectations. They also expect a product to operate satisfactorily, and safely, for a reasonable period of time. A major cause for customers to change brands or suppliers, other than price, is poor service.[8] It seems paradoxical that most producers go to great lengths to define and provide warranties but don't back them up with convenient or effective service. It is short-sighted not to implement activities that satisfy customers and contribute to their loyalty because it is usually more costly to obtain new customers than to retain old ones. A weak seller-customer interface is perceived by customers as a lack of interest in them once the sale is made.

Existing customers are also lost through the following:

- Noncompetitive pricing or delivery service
- Failure to resolve customer complaints or answer their questions
- Providing warranties or guarantees with all kinds of exclusions
- Having improperly trained customer interface employees
- Allowing an initially good relationship to fade away because of a lack of follow-up

Key Ideas—Chapter 4

1. A customer can be external or internal. A customer is the next-in-line receiver of a product or service.

2. A customer-driven organization will recognize the importance of intangibles, such as employee knowledge, courtesy, responsiveness, and trust, as well as tangibles, such as cleanliness.

3. Customer expectations and needs are continually evolving, and to stay competitive an organization must continually listen and challenge its previous assumptions.

4. A customer-driven organization realizes that complaints are opportunities. They are a golden chance to learn, grow, improve, and gain crucial market differentiation data. Such an organization will actively solicit and use feedback data from all customers, internal and external, in the drive to continually improve and satisfy its customers.

References

1. Whiteley, R. C. 1991. *The Customer-Driven Company: Moving from Talk to Action.* Reading, Mass.: Addison Wesley.

2. Hart, C. W. L. 1993. *Extraordinary Guarantees: A New Way to Build Quality.* New York, N.Y.: AMACOM.

3. Collins. E. G. C, and M. A. Devarma. 1994. *The Portable MBA.* New York, N.Y.: John Wiley & Sons.

4. Ibid.

5. Ibid.

6. Ibid.

7. Ibid.

8. Markel, A. 1995. "ASQC Customer Survey Results." *Wall Street Journal.* 7 November.

Related References

Brocker, E. J. 1989. "Build a Better Supplier-Customer Relationship." *Quality Progress* (September).

Conway, W. 1994. "Partnership for Quality Improvement." *Quality* (April).

Drew, J. H., and T. R. Fussell. 1996. "Becoming Partners With Internal Customers." *Quality Progress* (October).

Edosomwan, J. A. 1993. *Customer and Market-Driven Quality Management.* Milwaukee, Wis.: ASQC Quality Press.

Erickson, K., and A. Kanagal. 1992. "Partnering for Total Quality." *Quality* (September).

Fredrick and Salter. 1995. "Beyond Customer Satisfaction." *Management Review* (May).

Juran, J. M., and F. M. Gryna. 1988. *Juran's Quality Control Handbook,* 4th ed. New York, N.Y.: McGraw-Hill.

Levitt, T. 1993. "The Globalization of Markets." *Harvard Business Review.*

Reichheld, F. F., and W. E. Sasser. 1990. "Zero Defections: Quality Comes to Services." *Harvard Business Review* (May).

Schruing, E. E., and W. F. Christopher, eds. 1993. *The Service Quality Handbook.* New York: N.Y.: AMACOM.

Tompkins, J. 1995. *The Genesis Enterprise: Creating Peak-to-Peak Performance.* New York, N.Y.: McGraw-Hill.

Van Mieghem, T. 1994. "Implementing Supplier Partnerships." *Quality* (April).

Webster, F. E. 1994. *Market-Driven Management.* New York, N. Y.: John Wiley.

Zemke, R., and K. Anderson. 1991. *Delivering Knock-Your-Socks-Off Service.* New York: N.Y.: AMACOM.

Chapter 5
Continuous Improvement (CI)

5.A. Improvement Tools

Continuous improvement, discussed briefly in Chapter 1, is an objective as well as a policy for the overall organization. The primary focus is inward: improving the processes of an organization. A key factor in operating as a TQ organization is the understanding and use, by all organization members, of the appropriate improvement tools. These tools are primarily used by improvement teams to conduct problem and process analysis leading to problem solutions. CI is not something that can be left to specialists.

Management should fully understand the tools' principles and applications. CI is an important element in modern management theory. These relatively simple tools are fundamental to conducting structured, objective, process improvement activities and also lead to a critical way of thinking about how organizations actually operate. If an organization is to improve, its work processes must improve.

Applications for these tools are included in the references.

5.A.1. Quality Control Tools[1,2]

Team Decision-Making Tools. Teams need methods to identify problems and solutions in an orderly and efficient way as they progress.

Brainstorming—Brainstorming is an organized or formalized method of soliciting the best ideas from team members for making decisions at any stage of operation. Without order and a methodology the best ideas will not always surface or problems will be poorly identified. Before making decisions, such as problem cause or solution, a team should examine all the options. One of the most effective ways to generate ideas or theories is by brainstorming. Properly managed and facilitated, it allows people to be as creative and free-thinking as possible.

The rules for conducting brainstorming sessions are key to its successful use.

1. Encourage everyone's contribution. The objective is to collect all the ideas members can think of. (It takes new teams several sessions before members are comfortable with this approach.) This is the essence of brainstorming.

2. No one is allowed to comment or show any negative reaction during the idea generation period.

3. Build on the ideas of others. This is one of brainstorming's sources of power. Quite often an impractical idea has the seed of a solution or directs thought in a new way that provides the answer. (This is also the reason for rule 2.)

4. Record and post all ideas as they are offered. If some ideas are irrelevant or negative, record them in a separate category to be reviewed later. Do not discard any idea.

5. Have members reduce the total list to one or a few key items and then select other tools to continue the problem-solving process.

There are several variations to this procedure that have been developed. The experience of the facilitator is very important in determining group dynamics and helping select the best way to operate.

Problem or Solution Selection

Multivoting

1. Reduce the initial idea list to the key items and number each. This is done using a series of straw votes.

2. Have each member choose the item number he or she would like to discuss. Limit the team's selection to about a third of the total.

3. Tally and post the results, using a show of hands or a secret ballot.

4. Reduce the list further by dropping items with the fewest votes.

5. Continue to vote and cut, using discussion by the team, until one top-priority item is selected for action.

Crawford slip method[3]—This is a method to gather and condense ideas in a structured but flexible way. Information is gathered anonymously and quickly, without group interaction. It is particularly useful in large groups. Briefly, it involves

1. Writing ideas on slips of paper(one idea per paper).

2. Collecting and sorting ideas into general categories.

3. Looking for patterns and similarities and consolidating ideas into a few main categories. (This is analogous to the affinity diagram, discussed in section 5A2.)

Nominal group technique—This is a structured approach. It involves little (nominal) team interaction in generating a list of ideas or options and then narrowing it down. It's a good technique when handling new teams, controversial subjects, or when a team can't agree. Briefly, it includes the following steps.

1. Propose the task as a question to the group. The question is often proposed to members before the meeting.

2. At the first meeting, discuss the purpose of the subject selected and establish the operating rules to be followed.

3. Post the question and allow discussion only for clarification.

4. Have members, silently, write their ideas or questions on paper. Set a reasonable time limit. Have them prioritize their lists.

5. Have each member, in sequence, read his or her ideas in order of priority. List them on a flip chart. Continue the rotation until everyone has read his or her list (or just the top five ideas from each list). There is no discussion during this exercise.

6. Discuss and clarify ideas. An idea's wording can be changed if the originator agrees.

7. The facilitator or leader condenses the list to a minimum number of items.

8. Use the procedure in step 5 to reduce the list to the main items.

9. Give each member four to six cards. Have everyone write one item per card from the final list.

10. Have members mark each card by rank. If there are six cards per person, the highest rank is 6.

11. Collect cards and tally votes. The item with the most votes is the team selection.

12. If there are two or three items receiving a high number of votes, the group may elect to repeat the voting or investigate all the items.

Delphi method—This is a method of collecting ideas from a group of experts, frequently geographically dispersed, using a leader to prepare questions and collect responses, whether written, by phone, or by fax. It is a way to reach consensus without direct conversation. A common variation is to give the responses of each expert to the next one in line. This is a useful technique to avoid having strong personalities dominate. Except for its methodology, it is similar to other consensus-reaching techniques. It is often used to get a quick overview of the opinions of a group on some subject.

Flowcharts. Flowcharts are a graphic description of the activities in a process. They can vary from elementary, identifying just the order of key process activities, to complex, including information feedback paths and activity performance measures (metrics).

Flowcharts also display the supplier-customer concept of a process. Charting is usually the best first step in the continuous process improvement activity. It frequently makes some improvements obvious. For example, redundancies or nonvalue-added steps are visually identified. Work procedures written based on current process flowcharts are the most usable and effective. Figure 5.1 represents the basic flowchart module.

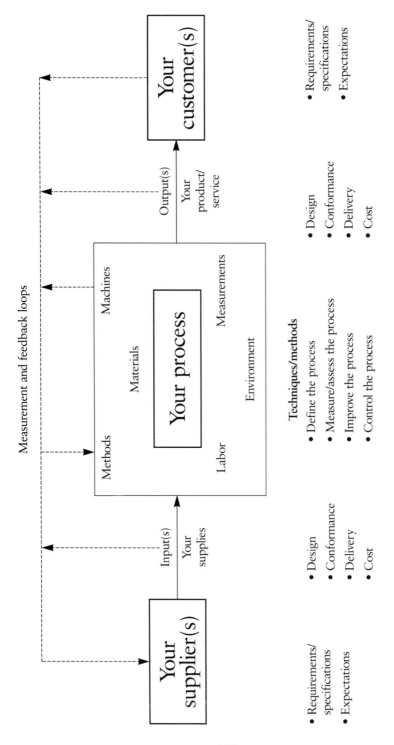

Figure 5.1. Basic flowchart.

127

Process Mapping.[4] A process map is a comprehensive flowchart. It is the visual representation of a process, showing the sequence of tasks in detail. The purpose in mapping is to define the practices being used, then look for better alternatives. Mapping is most useful when conducted by a team of people in, or closely associated with, the process under scrutiny.

In addition to providing process improvements the mapping activity has value in improving team communications and gives members an understanding of other points of view. Mapping is applicable to internal and external processes in any organization; for example, the selling process, order entry, and budgeting.

Types—Macro processes are identified from the top down. They are usually broad in scope and identify many smaller processes. An example would be the process from order entry to delivery of a product or service, with only the major steps noted. Even at the top level it can get complex, since important processes involve almost all internal organizations. Macro mapping is useful to identify key processes but difficult to analyze in detail. The usual methodology is to break down the macro map into manageable segments. If cycle time and costs can be established at the macro level the results can be used to prioritize the use of resources.

Micro processes are the detailed elements of the macro processes. The real process analysis and improvement work is done at the micro level and its effect measured at the higher level.

Application—Process mapping is a good place to begin work on the improvement process team activity. Oftentimes, even when team members have worked in the process under analysis, they encounter the fact that they all don't have the same perspective or conception of how the process works. Clarifying these differences opens the participants' minds to new improvement ideas.

An overview of the steps in process mapping includes:

1. Defining the process. Identify suppliers and customers, the inputs and outputs, and the process owner (usually the first stopping point because it is usually found that none exists—one reason the process needs improving). Identify process boundaries.

2. Mapping the process. Identify the major elements. Put the operation in sequence. Add arrows to show direction of work flow. Include parallel processes that occur simultaneously. Establish the cycle time from boundary to boundary.

3. Analyzing. Group tasks that are related, question and understand each step, rank frequency of doing each task, separate tasks that must be done from those sometimes done.

4. Mapping alternatives. Add flexibility to process paths. Identify decision points. Choose between alternatives.

5. Mapping inspection points. Show pass-fail paths and rework loops.

6. Evaluating and improving the process. Reduce nonvalue-added steps.

There are no standardized rules for drawing a process map. As long as the participants agree, it makes little difference. For organizations with several improvement teams at work, however, some general standards should be set so that all the teams can understand every map. Figure 5.2 is an example of one approach. It identifies one process, the steps in getting a part from receiving to storage. One objective would be to reduce the number of steps and the nonvalue-added time.

Cause-and-Effect Diagram. The cause-and-effect diagram is also known as the fishbone or Ishikawa diagram. It is used to identify the variables acting in and on a process. Organizing the variables into causes and effects can lead to the identification of the main causes of process variation and effective solutions toward reduction. It is a powerful tool when used in team brainstorming session.

The basic, or typical, diagram is shown in Figure 5.3. Note the hierarchical relationship of the effect to the main causes and the main causes to subcauses. For example, main cause A has a direct relationship to the effect (problem). Each subcause in A has an influence on the main. A main cause is a basic factor, such as machines, labor, or materials, as shown in Figure 5.4.

Another type of cause-and-effect diagram is *process classification*. In this type, the flow of the process to be analyzed is identified, then the key quality influencing factors at each step are listed. See Figure 5.5.

Tracking a part from receipt

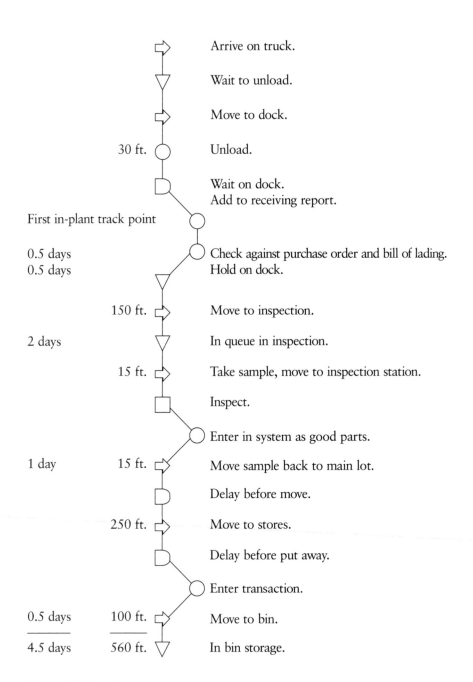

Arrive on truck.

Wait to unload.

Move to dock.

30 ft. Unload.

Wait on dock.
Add to receiving report.

First in-plant track point

0.5 days Check against purchase order and bill of lading.
0.5 days Hold on dock.

150 ft. Move to inspection.

2 days In queue in inspection.

15 ft. Take sample, move to inspection station.

Inspect.

Enter in system as good parts.

1 day   15 ft. Move sample back to main lot.

Delay before move.

250 ft. Move to stores.

Delay before put away.

Enter transaction.

0.5 days   100 ft. Move to bin.

4.5 days   560 ft. In bin storage.

Figure 5.2. Sample process map.

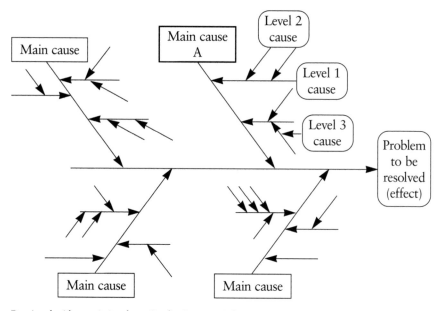

Reprinted with permission from *Quality Progress*, July 1990.

Figure 5.3. Basic cause-and-effect diagram.

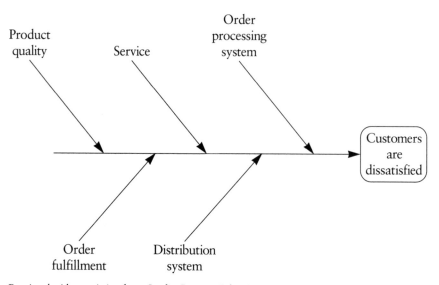

Reprinted with permission from *Quality Progress*, July 1990.

Figure 5.4. Main cause headings.

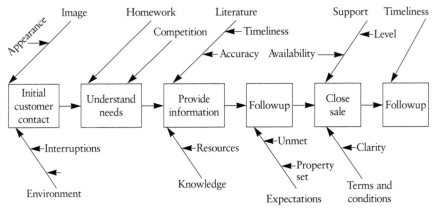

Reprinted with permission from *Quality Progress,* July 1990.

Figure 5.5. Completed process classification diagram.

Team analysis results are converted to action by assigning responsibility to members to prepare a plan, implement the prioritized solutions, and report results to the team. Another approach is to quantify the key variables in the main causes and measure the effect of implementing solutions. This is a desirable but not always practicable approach.

Checksheets and Histograms. Checksheets are designed, structured formats for recording process data in a manner that can reveal underlying patterns. They can, for example, give a picture of the data distribution (a histogram), such as that shown in Figure 5.6.

Data collected on a properly designed checksheet can be a simple quick check on a process (without calculations) to determine

- Process distribution—how widely the process varies.
- Existence and proportion of output outside of requirements.
- Skew of the output distribution—an unbalanced distribution.
- Whether further process measurement and analysis are needed.

Histograms are a graphic means of summarizing variation in a set of data. They are used when process variables can be measured (grams, millimeters, volts, dollars). The pictorial nature of a histogram exposes

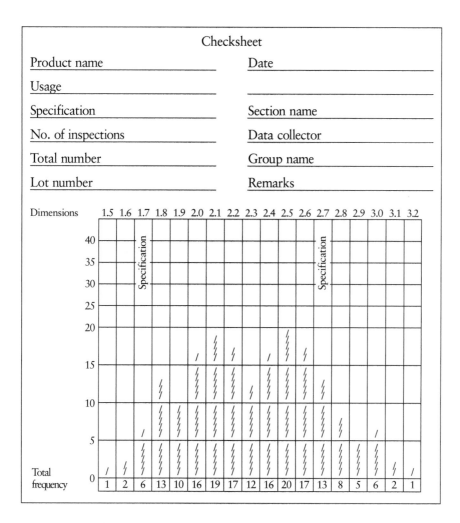

Figure 5.6. Checksheet to collect data.

patterns of the data, such as its range (horizontal axis) and frequency of occurrence. Figure 5.7 shows a typical form.

The horizontal axis is in terms of the data metric. The vertical bars indicate the frequency of occurrence of the collected measurement. The pattern of a histogram provides a good indication of how a process was operating at the time samples were taken.

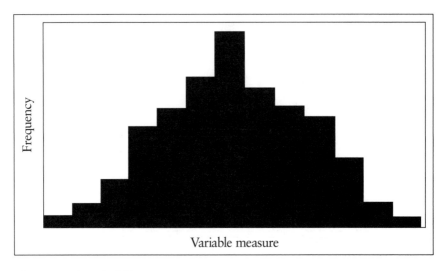

Figure 5.7. A typical histogram.

Different patterns illustrate how varied a process operation can be. A bell shape describes a process fairly balanced around some central average value. These data approximate a normal distribution (described later in this chapter), which is the most desirable. Further analysis is needed to determine whether this process operating range is adequate to meet specifications all the time. The other patterns suggest that further analysis is needed to determine the cause of their abnormality.

Pareto Diagrams. This tool is a ranking system to identify which of the variables being measured is the most significant of the total. Common measurements used are frequency of occurrence and cost (see Figure 5.8). Also shown is the cumulative percentage of all items.

If diagrams are made periodically of the process they will show any changes in rank.

The most effective process improvement can usually be made by first addressing the highest-ranked variable

Scatter Diagram. This is a plot of paired data illustrating their relationship to each other. It can provide a deeper understanding of process behavior, particularly in process experiments using the design of experiments technique. Figure 5.9 shows this relationship in a process.

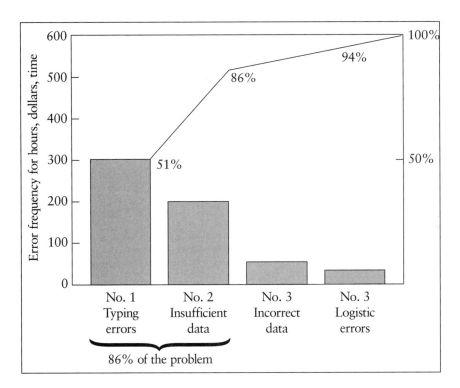

Figure 5.8. Typical Pareto diagram.

The strength of the relationship can be expressed in terms of correlation. The measure is the coefficient of correlation (r). It is expressed as a number from +1 to −1. Zero means no correlation (widely scattered points). 1 is a maximum correlation (a 1-to-1 change between two variables). If the line of best fit slopes up, the correlation is positive. If it slopes down, it is negative. Relationships are not always linear; sometimes the line of best fit is a curve. A precise coefficient can be calculated, but a visual approximation is usually sufficient for process improvement applications. Technical knowledge of the process variables is needed to accurately assess the correlation.

Run Charts. This is a chronological plot of sample measurements from a process. It indicates process variation, range, and trend. The horizontal measurement is a unit of time. Figure 5.10 shows a typical run chart.

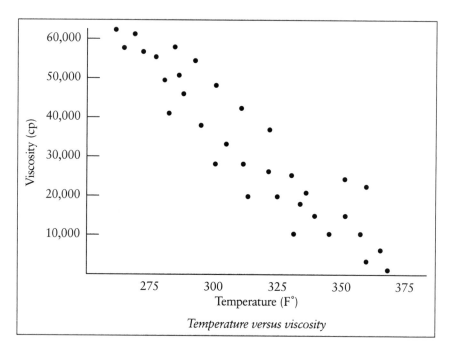

Figure 5.9. Scatter diagram showing the relationship between two variables with a dependent relationship and good (negative) correlation.

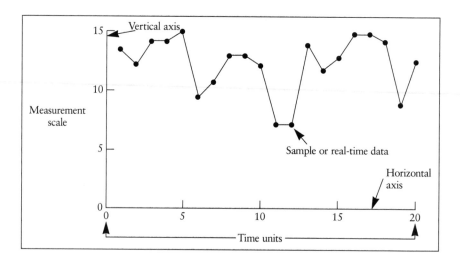

Figure 5.10. Sample run chart.

The vertical measurement scale can be any kind of data, such as a count of errors or defects (attributes data), or measurements (variables). This makes the run chart a simple and widely applicable tool for process analysis, as it visually indicates changes over time.

Control Charts. Control charts are a major tool for process improvement and the first tool in this discussion requiring statistical calculations. Figure 5.11 shows the sequence in getting a process in statistical control and then improving it. Calculating control limits for a run chart converts it to a control chart. Control limits and specification limits (tolerances) are not the same thing. Control limits are calculated from the process data. They bracket an area of ±3 standard deviations from the mean and are the area of random process variation. Specification limits are the design tolerances established by the engineer. A sufficient number of samples must be plotted before the chart can be used to determine whether the process is in statistical control (one of the major uses of control charts). When a process is in control its output operating range is known with great certainty. Its capability to produce acceptable products can be determined. The calculation of control limits for different kinds of process data as well as tests for statistical control are in Appendix A.

The form of a control chart is shown in Figure 5.12. It shows the vertical measurement axis and the horizontal time axis.

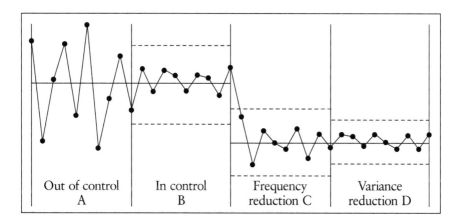

| Out of control
A | In control
B | Frequency
reduction C | Variance
reduction D |

Figure 5.11. Four stages of statistical quality control (SQC).

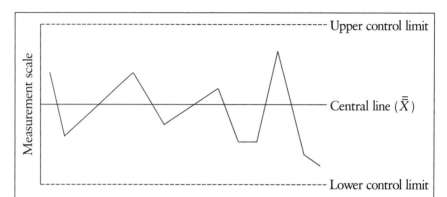

Measured scale—information on some identified process output or characteristic

Control lines
* Upper control limit (UCL) is the highest value a process should produce.
* Central line ($\bar{\bar{X}}$) is the average value of consecutive samples.
* Lower control limit (LCL) is the lowest value a process should produce.
* There is no relation between control limits and specification limits.`

Figure 5.12. Elements of a control chart.

Terms for Control Charts. The following terms are the most commonly used in preparing and interpreting control charts. They are also listed in the glossary.

* *Sample average* ($\bar{X}$). The arithmetic average of a sample. Each plotted point is a sample average, X.

* *Process average* ($\bar{\bar{X}}$). The arithmetic average of the sample averages.

* *Range.* The difference between the highest and lowest sample measurement.

* *Standard deviation* (σ, *sigma*). A calculated measure of the dispersion of average sample data around the process average.

* *Control limits.* Calculated limits for signaling the need for action or whether a set of data indicates a state of statistical control. For an $\bar{X}$ and R chart they are $\pm 3\sigma$ around centerline $\bar{\bar{X}}$.

- *Statistical control.* A process is in a state of statistical control when only common (process inherent) variation causes are present. A process is not in control when special causes of variation are present. The state is determined using control charts.

- *Normal distribution.* A term used to describe the pattern of variation of data. Its charting parameters are frequency of occurrence (vertical) and standard deviation (horizontal). It is applicable when there is a concentration of observations about the average and there is an equal chance that observations will occur on either side of the average. *Equal chance* is another way to say that the data are from a process in which the variation is occurring in a random manner. In quality control it is viewed as the inherent process variation natural to that process. It can only be reduced by changing the process elements. Statistical methods for measuring the effect of process changes are discussed in section 5E2.

  Figure 5.13 depicts the normal distribution and its key characteristics, which are as follows:

  —In a process meeting the normal distribution criteria, 99.73 percent of measured data will occur between $\pm 3\sigma$ (which corresponds with the upper and lower control limits).

  —For a process in statistical control there is a 100 percent probability that 95.65 percent will fall within $\pm 2\sigma$ and ± 68.26 percent will fall within $\pm 1\sigma$.

  —Data will vary randomly around the center value (the average) in these proportions.

- *Process capability.* The comparison of a process average and its $\pm 3\sigma$ limits to a design tolerance range. A stable process is capable if its $\pm 3\sigma$ limits do not fall outside the tolerance limits. A highly capable process is one with its $\pm 3\sigma$ limits significantly narrower than the tolerance and its average close to the tolerance center. (Process capability is discussed in more detail in Section 5E.)

- *Six-sigma* (6σ) *capability.* A process in which the design *tolerance* is $\pm 6\sigma$ around the *process average* with the centered process variation at $\pm 3\sigma$.

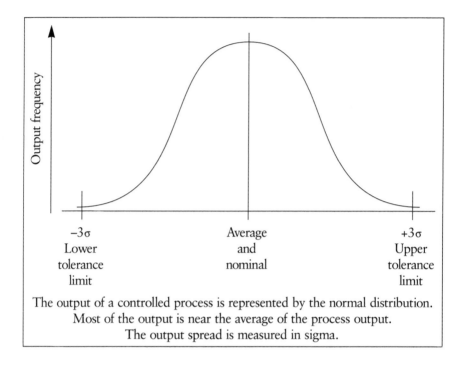

The output of a controlled process is represented by the normal distribution. Most of the output is near the average of the process output. The output spread is measured in sigma.

Figure 5.13. The normal distribution.

Common Types of Control Charts. Formulas for construction of these charts are in Appendix A.

- *Variables* $(\overline{X})$. When data measures are of the continuous type, such as millimeters, inches, or dollars. The control chart shows the average process output and whether the process is in statistical control. One such is shown in Figure 5.14.

- *Range.* This is the process variation between the highest and lowest sample measurement (see Figure 5.14). This chart indicates the stability of the process when it has shifted.

- *Attributes (discrete measures).*

   —*p* chart—A plot of the fraction, or percent, of defective items in a sample. It is used when sample sizes are equal.

   —*np* chart—A plot to show the number of defectives in a sample of equal size.

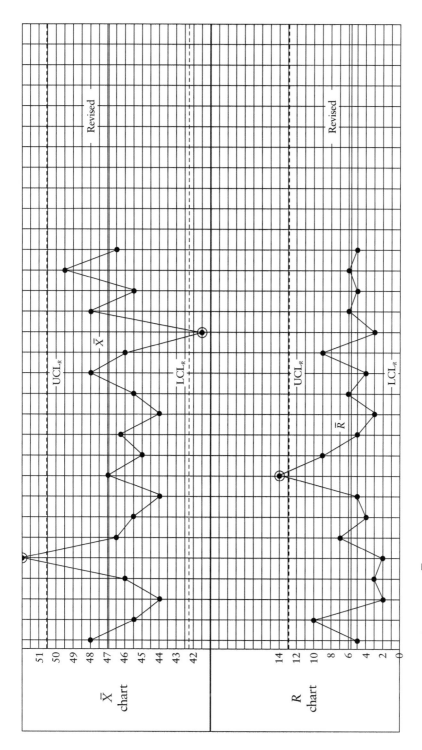

Figure 5.14. Sample average ($\overline{X}$) chart and range (R) chart.

—*c* chart—A plot showing the number of defects or errors in a sample, of the same classification, of equal size.

—*u* chart—A plot of the average number of defects per sample, for varying sample size.

Control Chart Interpretation. Control charts are interpreted by comparing them to the test patterns shown in Appendix A. Charts indicate whether a process is operating in statistical control (varying randomly, no special causes present) and when corrective action should be taken, or at least investigated. They also provide feedback on the effect of process changes or corrective actions. The kinds of errors or defects plotted in attribute charts can be categorized using Pareto analysis.

Control Chart Limitations. Used correctly, charts may indicate where to look for a problem, but they don't provide the assignable cause of an out-of-control operation. A chart can only tell you when, where, and what; it cannot tell you why and how.

Charts provide objective data. They don't indicate if the detected total variation is good or bad. This is a judgment made by comparing the data to the requirements.

Control Chart Applications. Figure 5.15 summarizes the different control chart applications, which are dependent on the type of process data.

Factors in Managing Statistical Process Control (SPC). A successful SPC program must consider the following factors.

- Management must show support for personnel time, responding to corrective actions, and implementing improvements. It must also show support by scheduling periodic reviews.

- Participants must have proper training both in the classroom and, more important, on the job.

- Process operators must be involved in the application, development, and implementation of SPC and the interpretation of results, as well as changes. Once a process is in control no change can be made without recognizing that it will most likely drive the process out of control.

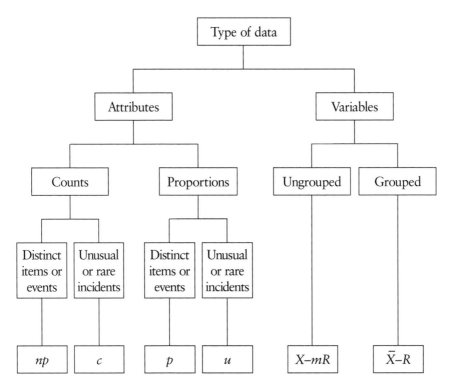

Figure 5.15. Relationship between the type of process data and the appropriate control test.

- SPC is not developed and installed by the quality organization, but driven by the need for information on how to monitor and improve.
- Start slowly and develop support. Begin by charting no more than two or three characteristics.

5.A.2. Quality Management Decision and Planning Tools[5,6]

There are seven basic management tools used for exploring problems, organizing ideas, and converting concepts into action plans or design criteria. While the QC tools in the previous discussion are graphic means to display and analyze data, the management tools are more linguistic, with applications in planning (in any kind of organization), research and development, designing, and selling products. These tools were developed in Japan and have been translated and modified to fit American applications.

Affinity Diagram. Facilitates the definition of a problem by organizing ideas according to a recognized relationship, or affinity. It is a form of brainstorming.

In application, items are listed on separate cards that are then arranged in groups by relation. Affinity diagrams are very useful in turning concepts into plans, which are further defined using other management tools.

Some advantages of this method include

- It encourages open, creative thinking.

- It suggests new connections between ideas and issues.

- It provides a climate for breakthrough thinking.

- It helps establish new communication links between functions.

Relationship Diagram (Interrelationship Digraph). Aids the problem-solving process by showing the relationship between problems and ideas in complex situations. It is useful when relationships between ideas are difficult to recognize. It is often used in conjunction with the affinity diagram.

In using this tool, the team writes each idea and circles it, then clusters the circles. It then identifies which ideas strongly influence others by drawing arrows between them. The results are evaluated by counting the ideas that have the most arrows entering or exiting the circle. Circles with the most entering arrows are the important ideas and problems. Using these tools can

- Stimulate team members to think in multiple directions.

- Examine the cause-and-effect relationship between issues not normally examined.

- Maintain a balance within teams. Every member can offer ideas.

Tree Diagram. A diagram that identifies the tasks and methods needed to solve a problem and reach a goal. It starts with the problem and breaks it down into its subelements, using the tree structure to display the relationship. It can also be used to plan the elements of a product or service design.

The tree diagram can be used to

- Keep team solutions tied to original problems or objectives.
- Provide assurance that all important links have been considered.
- Clarify complex problems.

Process Decision Program Chart. This tool is used to plan the implementation of complex tasks. Its application results in a map of all conceivable events that can go wrong and identifies contingencies for each. The contingencies, or countermeasures, are included in the final plan.

Matrix Chart (Diagram). A chart to yield information about the relationship and importance of elements in the subject under study. It typically is used to weight and rank the problem causes identified through other planning tools.

Prioritization Matrix. This is a tool dependent on statistical analysis. It is a technique used to prioritize options through a systematic approach of comparing choices by selecting, weighting, and applying criteria.

Activity Network Diagram (Arrow Diagram). A scheduling design technique used to schedule sequential and simultaneous tasks in order to define the most efficient path to achieve an objective. It incorporates many PERT and CPM techniques (these scheduling techniques are discussed in Chapter 8).

5.A.3. Plan-Do-Check-Act (PDCA)

The continuous process improvement concept can be depicted using the plan-do-check-act sequence developed by Shewhart and now commonly referred to as the Deming cycle. It is based on the scientific method.

Plan—Identify what is going to be done as a process improvement, plan who will do it, and when.

Do—Introduce the change or conduct the experiment.

Check—Study and evaluate results. Determine effectiveness.

Act—Adopt or drop the change, or modify it, and repeat the cycle.

Figure 5.16 illustrates the method. PDCA is a good structure for solving any organization problem. In its use it becomes an iterative methodology, as one enters and leaves the circle at various places, directed by the results. More complex problems may require the use of some of the managerial planning tools or advanced SPC methods.

5.A.4. Quality Function Deployment (QFD)

Quality function deployment is a team planning tool to incorporate the voice of the customer and customer requirements throughout the design, from the production process to the delivered product. It has also been used more broadly to plan activities in which there are requirements, a process, and a specific result. Examples of this include software development[7] and other internal development activities.[8] To use QFD effectively, team members must have an accurate understanding of organization practices and a knowledge of the processes that will be involved.

The value of QFD is that it forces early answers to important design, process, and control issues that seriously affect final product quality, reliability, and customer satisfaction. Without the discipline required by this tool, many important production decisions are postponed in the interests

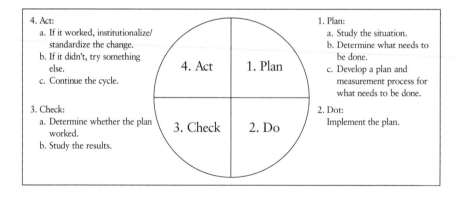

Figure 5.16. The plan-do-check-act (PDCA) cycle.

of getting a product into production, resulting in changes, delays, higher costs, and often a compromised design.

QFD is an ideal tool for concurrent engineering (CE). CE is a methodology for establishing product design parameters and tolerances in conjunction with production process design and definition. CE is discussed in section 5F. QFD is the planning tool that ensures customer needs, initially identified, are not diluted as product and manufacturing processes are defined. The use of QFD results in reduced development-to-market cycle time, with higher quality and lower costs. The Japanese developed this tool and successfully shortened cycle times in the automobile industry.

QFD is an important TQ tool because it is team based and process oriented. Organization functions are secondary to planning the integration of activities in technical detail. In this respect QFD can be classified as an organization development tool. Not only do functions have to become process oriented (the matrices QFD uses are analogous to process mapping) but its application demands useful information from the cost, information systems, and support functions. Teams using it also routinely apply quality control problem-solving tools and, in the initial product definition stage, quality management tools.

Application. The technique of QFD is to convert customer needs, expectations, and requirements into design characteristics, right down to the parts level, and then translate these to manufacturing techniques, processes, and controls before production begins. QFD displays the completed, detailed design, production, and quality plan as a series of interconnected matrices, as shown in Figure 5.17.

Factors in successful QFD application include

- Recognizing that the implementation of QFD requires a significant multifunction effort in producing a plan before release to production. Management must accept this longer front-end effort to save overall time and cost and achieve greater customer satisfaction.

- Beginning with a simple pilot program.

- Not trying to maximize the number of charts and define everything at the outset. It should be used as an iterative process.

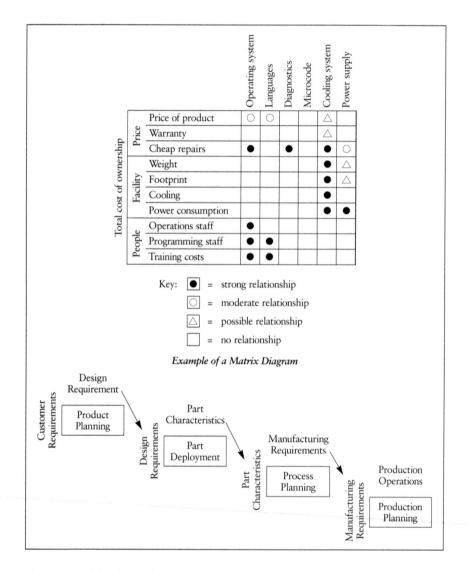

Figure 5.17. The QFD planning matrix and interconnected matrices.

- Providing training in QFD principles and practices to every team member before using it.

Further sources on application methodologies are provided in the references.

5.B. Cost of Quality

Cost is a fundamental measure of activities in every organization. The cost breakdown is usually most comprehensive in industry. Figure 5.18 illustrates the major cost categories. Also noted are the cost items of most interest to quality management (useful quality cost data can be identified for most organizations). Using quality costs to determine what needs improvement, and the results of improvements, is an important signal to management that the improvement process has a business basis.

Quality cost data are a fundamental measure to identify where costs are commonly expended in the three general categories of prevention, appraisal, and failure.

Prevention—Those costs expended in the prevention of errors, including process improvement and the cost of maintaining the quality system. Other activities include design review, supplier management, planning, training, and instrument calibration.

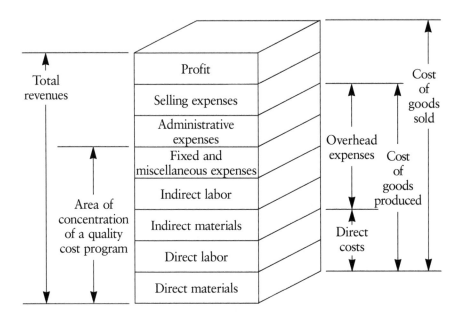

Figure 5.18. Common product cost breakdown.

Appraisal—Those costs associated with measuring, evaluating, auditing, and inspecting.

Internal failures—Assignable cause, error costs, defects in products, or services that fail to meet requirements. Some of these costs include scrap, rework, repair, replacement, and documentation errors.

External failures—Costs generated by defective products or services in the hands of the customer. These include warranties, complaints, replacements or recalls, repairs, packaging, handling, and field service.

The Economic Model Concept. The historical economic quality cost model is shown in Figure 5.19. It shows the relationship among the basic quality costs of prevention, appraisal, and failure. It shows appraisal and prevention costs rising toward infinity as quality of conformance approaches 100 percent (perfection). Total quality costs are also higher as

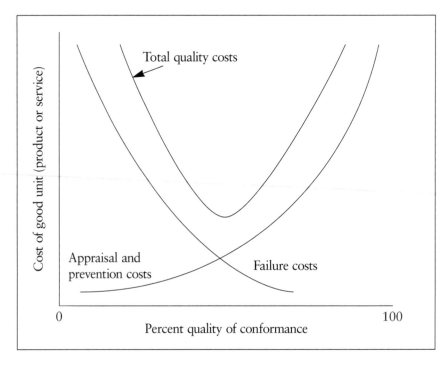

Figure 5.19. The historical quality cost model.

failure costs increase. Total costs are optimized at some point when the sum of the two costs is at a minimum.

This illustration is used to identify the relationship among the different quality costs. Before TQ it was common to find that appraisal costs were the larger factor in the appraisal-prevention combination. The problem has been that these relationships only appeared in quality control textbooks. Typically, general management considered appraisal (inspection, testing) costs as preventive. It relied on appraisal to prevent defects from reaching the customer. Preventing defects from occurring was not considered feasible; controlling and integrating all organization processes was an unknown concept. TQ organizations realize that process control and continuous improvement reduce all quality costs. TQ is a focus on prevention. Initially prevention costs will be high, but they will decline as control is reached and improvement becomes the way of life.

Service Organization Costs. J. Gray[9] reports an estimated 30 percent to 50 percent of service companies' operating expenses are spent on quality costs, with about 70 percent of that allocated to failure costs. Yet few service companies pay attention to such costs. The basis for such costs is identified in Table 5.1. Related failure costs are such things as customer and employee turnover, lost productivity, and the various forms of rework.

Useful quality cost systems do not require exact cost measurements. Starting with good estimates as a basis, the cost effect of improvements can be determined. (A before-and-after quality cost comparison would be interesting in organizations downsizing and restructuring. They may well find that many of these actions are counterproductive in achieving the desired short-term savings.)

Managing Quality Costs. An objective of managing quality is to minimize or eliminate quality costs and ensure customer satisfaction through continuous reduction in variation in all organization activities, products, and services.

The strategy is to

1. Plan and implement a quality cost collection system.

2. Implement a quality cost reporting system.

Table 5.1. Quality costs: jobs, activities, and expenses.

Prevention	Detection	Correction
Market research	Internal auditors/	Complaints
Customer/internal user	audits	Worker's compensation
surveys	Review of work	Error correction
Training and education	Proofreaders	Service guarantees/
Account reconciliation	Running spell	warranties
Quality director, staff,	check function	Interest penalties
and expenses	Fire alarm	Disability payments
Quality system audits	equipment	Equal Employment
Quality planning	Inspectors	Opportunity lawsuits
Supplier qualification	Appraisers	Returns
program	Checkers	Replacements
Preventive maintenance	Approvals	Penalties
Cross-functional design	Authorizations	Rework
teams	External appraisal	Troubleshooting/repair
Customer service	costs	Liability
training		Hidden costs

3. Implement a quality cost reduction program using the tools of TQ.

4. Study the results and change systems and procedures as needed.

5. Continuously reduce variation in all processes and activities and identify and report the effect on quality costs.

Some other activities to reduce quality costs include:

• Review requirements specifications for currency and accuracy.

• Simplify and effectively integrate processes.

• Maintain and raise process capabilities.

• Ensure adequacy of employee training.

• Maintain quality audits and use results to determine quality cost drivers.

• Don't make major organization or process changes before the new model is defined.

Life Cycle Costs. The life cycle cost concept began in the U.S. Department of Defense in the 1950s, but it has not been successful there or in many companies. Several reasons for this can be identified.

- Lack of management interest
- Lack of a useful model
- Failure to understand the concept and its potential value
- Organization preoccupation with other activities
- Little customer demand

The life cycle cost concept can be applied to any product. It is the optimum cost that meets the needs of both supplier and customer. For example, there are light bulbs on the market for $12 that last 10 times longer than a $1 bulb and use about $50 less electricity. But people don't buy them. The consumer needs education before these bulbs will sell well.

5.C. Process Improvement

The objective of process improvement is to provide higher quality and value to the customer and achieve competitive leadership. The value most often of concern is that perceived by the customer. One viewpoint expressed by Genichi Taguchi[10] is that

1. Quality should be designed into the product.
2. Quality is producing products close to the target value (dimensionally, the nominal). Products should be robust and little influenced by their environment. That is, they should be insensitive to the stresses of manufacturing and end use. On-line quality control is achieved using SPC. Off-line relates to the product multi-variable testing (a variation of design of experiments) methodology Taguchi developed.
3. The cost of quality should be measured as a function of the deviation from the target value. This cost should include all the life cycle costs related to not achieving target values. Taguchi called them a loss to society. This loss concept is depicted in Figure 5.20.

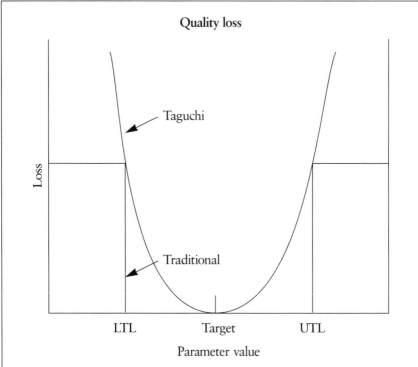

In the traditional understanding of quality, everything between the upper tolerance limit (UTL) and lower tolerance limit (LTL) was good. In the Taguchi concept, quality deteriorates at an exponential rate as it varies from the target nominal value.

Figure 5.20. Quality, variation, and the loss concept.

The traditional viewpoint is that anything within tolerance limits is good. Taguchi's thesis is that the greater the deviation from the target, or nominal value, the poorer the quality. Products made close to the tolerance limits will often not perform as well or as long as those near target. Normal use and wear, for example, might result in products drifting outside tolerance limits in a relatively short time. The result is customer dissatisfaction or perhaps a lost customer. Losses due to warranty costs are a loss to society in that poor quality products are wasteful, in the same manner as poor quality in a business process is wasteful.

The Context of Improvement. The concept of continuous process improvement (CPI) was discussed in Chapter 1. This chapter discusses the approach and tools to use in achieving it.

A process is improved by reducing three measurable values: variation, cycle time, and nonvalue-added activities. For processes providing a variables measurement, reducing variation means reducing the output dispersion around the process average and keeping the process near the tolerance center. For attributes, reducing variation means, in practical terms, driving the trend toward zero and reducing dispersion. Improving cycle time means simplification, technological improvement, and reducing nonvalue-added activities. Attributes and cycle time improvements are particularly applicable to both internal and external processes.

The factors mentioned can be improved using an incremental approach (small, steady improvements) or, as many leading companies do, combining them with breakthrough improvements.

Approach. Process management is not a procedure or a canned approach that can be given to an organization. In considering its use, management must first understand its theory, practices, and implications for management and the entire organization. It requires a significant change in the way the organization is managed at every level and, in particular, the role of all employees. Process management

- Takes years to implement fully.
- Means additional work for an organization.
- Requires an investment of resources to implement and operate.
- Changes responsibilities and organization relationships.
- Permanently changes the way organizations function (culture).

The chart in Figure 5.21 depicts a methodology that, as explored, will suggest the manner and scope of the process improvement methodology. This model suggests a procedure that could be used after overall quality objectives have been set and are ready to flow down through the organization.

Step 1. Prioritizing is done at several levels. The first priorities are the strategic quality objectives. (See Chapter 3 for more on setting objectives.) In consonance with these, functional

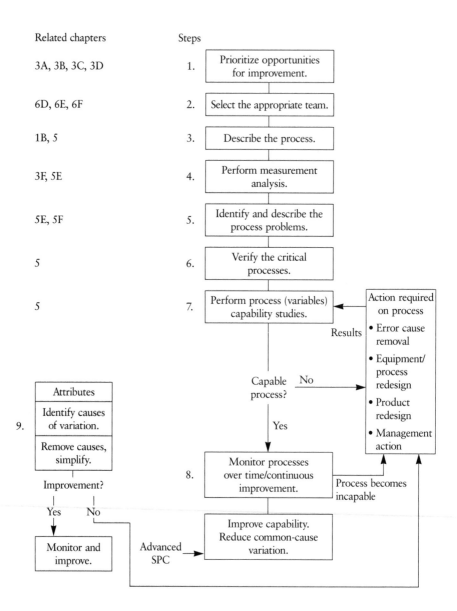

Figure 5.21. Generalized product/process improvement methodology.

organization short- and long-term objectives are defined. This will provide several objectives for the multifunctional teams. The functional level managers next prioritize these objectives.

2. After key process identification, managers select and prioritize the objectives for these processes and select the improvement teams. This requires consideration of the level of knowledge and skills required. If pursuing an opportunity involving product and process design, a concurrent engineering team may be the best approach. If reducing cycle time, an entirely different team may be assigned.

3. Describe the process. The core of the team should be those who are knowledgeable of the process and those from important peripheral activities that have significant inputs or are customers. (A peripheral activity could be an outside supplier or a quality control function that has pertinent records.) The tools for adequate process description are the flowchart and its extended methodology, process mapping.

4. Perform measurement analysis. Before process analysis and improvement are pursued some critical process performance measures should be established, as well as the place in the process where they are to be measured. These measures are needed to establish a baseline against which improvements will be compared.

5. An initial part of the team action, along with the process definition, is to clarify/define the process output and identify the process problems.

6. Output requirements must be verified and explicitly described. Verifying the process involves detailed descriptions and analysis to the degree necessary.

7. The team must describe how the process is operating with respect to requirements. When the process involves variables measurements a definitive process capability must be established. If the process is capable, further improvements

should be identified and quantified and their value and cost estimated. Pursuit of improvements will depend on this cost as well as the priorities in the expenditure of resources. It might be more valuable to work on another process first.

When a process is measured using attributes, the same capability concept is inappropriate. The measures in such a process are usually errors or defects, good/bad, cost, and cycle time. Control limits can be calculated for the process to show what it will continue to do if improvements are not made. Many such processes can be brought into statistical control at some average defect level. This would at least indicate stability and provide a baseline to measure the effects of changes. The objective in improving these processes is to drive poor quality to the lowest level that is economically justifiable.

8. The first seven steps describe the decision-making methodology based on whether a process is capable. The last condition describes actions involved in continuous improvement. Processes that are capable are further improved. Those that require remedial action are shown in Figure 5.21 as the feedback paths. Processes in statistical control and capable will require the reduction of common-cause variation to obtain further improvement. Technological changes or advanced statistical techniques such as DOE will be required.

9. Attributes processes require basically the same approach, except the process capability measure does not apply.

5.C.1. Reengineering

The technology revolution has resulted in a rapid increase in the options for how to do work. There are many new products that can tap human potential to work more creatively. Organizations in all economic sectors, however, have been trying to exploit this phenomenon with traditional structures and work organization. American business has traditionally met new challenges by reorganizing,[11] adding, or removing functions and changing responsibilities, but doing so under traditional concepts of management and structure. It's an ancient activity, as can be seen from the writings of Gauis Petronius on changes in the Roman Empire.

> We trained hard to meet our challenges but it seemed as if every time we were beginning to form into teams we would be reorganized. I was to learn later in life that we tend to meet any new situation by reorganizing; and a wonderful method it can be for creating the illusion of progress while producing confusion, ineffectiveness and demoralization.

It is also common for management to adopt new technological solutions to improve productivity and quality. But management has found it difficult to integrate this with a coherent strategy in its application. Also, in many cases, only focusing on internal customer-supplier relationship process improvement has enabled the barriers created by functional hierarchies to remain intact.[12] The poor success record has led to the organization reengineering approach: starting over from scratch to find a structure that fits today's needs. The term implies a rational, information-based analysis and decision-making process to determine what the organization should be and how it should operate in the modern marketplace.

Reengineering is a popular activity and is another name for making major organizationwide improvements. It is more than just business process improvement and simplification. It is not restructuring or downsizing; those are decisions made by management based primarily on cost reduction.

Within reengineering there are two expert methodologies. Hammer and Champy[13] describe it as starting all over, from scratch. The existing process configuration baseline is not used. Reengineering uses only a high-level understanding of the *what* and *why*, not the *how* of a process (the *how* is going to change as a result of the reengineering). They define reengineering as the fundamental rethinking and radical redesign of business processes to achieve dramatic improvements in critical contemporary measures such as cost, quality, service and speed."

Harrington[14] and Morris and Brandon[15] emphasize process simplification and improvement, determining where processes are and then improving them from that point. This is analogous to TQ continuous improvement.

Reengineering and TQ. There is some argument about the similarities and differences between TQ and reengineering. It is based on the differences in the accepted definitions in the two approaches. Table 5.2 illustrates key reengineering concepts.[16]

TQ is frequently interpreted as emphasizing incremental improvements and reengineering as emphasizing breakthrough improvements. The differences are a matter of degree. Juran has long emphasized both incremental and breakthrough improvements in his Trilogy concept. Also, benchmarking, which preceded reengineering, frequently yields breakthrough improvements. On the other hand, reengineering sometimes produces only incremental change. Most experts and practitioners

Table 5.2. Key reengineering concepts.

Topic	Concept
Reengineering	Fundamental rethinking Radical redesign Process Dramatic improvement Measures Return Risk
Process	Activities Customers Measures Work ordering Time Space Beginning Ending Inputs Outputs Structure Action Baseline
Redesign	Process configuration Design flows Process transformation Redesign alternatives

believe that both approaches are needed. For example, improved processes from reengineering can use an incremental, continuous improvement effort to refine them.

Methodologies reflecting both approaches might involve the activities listed in Tables 5.3 and 5.4.

Breakthrough redesign and process improvement, not reorganization, is the usual objective of reengineering. It is the reorganization of the work

Table 5.3. Critical redesign activities.

Understanding and improving existing processes
1. Describe the current process flow.
2. Measure the process in terms of the new process objectives.
3. Assess the process in terms of the new process attributes.
4. Identify problems with, or shortcoming of, the process.
5. Identify short-term improvements in the process.
6. Assess current information technology and organization.
Designing and prototyping a new process
1. Brainstorm design alternatives.
2. Assess feasibility, risk, and benefit of design alternatives.
3. Select the preferred process design.
4. Prototype the new process design.
5. Develop a migration strategy.
6. Implement new organizational structures and systems.

Adapted from Davenport (1993), pp. 139 and 154.

Table 5.4. High-level reengineering activities.

1. Identifying processes for innovation
2. Identifying change levers (that is, enabling or transformation technologies)
3. Developing process visions
4. Understanding and improving existing processes
5. Designing and prototyping the new process

Adapted from Davenport (1993), pp. 139 and 154.

people do in different organizational functions, into new methods, processes, and structure. Nothing is sacred. Companies may change structure in reengineering but only as a result of defining new processes and responsibilities. This is related to what has been discussed in other chapters; that is, clarifying the responsibility between organization functions about how work actually gets done, what processes are needed, and how they should relate. Reengineering eliminates work that does not contribute to goals.

A critical factor limiting the success of many reengineering applications is the failure to understand the effects on human resources. Reengineering often fails to change attitudes and culture. This requires a specific effort to support organization change and manage the resulting conflicts (this is discussed further in Chapter 6A).

5.D. Trend Analysis

Most managers have used trend analysis to determine the direction an activity is taking over time, to decide if corrective action is required. Trend analysis might be a plot of whether some costs are increasing or decreasing, whether errors are declining or increasing, cycle time changes, a process output behavior, or any number of factors being measured and plotted to visualize what is happening as time passes. The objective is to decide if any action is required to change the direction (trend). Graphic representations also give feedback on the effect of improvement actions. Newspaper financial sections, magazines, and trade journals contain a variety of trend charts.

One of the most common and useful evaluation techniques is trend analysis using some of the common QC tools. Run charts, for example, are plots of process performance data over time. They indicate the range of process variation and trend. Either variable or attribute data can be used. Examples are shown in Figure 5.22.

Trend analysis is used in variables $\overline{X}$ and R charts to interpret process behavior. This is discussed in Section 5A.

Attribute data plots are basically run charts; that is, data over time. For process improvement purposes the desired trend is negative—showing improvement. Upper and lower control limits can be established to indicate variation and a rough idea of capability if improvements are not

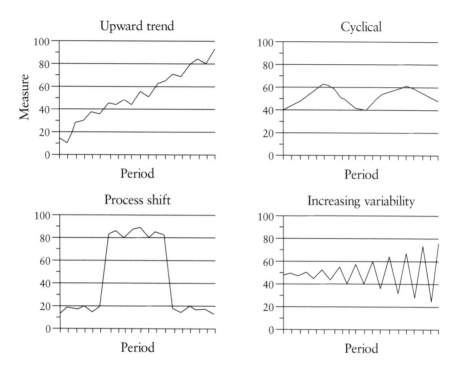

Figure 5.22. Examples of trend charts.

made. The process improvement effort is to drive the attribute value to zero, or at least to the lowest level economically attainable.

Statistical analysis methods exist for more technical analysis of trend data. One of the most common is the moving average. This is the average of the data over a selected number of periods, such as a three-month moving average. It is sensitive to changes in the trend of recent data or of recent performance. Other technologies, such as those used by stock market analysts, are beyond the scope of this book.

Trend analysis can be used at various stages in the improvement process: to set priorities, to depict the effect of process changes, and to monitor process behavior. It is a useful tool to track a process parameter for a short time. Determining the correlation between two variables by finding the best fitting line to a set of variables data is a form of trend analysis (scatter diagrams).

5.E. Measurement Issues

5.E.1. Reliability and Validity

Satisfying the customer requires product or service measurements with as high an accuracy as feasible. The measurements must also be reliable and valid. Product quality measurements during manufacture can be classified, for discussion purposes, as *hard,* yielding objective data and represented by units of measure. These data are then used to evaluate the process and product. These measures indicate conformance to the design. They also indicate to management how the business processes are working and what the effects of changes or improvements are. Process quality measures are discussed in Sections 5A1 and 5C.

Measurements of products in use, or of services, can be referred to as *soft.* These measurements are subjective and measured differently. The objective of both types of measures is to find out if the product features or services are what the customer needed or expected and, if not, what they do want. For example, a business may improve its cycle time to the point that it leads its competitors, only to learn that it's customers don't think its all that great.

Hard System Measurement. Measurement using physical tools and instruments can be made to very high orders of accuracy. This yields the hard data used to make accept/reject decisions.

Using such highly accurate instruments will provide accurate measurements that can be repeated. Repeated measurements of the same characteristic on the same piece, however, will not yield exactly the same value. This is the *error of measurement;* it is the random variation of factors in the measurement system, such as the instrument, user, and environment. Like any process there is inherent random variation, which is best expressed in terms of the standard deviation of the measurement(just like process variation). Characteristics of instrument variation are *accuracy* and *precision.*

Accuracy is the difference between the true value and the average of the measurements. If, for example, an instrument was checked against a standard, the difference between the average of the measurements and the standard (the true value) would be the amount the instrument was out of calibration (the inaccuracy). But, measurement variation would still exist.

A further complicating factor is that the instrument can only be expected to measure within its design tolerance, so accuracy depends on consideration of all these factors, as well as precision.

Precision does not imply accuracy; an instrument can be very precise but not calibrated. Also, an instrument can be calibrated perfectly yet be so imprecise that measurements are meaningless. Precision is the degree to which the instrument will repeat itself when taking the same measurement. Precision can be quantified in terms of the standard deviation of replicated measurements. Unacceptably high variability can sometimes be overcome by averaging several measurements. *Repeatability* is another name for precision.

So even though hard data are obtained by product measurements there is always variation (error), and it can be quantified so that it can be considered in evaluating the accuracy of such measurements.

Reproducibility adds to measurement error. It is the increased variability when several people use the same measuring equipment. The combined estimates of repeatability and reproducibility, in practice, should be less than 10 percent of the design tolerance.

In hard measurement systems, all or at least final product acceptance systems should be validated. That includes determining whether the measurement system is measuring what it is supposed to measure.

Processes are validated when they are in statistical control and are capable ($C_{pk} = 1$). Reliability in hard systems is primarily a measure of the design capability to meet requirements over time. It is expressed in terms of a probability—the probability that a product will perform a required function, under stated conditions, for a stated period of time. Reliability is measured in terms of the mean time between failures (MTBF). Reliability is predicted during the design phase using the failure rates of the product parts, using probability analysis techniques to calculate the MTBF.

The true reliability can only be determined if the total operating time of a product is known at the time of every failure. Good estimates of the true reliability can be made by periodic testing of product samples under simulated use conditions.

Soft Systems. The major objective of a total quality system is to satisfy the customer. It is a major factor in the Baldrige Award assessment. For example, in 1990, the Cadillac Division of General Motors, to the surprise of many, won the Baldrige Award. Many automotive experts were critical because they did not think that the Cadillac was the best luxury car. Perhaps not, but it did well in all the assessment criteria and was outstanding in customer satisfaction with the product and service.

This leads to the issue of how to measure customer satisfaction; that is, how to measure customer perceptions and attitudes toward the quality characteristics of products or services. The value of knowing this is obvious. Conversely, not knowing, or basing decisions on inaccurate information, could be disastrous. Some customer information can be gleaned from competitor sales figures or competitor product or service features, but this is of limited value and can even be misleading.

Quality characteristic measurements in soft systems have some similarities to hard systems in that there is error between measurements and the true value. There is also a consideration of reliability and validation, but these have different meanings.

Assessment, Measurement, Issues of Reliability and Validity. The objective is to measure the customer level of satisfaction, find undetected problems in the relationship, or influence customer opinions. To gather the necessary data a measurement is needed to assess customer attitudes and opinions. The measures are then used to make inferences about the states of satisfaction. The other knowledge sought is the relationships between customer requirements.

Measurement issues are as important as the repeatability and reliability factors in product measurements described earlier. Statistical analysis can provide indicators of the quality of satisfaction questionnaires. The data collected must be reliable and valid.

Reliability in soft data has a meaning different from that used in hard data (equipment reliability). As discussed before, there is an error in measurement due to random factors in the measurement system. In other words, the measurement does not precisely reflect the true value. In application to questionnaires it means that the score given on a questionnaire doesn't reflect the true score. Errors of measurement are considered in the context of this reliability. Stating it another way, reliability is the extent to which questionnaires are free from bias. Statistical analysis techniques include correlation studies (scatter diagrams) to determine the degree of agreement between observed and true scores. A form of reliability would be the correlation coefficient. High correlation–high reliability would mean a good agreement between the questionnaire characteristics in determining customer satisfaction. As stated earlier, the true values cannot be known, so the correlation cannot be directly calculated. There are formulas, however, to estimate the reliability. Hayes[17] presents a detailed methodology for preparing and analyzing customer satisfaction questionnaires.

The other component of quality is *validity*. Validity refers to the degree to which evidence supports the inferences made from scores derived from the measures established. In other words, if it is inferred that scores on a measure do reflect customer satisfaction, information is needed to asses how well that inference is supported. Hayes presents methodologies and strategies to obtain evidence to support inferences made from scores. He also points out the usefulness of control charts to track the level of quality of the important quality dimensions.

5.E.2. Sampling Plans and Other Statistical Techniques

Sampling is an inspection procedure for making a decision on the acceptability of a lot, group of items (hardware or data), or a process based on a sample from the whole.[18] It is also used in surveys, opinion polls, and administrative applications.[19] Its advantages include

- It is economical and fast. A decision can be made without inspecting the entire lot.

- It can be used while a process is in operation rather than producing a large volume of unknown acceptability.

- It is applicable to hardware, software, services, and paper systems.

- It can provide a decision as accurate as 100 percent inspection.

- It provides an incentive for the producer to provide the quality level required to reduce the probability of having an entire lot rejected and returned.

- It is appropriate when inspection costs are high and on noncritical material or services.

- It can be used for variables or attributes measurements.

Its disadvantages include the following:

- Frequently, unacceptable lots are 100 percent inspected anyway because the material is needed to maintain schedule. Suppliers' knowledge of this may lead them to ship material and let the customer sort good from bad. Full-lot inspection may also be needed to identify the nature of errors or defects.

- Sampling plans allow some risk of accepting some materials or services that do not meet requirements.

- There is risk of rejecting some conforming orders when working with an acceptable defect level.

- Sampling is not always appropriate for complex products.

- It is often too expensive to be used when destructive testing is required.

- Some industries (such as U.S. automotive) no longer use sampling or use it in limited applications because of liability laws.

Sampling Plans. Acceptance sampling must be conducted using statistically valid plans, not rules of thumb, to provide assurance that the risks involved are known. Sampling plans have been published with stated sample size, selection procedures, accept and reject criteria, and the risks involved in each selection.

The most extensively used sampling plans (tables) for attributes are those contained in MIL-STD-105E (superceded by ISO TR 13425, *Guidelines for Selection of Statistical Methods in Standards and Specifications,* and ISO Handbook 3, *Statistical Methods*). This standard allows for single, double, or multiple sampling, depending on the circumstances. It is based on the concept of an acceptable quality level (AQL). Sampling plans for variables (measurable characteristics) are sometimes used. Although more complex, they can reveal useful information, such as how the process is operating with respect to the specification.

Terminology

AQL (acceptable quality level). The maximum percentage of items in a lot that are defective or contain errors that can be considered satisfactory, as a process average.

LTPD (lot tolerance percent defective). The lowest quality level in a lot that should be accepted. LTPD plans provide a low probability of accepting that percent defective.

Alpha. The producer's risk. The probability of rejecting a lot that is within the AQL.

Beta. The buyer's risk. The risk of accepting a lot that is worse than the AQL.

OC curve (operating characteristic curve). A pictorial view (a plotted curve) of the probabilities of accepting lots submitted at various levels of percent defective. The curve illustrates the risk in acceptance sampling for different sampling plans. This is illustrated in Figure 5.23.

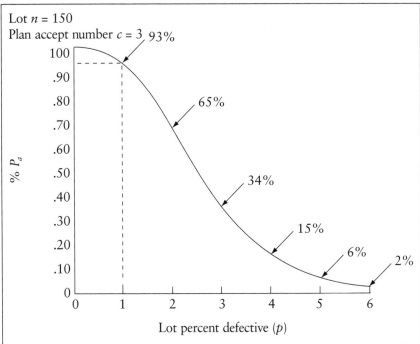

If a lot is 1 percent defective the probability of accepting it is 93 percent; if 4 percent defective, the probability is 15 percent. Conversely, there is a 7 percent and 85 percent chance that these two lots would be rejected.

Figure 5.23. OC curve for acceptance plan with accept number of 3.

Studies have shown that 100 percent inspection, on average, will find only about 85 percent of the defects. So there is a 15 percent risk of accepting or rejecting incorrectly. Sampling also involves risk, but statistical analysis has quantified those risks and depicts them as an OC curve. The ideal-shaped OC is a rectangle. If a lot was 1 percent defective the probability of acceptance would be 100 percent.

If a sampling plan could be devised to provide this curve, all lots above 1 percent defects would be rejected, and all below, accepted. But every plan has some alpha and beta risks. They are related to lot and sample size.

The curves for each sampling plan are included in MIL-STD-105E (and the ISO standard). In these the probability of accepting an AQL lot is 88 to 99 percent. Lot size has little effect.

Application. Acceptance sampling is a procedure developed for wide application. It is used widely in industry for making surveys and anywhere information is needed from a large number (population) of items. There is, however, argument about its applicability in TQ. The idea that there is an acceptable AQL conflicts with the philosophy of continuous improvement.

There are many applications, however, where there is a high volume of manufactured parts, or paper processes, that can only be evaluated economically using sampling, such as credit card entries from point of sale to billing, process sampling to identify improvement candidates, and in auditing.

Attribute Plan Types

- Single sampling. The accept-reject decision is made by drawing one random sample from the lot. The lot is accepted if the number of defects is equal to or less than the given (plan) acceptance number.

- Double sampling. First a small sample is drawn. If the number of defects is quite small the lot is accepted; if large, it is rejected. If it is in between, another sample is taken and the cumulative number of rejects is used to make a decision. If the lot is good, inspection time is less than for single sampling.

- Multiple sampling. A variation of double sampling. Several small samples are taken until a decision can be reached, based on the cumulative sample results.

Other Statistical Techniques. Techniques other than sampling and control charts (commonly considered the scope of SPC) are not new but have become recognized more widely as powerful tools to reduce variation. Many special processes that were thought of as requiring years of experience for an operator to control have succumbed to statistical techniques that identify the real, and unsuspected, process variables that control the output variation. These techniques are also useful to reduce the common causes of process variation.

It is not uncommon to find a process that is in statistical control (variation varying randomly) but not capable of producing products within specification limits (being in control only means that the process will probably continue to operate within the calculated control limits). To improve a process under control requires other statistical techniques. The most common approach has been to experiment with a process by holding one factor constant at a time and measuring process output. If variability is reduced, that factor is tightly controlled. This approach can sometimes yield useful results but nowhere near the maximum potential if more powerful statistical techniques are used.

What the one-factor-at-a-time technique misses is the often-critical interactions between some factors operating in a process that can cause most of the variation. Figure 5.24 is an illustration of the effect of different methods. The upper curve provides only a slight reduction in variation, while the lower curve shows that using other techniques can provide dramatic improvement. Some examples of factors that interact in a process are temperature, pressure, and outside temperature. In addition, there are many interactive factors that affect nonindustrial processes.

Figure 5.25 shows the usual relationship and common path for conventional versus statistical improvement methods. Only since the mid-1980s have techniques beyond control charts become widely used in industry, with profoundly valuable results. The most common is design of experiments (factorial experimentation). This is now also being referred to as multi-vari testing.

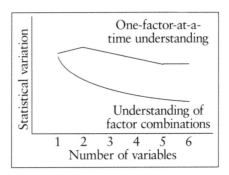

Figure 5.24. Reducing statistical variation through understanding variable combinations.

Design of Experiments (DOE). Sir Ronald Fisher invented experimental design in the early 1920s to provide better results in agricultural experiments. Farmers wanted to know how to better control the planting-growing process. Much like industrial processes, there are many variables that affect the output, such as seed, soil, temperature, sunlight, moisture, and fertilizer. It is intuitively obvious that these factors interact, but how much of each is optimum, and which has the most effect and in what proportions? Using DOE gave new insights into plant growth. The DOE technique has also been used for many years in food and drug industry research.

DOE is an experimental test technique that identifies and quantifies process variables that have the most effect on process output variation. Many variables can then be changed and tested at the same time, reducing the cost of testing. Common industrial processes like casting, forming, and injection molding have been improved significantly using DOE. It has also accelerated the product design cycle when used in conjunction with concurrent engineering. DOE is a strategic competitive weapon providing more reliable products, reducing concept-to-market time and lowering life cycle costs.

Definition. A planned, structured observation of two or more process input variables and their effect on the output variables under study.

Objective. To select important input variables(factors) and their levels which will optimize the average output response levels and variability.

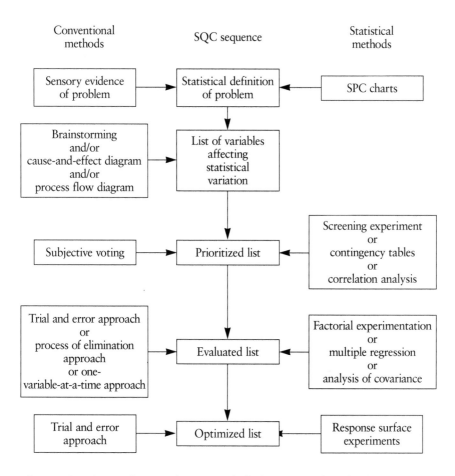

Figure 5.25. Comprehensive depiction of all the statistical methods available to reduce process variation.

Results. These experiments can provide process managers the data on selecting input variables which will make the output less sensitive (robust) to the process and product operational environments.

Methodology. The following steps are important in using DOE.

1. Obtain management support for the implementation of an experiment and approval for the required resources.

2. Organize the experiment team from people with both technical expertise and operating knowledge of the product and process to be studied. It is also necessary for someone to be fully competent in the application and interpretation of the statistical aspects of constructing the experiment and assisting in interpreting results.

3. Have the team establish objectives, kinds of data and measurements, and method of operating.

4. Perform the process analysis using appropriate QC tools to select the input factors for study. Choose responses to be measured. Select the factor levels.

5. Formulate a design and data sheets.

6. Manipulate the process—run the experiment.

7. Analyze the results. Draw conclusions. Identify the controlling factors and their levels.

8. Make an experimental conformation run and identify refinements.

Note that more than one experiment is frequently required to optimize the results.

Although the emphasis in the use of DOE has been on industrial processes, Koselka[20] describes some other applications. For example, a sneaker manufacturer that was planning an expensive, high-tech advertising display evaluated its plan against other lower-cost approaches using DOE. The result was a much less costly display that boosted sales by 35 percent. Another application was the successful improvement of Southwestern Bell service calls. DOE has application anywhere there are several variables that can affect the response.

Multi-Vari Chart. This analysis tool uses range data plotted with respect to time. It provides a picture (data) of what is happening to a piece in a production process to indicate the presence and nature of a problem. There are many separate causes of variation in the statistical variation of a product characteristic. A Pareto analysis would show that a few of the causes contributed most of the variation. The multi-vari chart is a way to visualize the contribution of these causes. There are some types of variation that cannot be seen on a control chart. This technique isolates variables contributing to variation by showing

- Within-piece variation
- Piece-to-piece variation
- Time-to-time variation

This variation is illustrated in Figure 5.26. Vertical lines show variation within a piece or sample. Averages are connected to show their variation. In this example there is little variation between averages but a large variation within pieces. The time variation is large from batch to batch or period to period. This method identifies candidates for future analysis or even experimentation and is relatively easy to apply.

In Japan, DOE became synonymous with Taguchi.[21] He modified the classical DOE approach to make it more practicable and economical. In brief, he developed some fixed experimental matrices that reduced the number of experiments required for various combinations of factors and levels. The tradeoff was an increased risk of not detecting some interactions.

Some have had difficulty accepting this shortcut approach. Taguchi's position was that it is better to do this less expensive level of experimentation than none at all. This approach was acceptable to engineers who frequently take risks for economic reasons.

5.E.3. Specifications, Calibration, and Process Capability

Specifications are written to establish product design criteria and systems performance. They are the requirements for a product, system, or service. Design criteria are the shape, size, materials, performance levels, tolerances, and environment-of-use details. They describe a design so that it can be consistently produced, inspected and tested, and satisfy the customer in its intended use. Properly setting all the criteria is critical to a product's manufacturability, cost, and reliability.

There is a direct relationship between design tolerances and process capability. If tolerances are set based only on successful product performance in development testing, without full knowledge and understanding of the manufacturing process capability, manufacturing will usually have

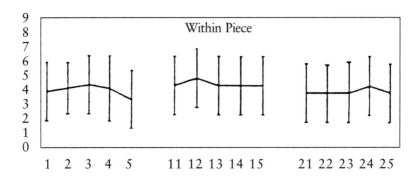

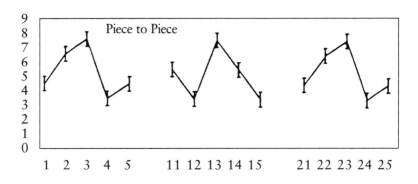

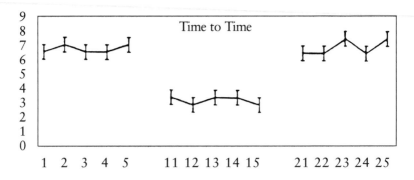

Figure 5.26. Types of variation in the critical or key characteristic of a price.

trouble eliminating defects and controlling costs and delivery. Such incompatibilities can also reduce design-level reliability. Design specifications can be set to reflect process variation using the DOE approach previously discussed. It also involves using concurrent engineering (discussed later) in the design and interpretation of the experiments and use of the results. This experimentation (testing) provides data that

- Allow designers to optimize the design characteristics (parameters) and set tolerances such that the product performance variation can be minimized in the manufacturing and use environments.

- Make products less sensitive to variations in their internal components.

- Identify the best materials, designs, or methods to provide adequate performance.

- Produce the lowest cost design.

Taguchi[22] refers to the first two steps in DOE as parameter design, which is critical to complete before tolerance selection. In other words, the designer will learn how the product will vary when subjected to the variables in the manufacturing process. These data are the basis for setting specification tolerances. If the experiments indicate unmanageable variation, the design must be changed. If, for example, the design proved sensitive to the factory temperature and humidity variations, it would be less expensive to change a new design than to put tight controls on the factory environment. This experimentation methodology leads to a robust design, one relatively insensitive to the manufacturing and use environment.

Statistical Tolerancing. Design engineers, in preparing product drawings and specifications for manufacturing, must specify tolerances around some nominal value. Tolerances that are too narrow raise manufacturing costs. Those that are too broad can result in poor product performance. Most products consist of several parts that must be manufactured so that they will fit well when assembled. Parts' dimensions will vary as the processes that make them vary. An economical but little-used way to set tolerances is to consider the probabilities of where in the tolerance range parts will most likely be produced, and draw dimensions accordingly (when processes are in statistical control). The drawing tolerance used would be

$$T(\text{overall}) = \sqrt{T^2_A + T^2_B + T^2_C + \ldots} \qquad T = \text{tolerances}$$

To safely use this method the process capability should be at least 1.

Calibration. *"Measurement rests on a highly organized, scientific base called Metrology, i.e., the science of measurement. This science underlies the entire systematic approach through which we quantify quality characteristics."*[23]

The accuracy of all measuring tools and instruments, in the design phase, production, or in service, can change with time and use. They must be accurate if the data they collect are is to be used for design, manufacture, field service, or process improvement. This requirement is particularly important in the case of medical equipment directly affecting lives and safety. An adequate control system to ensure equipment accuracy can also be important in product or service liability issues. The basic requirement for maintaining accuracy is that a system be maintained to ensure that measuring equipment is regularly calibrated against known standards. The physical calibration standards used are periodically calibrated and certified against primary standards maintained by the U.S. National Institute of Standards and Technology (NIST).

Calibration records are maintained to evaluate instrument accuracy and behavior with respect to time. Control chart techniques are a valuable tool for this activity. ISO 10012-1-1992, *Quality Assurance Requirements for Measuring Equipment—Part 1: Metrological Conformation System for Measuring Equipment,* describes calibration and control requirements. Similar requirements are described in the military standard MIL-STD-45662.

The accuracy and precision of measuring instruments should be better than 10 times the drawing tolerance. Instruments should be able to make accept-reject decisions at or near the tolerance limit. The instrument accuracy range should not be a significant factor in the measurement.

Management should be aware that the United States is the only country still using the English measurement system. The rest of the world uses the metric system. This can be a factor in buying or supplying to the world market. Some U.S. industries, such as automotive, have converted to the international system, which is referred to as the *SI system*.

Process Capability. One of the first objectives in continuous improvement, for a process where variables are measured, is the determination of how a process is operating. That is, how well does the output conform to what is needed, how stable is the process, and how much does it vary? Process capability is a statistical measure of the inherent ability of a process to continually meet a characteristic requirement. This is done using statistical techniques mentioned earlier in this chapter, such as histograms, trend charts, and control charts. The result of this analysis should be the important determination of the process capability. This measurement has many applications in industrial processes, as well as in services and administration. An example[24] is establishing control charts for sales volume, by salesperson, in different regions and evaluating the results to compare performance against the process capability. Does the process have the capability to allow individuals to meet their goals and objectives?

Process capability can be calculated when a process is in statistical control. It corresponds to the ±3σ control limits. If a process doesn't have the capability to produce output within the range of requirements, process improvement is required. Figure 5.27 presents some typical histograms that illustrate basic situations encountered in process measurement, as well as the most ideal, one that is highly capable. In application, several continuous samples would be required for an accurate process capability determination.

A brief summary of the concept follows.

- Determine if the process is in statistical control. Correct if it is not (remove special causes).

- Determine the relationship between the range of operation (the ±3σ limits) and requirements (the product specification limits for that characteristic).

- Calculate a process capability ratio or index to measure the relationship.

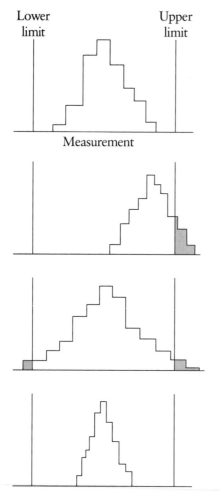

a. Process appears to be centered and capable of producing within required limits. Production outside limits will be infrequent.

b. Same process with a shift from center. It will produce some product outside the upper limit.

c. A process with a centered, balanced distribution of output but with a variation too wide for requirements.

d. A process with a narrow variation and a good margin between limits. It has a high capability.

Figure 5.27. Process capability as indicated by a series of histograms of process samples.

- If the relationship is less than 1, the process is not capable and corrective action is required.

    —The process center may need to be shifted closer to the tolerance center.

    —The tolerance may be increased. This is often possible on noncritical characteristics.

—The process operating range may have to be reduced (the standard deviation reduced).

—Some combination of the preceding may be needed.

Measures. The capability of a process is $\pm 3\sigma$ around the process average. That is, the span of output of a process in statistical control is $\pm 6\sigma$. The distribution of the characteristics being measured should conform generally to the normal distribution. The indication of the capability of a process to produce within requirement limits requires a few simple calculations.

There are two measures for this. One assumes the process average is at the center of the tolerance. In this case the process capability is called the *capability index* and is (for variables)

$$\text{Process capability } (C_p) = \frac{\text{Upper tolerance limit} - \text{Lower tolerance limit}}{\text{Process } 6\sigma}$$

Figure 5.28 illustrates the change in C_p as process improvements are made. To be capable, C_p must be at least 1. This requires tight control and frequent measurement. A C_p of 1 means that 99.73 percent of output will fall within $\pm 3\sigma$. For quality assurance the ratio should be greater than 1 because process performance is dynamic. It does not remain centered around the process average. (The process average is an approximation, it varies with time.)

Another capability measure takes into account the effect of the process average not coinciding with the tolerance center. It is called the process capability index (C_{pk}).

$$C_{pk} = \frac{\text{Tolerance center value} - \text{Process average}}{\dfrac{\text{UTL} - \text{LTL}}{2}}$$

Where LTL = lower tolerance limit

UTL = upper tolerance limit

- If the C_{pk} is 1 or greater, the process is producing within specification limits.

- If the C_{pk} is less than 1, it is producing products outside of specification limits.

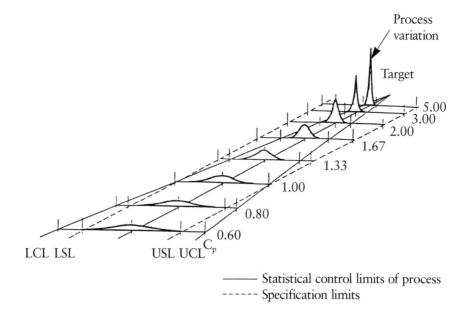

Figure 5.28. Effect on variation of improvements on the process capability.

Another index, C_{pm}, takes into account the target value of interest, which may not be the mean of the required limits (tolerance).

$$C_{pm} = \frac{C_p}{\sqrt{\dfrac{1 + (\text{mean} - \text{target})^2}{\sigma^2}}}$$

Application. Process capability measurement is an important concept as well as a basis for making improvement. It enables design engineers to know their organization's manufacturing capability. It must be, however, used with care. Summarizing what Gunter[25] states,

- C_{pk} is meaningful only when the process is in statistical control and the distribution is close to normal.

- It is meaningless in unstable processes not in control. Using it under those conditions can result in making totally wrong decisions.

- Its proper use requires understanding the principles of statistical process control.

The Six-Sigma Quality Goal. Some leading companies have a goal to achieve a 6σ capability in their key processes. This means they want a process that has a 6σ distance from the average, $\bar{\bar{X}}$, to *each* tolerance limit. It would be equivalent to a C_p of at least 4. Setting an objective of this kind is a way to quantify continuous improvement objectives. Depending on the tolerances and the process, it could take considerable time to get there.

Management must understand that the literal use of sigma assumes a normal distribution. Further, management adoption of a six-sigma quality program is intended to convey an objective of continuous process improvement, beyond just making processes capable. A six-sigma capability has meaning only in variables measurements, not attributes, many of which are important in organizationwide improvement, and all of which can affect quality, cycle time, and cost.

A defect rate objective of 2 per million is also used in describing a six-sigma quality program. Again, this only has meaning for variables.

Also, six sigma is not economically achievable in all processes. When used broadly, it is a slogan that helps quantify the program objective rather than just saying higher quality. Before adopting a six-sigma program management should define how it will measure and report it.

5.F. Concurrent Engineering (CE)

Sometimes also referred to as simultaneous engineering, concurrent engineering is a methodology for the design, development, and manufacturing of products that meet customer demands for high quality, low cost, and a shorter development-to-delivery cycle. This last aspect has become a big factor in competitive strategy. Engineering considerations for design, manufacturing, and delivery occur in parallel from the beginning. In a nonindustrial application CE could be considered the activities of a multifunctional team involved in process redesign or improvement.

The key element of CE is the use of multifunctional teams, including suppliers, from product conception to manufacturing stability. It involves parallel functional activities versus the older serial methodology (see Figure 5.29).[26]

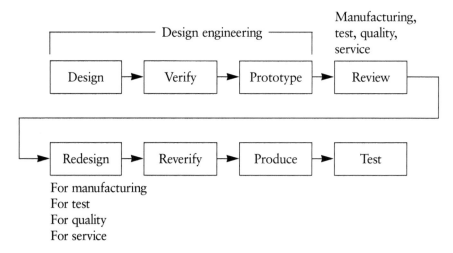

Serial engineering is characterized by departments supplying inputs to design only after a product has been designed, verified, and prototyped.

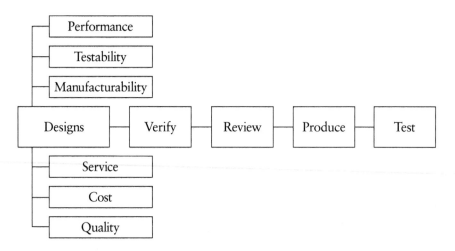

During product design, concurrent engineering draws on various disciplines to trade off parameters such as manufacturability, testability, and serviceability, along with the customary performance, size, weight, and cost.

Figure 5.29. Serial engineering versus concurrent engineering.

All organization functions have a role without time-phased boundaries on their contribution. Participation continues until the product is in production and stable. In CE there is analysis, give-and-take, compromise, modification, and risk taking early in the product cycle so that each function has input from its specialty and is kept up to date on decisions that will affect the members and their work. CE provides better matched product and processes. Organizations can then do early and effective planning and process design concurrently with product design. Modern techniques like computer-aided design and manufacturing tool automation are factors that make it practicable.

The use of CE has a profound effect in reducing costs and improving customer satisfaction as a result of the following:

- Major reductions in design changes in production (lower costs)
- Reduction in concept-to-delivery cycle time by as much as one-third
- Higher production process yields
- Reduction in required resources
- More reliable products
- Earlier break-even point

Concurrent engineering can have a major impact on how organizations are managed because it can aid in breaking down functional barriers. Effective CE requires teamwork, cooperation, information sharing, and open communication. Project management can also be affected; risk is increased because the concurrent activities begin before planning is complete. Scheduling is very difficult during the early concurrent stages. Many critical activities and decisions are made simultaneously and interactively. Also, the work breakdown structure becomes more complex and difficult to establish. CE can create multiple critical paths, making it difficult to define scope and control. With CE, project resource expenditures will be higher earlier, compared to the traditional design-manufacture sequence. With CE, the project manager's primary skill is multidisciplinary knowledge. The secondary skill is the ability to analyze and assess risk. Similar skills are needed by the project team. Behavioral skills are of less importance than in a traditional project.[27] Procurement usually begins before all design parameters are set and before there is a complete bill of material. As a result, project contingency planning becomes more complex.

5.G. Total Productive Maintenance

As an expansion of the responsibilities of production teams, the Japanese developed the concept of *total productive maintenance* (TPM).[28] It involves team members taking responsibility for the condition and maintenance of their work areas and equipment, which includes lubrication, adjustment, and minor repairs. This can also be considered an expansion of the concept of cell manufacturing where a production team performs all or nearly all of the operations on a product in its work area. Adding TPM gives workers more control of all the factors affecting their ability to improve quality and cycle time. They have more control of the process and some of its variables.

Implementing TPM requires team training on equipment maintenance, particularly preventive maintenance. A separate maintenance organization may still exist to do more complex work, but it is at the call of the teams.

The benefit of TPM, in addition to keeping tools and equipment from creating defects, is motivational. Teams feel that they have more control of their work and thus take ownership of the production process. The General Electric Company uses its version of TMP in its Appliance Division teams. TPM is a common factor in the performance of America's best plants.[29] It provides critical support of defect-free processes and is religiously practiced. Workers take much of the responsibility for the smooth, defect-free operation of their machines and equipment.

Key Ideas—Chapter 5

1. Several different tools can be used at each stage of the improvement process to define, measure, and manage.

2. Generally speaking, there are two groups of tools: those that manage data and the process, and those that manage people and the organization as a whole (the seven management tools).

3. QFD keeps the organization's purpose—the customer view—in the forefront of planning.

4. There are three basic categories of cost: prevention, appraisal, and failure. TQ will produce initially higher preventive costs to lower the appraisal and failure costs.

5. There are two groups of data that may require different statistical analysis to monitor: hard data (product, dimensional, objective) and soft data (service, customer perception, satisfaction).

6. Design specifications and process capability to meet those designs are two interrelated issues that must be considered to control a process.

References

1. *Memory Jogger II.* 1995. Methuen, Mass.: GOAL/QPC.

2. Juran, J. M., and F. M. Gryna. 1988. *Juran's Quality Control Handbook,* 4th ed. New York, N.Y.: McGraw-Hill.

3. Fiero, J. 1992. "The Crawford Slip Method." *Quality Progress* (May).

4. Galloway, D. 1994. *Mapping Work Processes.* Milwaukee, Wis.: ASQC Quality Press.

5. *Memory Jogger II.*

6. Tague, N. R. 1995. *The Quality Toolbox.* Milwaukee, Wis.: ASQC Quality Press.

7. Zultner, R. E. 1989. "Software QFD: Applying QFD to Software." *Rocky Mountain Conference Proceedings,* Milwaukee, Wis.: ASQC.

8. Gopalakrishnan, K. N., B. E. McIntyre, and J. C. Sprague. 1992. "Implementing Internal Quality Improvements With the House of Quality." *Quality Progress* (September).

9. Gray, J. 1995. "Quality Costs: A Report Card on Business." *Quality Progress* (April).

10. Taguchi, G. 1986. *Introduction to Quality Engineering.* Dearborn, Mich.: American Supplier Institute.

11. Ouchi, W. 1981. *Theory Z*. Reading, Mass.: Addison-Wesley.

12. Gadd, K. W., and J. S. Oakland. 1996. "Chimera or Culture? Business Process Reengineering for TQM." *Quality Management Journal* 3, No. 3.

13. Hammer, M., and J. Champy. 1992. *Reengineering the Corporation: A Manifesto for Business Revelation*. New York, N.Y.: Harper Business.

14. Harrington, H. J. 1991. *Business Process Improvement*. San Francisco: Ernst & Young, L.L.P.

15. Morris, D., and J. Brandon. 1993. *Re-engineering Your Business*. New York, N.Y.: McGraw-Hill.

16. Gadd and Oakland. "Chimera or Culture? Business Process Reengineering for TQM."

17. Hayes, B. 1992. *Measuring Customer Satisfaction*. Milwaukee, Wis.: ASQC Quality Press.

18. Juran and Gryna. *Juran's Quality Control Handbook*.

19. Glasser, G. T. 1985. "Quality Audits of Paperwork Operations." *Journal of Quality Technology* 17, No. 2.

20. Koselka, R. 1996. "The New Mantra: MVT." *Forbes*. 11 March.

21. Lochner, R. H. and J. E. Matar. 1990. *Designing for Quality: An Introduction to the Best of Taguchi and Western Methods of Statistical Experimental Design*. Milwaukee, Wis.: ASQC Quality Press.

22. Taguchi. *Introduction to Quality Engineering*.

23. Juran and Gryna. *Juran's Quality Control Handbook*.

24. Nolan, T. W., and L. P. Provost. 1990. "Understanding Variation." *Quality Progress* (December).

25. Gunter, B. H. 1989. "The Use and Abuse of C_{pk}." Series. *Quality Progress* (January, March, May, June).

26. Kerzner, H. 1995. *Project Management*. New York, N.Y.: Van Nostrand Reinhold.

27. Turino, J. 1991. "Concurrent Engineering: Making It Work Calls for Input from Everyone." *IEEE Spectrum* (July).

28. Turbide, D. A. 1995. "Japan's New Advantage: Total Productive Maintenance." *Quality Progress* (March).

29. Kinni, T. B. 1996. *America's Best: Industry Week's Guide to World-Class Plants*. New York, N.Y.: John Wiley & Sons.

Related References

Adair, C. B., and B. A. Murray. 1994. *Breakthrough Process Redesign*. New York, N.Y.: AMACOM.

Andrews, D. C., and S. K. Stalick. 1994. *Business Reengineering: The Survival Guide*. New York, N.Y.: Yourdon Press.

ASQC Automotive Division Process Control Manual. 1986. Milwaukee, Wis.: ASQC.

ASQC Quality Costs Committee. 1987. *Guide for Reducing Quality Costs*. Milwaukee, Wis.: ASQC Quality Press.

———. 1989. *ASQC Quality Costs: Ideas and Applications*, Vol. 2. Milwaukee, Wis.: ASQC Quality Press.

———. 1990. *Principles of Quality Costs: Principles, Implementation, and Use*, 2d ed. Milwaukee, Wis.: ASQC Quality Press.

ASQC Statistics Division. 1996. *Glossary and Tables for Statistical Quality Control*, 4th ed. Milwaukee, Wis.: ASQC.

Atkinson, H., and J. Hamburg. 1994. *Linking Quality to Profits: Quality-Based Cost Management*. Milwaukee, Wis.: ASQC Quality Press.

Barber, T. B. 1985. *Quality by Experimental Design*. New York, N.Y.: Marcel Dekker.

Blake, S., R. G. Launsby, and D. C. Weese. 1994. "Experimental Design Meets the Realities of the 1990s." *Quality Progress* (October).

Bossert, J. L. 1990. *Quality Function Deployment: A Practitioner's Approach*. Milwaukee, Wis.: ASQC Quality Press.

Cartin, T. J. 1993. *Principles and Practices of TQM*. Milwaukee, Wis.: ASQC Quality Press.

Cohen, L. 1995. *Quality Function Deployment: How to Make QFD Work for You.* Milwaukee, Wis.: ASQC Quality Press.

Collins, B., and E. Huge. 1993. *Management by Policy.* Milwaukee, Wis.: ASQC Quality Press.

Daniel, W., and J. Terrill. 1992. *Business Statistics for Management and Economics.* Boston, Mass.: Houghton-Mifflin.

Davenport, T. H. 1993. *Process Innovation: Reengineering Work Through Information Technology.* Boston, Mass.: Harvard Business School Press.

Deming, W. E. 1982. *Quality, Productivity, and Competitive Position.* Cambridge, Mass.: Massachusetts Institute of Technology, Center for Advanced Engineering Study.

Evans, J. R. 1993. *The Management and Control of Quality.* Minneapolis, Minn.: West Publishing Co.

Futnell, D. 1995. "When Quality Is a Matter of Taste, Use Reliability Indexes." *Quality Progress* (May).

Godfrey, A. B. 1996. "Life Cycle Costs." *Quality Digest* (November).

Griffith, G. K. 1996. *Statistical Process Control Methods for Long and Short Runs,* 2d ed. Milwaukee, Wis.: ASQC Quality Press.

Hartley, J. R. 1992. *Concurrent Engineering.* Cambridge, Mass.: Productivity Press.

Hunter, M. R., and R. D. Van Landingham. 1994. "Listening to the Customer Using QFD." *Quality Progress* (April).

Ishikawa, K. 1974. *Guide to Quality Control.* Tokyo: Asian Productivity Organization.

Juran, J. M., and F. M. Gryna. 1988. *Juran's Quality Control Handbook,* 4th ed. New York, N.Y.: McGraw-Hill.

Kelada, J. N. 1996. *Integrating Reengineering with Total Quality.* Milwaukee, Wis.: ASQC Quality Press.

Knowlton, J., and R. Keppinger. 1993. "The Experimental Process." *Quality Progress* (February).

Kotter, J. P. 1996. *Leading Change*. Boston, Mass.: Harvard Business School Press.

Leach, L. P. 1996. "TQM, Reengineering, and the Edge of Chaos." *Quality Progress* (February).

McFadden, F. R. 1993. "Six-Sigma Quality Programs." *Quality Progress* (June).

Morgan, M. W. 1996. "Measuring Performance With Customer-Defined Metrics." *Quality Progress* (December).

Nissen, M. E. 1996. "A Focused Review of the Reengineering Literature: Expert Frequently Asked Questions." *Quality Management Journal* 3, No. 3.

Pennella, C. R. 1992. *Managing the Metrology System*. Milwaukee, Wis.: ASQC Quality Press.

Pyzdek, T., and R. W. Berger. 1992. *Quality Engineering Handbook*. Milwaukee, Wis.: ASQC Quality Press.

Scholtes, P. 1989. *The Team Handbook*. Madison, Wis.: Joiner Associates.

Snee, R. D. 1993. "Creating Robust Work Processes." *Quality Progress* (February).

Sullivan, L. P. 1986. "Quality Function Deployment." *Quality Progress* (June).

Tadikamalla, P. R. 1994. "The Confusion Over Six-Sigma Quality." *Quality Progress* (November).

Zaciewski, R. D., and L. Nemeth. 1995. "The Multi-Vari Chart: An Underutilized Quality Tool." *Quality Progress* (October).

Chapter 6

Human Resource Management

Prior to the introduction of TQ organizations, a discussion of human resource management would primarily involve the functions of a human resource specialty organization, or personnel department. Most organizations still have such functions, but human resource management in a TQ organization is a different concept. It involves using leadership as well as management to guide organizations through change to a new management philosophy and organization structure, particularly through the use of teams. The organization focus becomes both outward, with its objective of customer satisfaction, and inward, toward continuous improvement. This requires a management style far different from the traditional (management styles are discussed in Chapter 2).

The resulting structure change has been to reduce the layers of management. Many of the functions of lower management, those directly related to managing work as a process, have become the responsibility of process teams. Employees become more in partnership with management, with a common goal of greater customer satisfaction. Managers function more as facilitators to assist teams, helping teams work together, scheduling the proper training, supporting team requests for resources, and providing communication throughout the organization. This is a management role different from the direct-and-control model, and it requires different knowledge and skills.

The role of the quality manager and the mission of the quality function also change, generally in the same direction, but with some unique differences (this is discussed in Chapter 3). The broader responsibilities of quality management now include the following:

1. Participation with upper management in setting quality improvement objectives for the overall organization as well as for any special quality function.

2. Maintaining a supportive work environment.

3. Managing work processes to improve quality.

4. Providing quality improvement expertise to the overall organization, managers, and teams.

5. Maintaining a focus on the external customer. Participating in or leading system improvements and corrective actions.

6. Managing organizationwide management systems and process audits.

6.A. Leadership Roles and Responsibilities

A requirement of managers today is to lead as well as manage. This need results from the adoption of the continuous improvement paradigm; that is, managing processes and employee empowerment. These factors require a change in organization responsibilities and structure and require new skills, work methods, and attitudes about and of employees and their role in the organization's success. Success in making such significant changes requires managers to demonstrate leadership. They must clearly define what is needed, how the organization will go about making the changes, what the role of management will be, and what is expected of all employees. Leaders are believed and followed when their actions consistently support their words. One of the strongest supportive actions upper management can take is to replace managers who don't accept the new direction and their new role. Actions such as this will go a long way to make employees believe in the need for them to change.

Leadership and Management Compared

Managers	*Leaders*
Administer	Innovate, energize, inspire
Use systems and structure	Focus on people
Maintain the status quo	Produce change; align people and the organization with the vision
Control	Trust, guide, coach
Take a short view	Focus on the future (long view)
Ask how and when	Ask what and why
Are bottom-line oriented	Are forward looking (vision and strategies)
Focus on doing things right	Focus on doing the right things

Of course this list isn't an either/or categorization. It's a matter of dominance and emphasis. Traditional management stresses the left column. Leading and managing an organization through the tough changes required in the present and future operating climate requires more of the behavior in the leadership column.

Kotter[1] discusses the most common management mistakes and errors in change efforts that limit or prevent the meeting of goals. Summarized, they are

- Failure to establish a sense of urgency.

- Not developing a significant and powerful coalition of managers to guide and sustain change.

- Providing an unclear vision; that is, where the change will take the organization.

- Failure to communicate the vision to the lowest levels. Words and deeds do not correspond.

- Not removing all obstacles, personal and organizational, that limit following the vision.

- Not providing short-term successful experiences.

- Setting and expecting cultural change in less than three years.

- Removing the force for change before the changes sought have become the way things are done.

The factors in quality management leadership are similar and usually have a broad scope since the quality manager deals with most, if not all, of the organization functions:

1. Communicate ideas and information to and from a variety of teams and organizations as well as to and from other managers.

2. Recognize actions and activities that can lead to conflict and take action to avoid, resolve, or minimize them. Quality managers should be sensitized to this if they have had audit experience.

3. Exhibit leadership traits that will motivate subordinates to reach objectives.

4. Demonstrate communication and negotiation skills in dealing with internal and external customers and suppliers.

5. Maintain knowledge of upper management planning and organization development directions.

6. Champion all the quality improvement initiatives by contributing any useful personal skills and knowledge.

6.A.1. Conflict Resolution

Conflicts develop from differences in opinion, attitudes, personalities, goals, information, language, organization culture, new or unresolved problems, and management inadequacies. Conflicts occur in every organization, and the ability to handle them requires an understanding of why they occur. The cause has to be identified before resolution or progress can be made (this is true of any kind of problem).

The quality organization has traditionally been involved in conflicts and their resolution because the position typically interacts with other functions. Quality has played the role of judge and police officer, evaluating other people's work and requiring corrective action. In the traditional role of monitoring, it has also produced data that sometimes put other people in an unfavorable light. The result in a traditionally managed organization meant, at a minimum, being blamed for something.

In a TQ organization, quality issues are primarily resolved at the team level. In the proper climate, teams view problems as opportunities to improve. This focus can reduce the conditions for conflict. One caveat is that conflicts tend to be more frequent and severe during the transition period from the traditional to the TQ organization. Conflict is something management should expect and prepare to act on quickly.

Some sources of conflict include

- Personality differences—likes and dislikes
- Ambiguous or incorrect communications
- Limited resources
- Policies
- Inadequate documentation
- Poor system design
- Inadequate training
- Time conflicts
- Poor goal setting
- Lack of management support or leadership
- Lack of team member commitment
- Conflicting priorities
- Regulatory requirements

Conflicts can occur in teams, particularly those composed of representatives of several functions (multifunctional). The source of conflict can be differences in educational level or the different goals of each function, particularly in the earlier stages of team management. This accentuates the need for competent team facilitators and leaders. Setting adequate rules of behavior and using structured problem-solving tools can help control strong differences in opinion and behavior.

Another source of team conflicts is the decision-making process. When decisions are made by more than one individual there are two possible approaches, majority voting or group consensus. Voting may be quickest but it results in winners and losers. The residual resentments can make team building more difficult. Consensus is the preferred method for group decision making, at least for issues that are not simple. It is not the quickest or easiest and it takes skill to achieve, but it will result in greater support for the result.

Quality managers and team leaders must consider the following factors in team dynamics and decision making.

Participation. Team members must understand that participation is required and must be kept in balance between members to prevent anyone dominating the group.

Selling. Ideas should be presented logically, with a minimum of emotion.

Relinquishing. When a member has sold an idea to the best of his or her ability, but is not convincing or influencing members, the individual must accept and support the team direction.

Evaluating. All members should take part in evaluating team operation and project results.

Relationship. Each member must be encouraged to resolve conflicts with other team members.

Task accomplishment. Every member must understand his or her task responsibilities, including what has to be done, when, how, and by whom.

The manager or leader, as facilitator, can encourage and guide the team in the use of the following:

Withdrawing. When a position can't be won, when the stakes are low, to preserve neutrality or reputation. It is a way of relinquishing in the decision-making process.

Smoothing. To help achieve the overall objective, to create an obligation for a tradeoff at a later date, to maintain harmony and create goodwill, or when any offered solution will do.

Bargaining. Also called conflict negotiation. When two parties need to be winners, when there are several strong parties, or to maintain a relationship with an opponent. When an individual is uncertain of his or her position, or when it looks like it is necessary to get at least something out of the settlement.

Collaborating. To create a stronger power base when skills and knowledge are complementary and can achieve more than each skill alone, when there is enough time and where there is trust.

Forcing. When a do-or-die situation exists, when important principles are at stake, when one position is stronger, when trying to gain status or power, or when the relationship is unimportant.

Frequently, organization conflicts can be attributed to the inadequacies of management. The source of conflict is mainly the control factor. Most managers still manage by direction and control. Even when teams are introduced, managers have great difficulty giving them the power and information necessary to operate without close supervision. This not only results in conflict and sets teams up for failure, but spreads cynicism throughout the organization. The only resolution to this kind of conflict is for upper management to replace managers who can't or won't change.

6.A.2. Professional Ethics

Buban,[2] in her article "Factoring Ethics Into the TQM Equation," emphasizes that TQM is most effective when the organizational environment encourages openness, trust, and ethics. She includes discussions regarding a company's obligation to its employees, to support their right to be treated fairly and provide employees the opportunity to reach their potential. Likewise, employees have an obligation to do what is right. Buban also includes a definition of ethics by former Supreme Court Justice Potter Stewart: "knowing the difference between what you have a right to do and what is the right thing to do." Probably the most commonly known code of ethics is the Hippocratic oath for physicians. A caution attributed to Hippocrates is, "abstain from whatever is deleterious and mischievous." This is also an appropriate moral basis for behavior in business.

It is useful and necessary to have a written code of behavior that goes beyond the letter of the law. Ethical behavior is more than just legal behavior, although that is paramount. Laws don't cover all behavior that is considered unethical. For example, it is not illegal if management doesn't take all reasonable steps to ship nondefective products, but if management knows that it is shipping defective material and takes no action, that is unethical as well as shortsighted. It nevertheless happens when a monthly billing must be met.

An important element of leadership is doing the right thing, not just in management decisions but in overall behavior and the treatment of employees. Business ethics, or the lack of them, have been given a lot of public exposure in recent years. The subject has gained such importance that it is now taught as a separate course in most business schools, although it was rarely mentioned before the mid-1980s.

Quality managers often play an important role when an ethical question is identified regarding some management actions or decisions. A manager may observe some questionable agreements between purchasing management and a supplier, for example. Once this is confirmed, he or she has a responsibility to inform upper management. The quality manager's role is different from that of others in that the manager plays a dual role on quality issues, as a trustee of both the company and the customer. The quality manager must develop a clear understanding of what ethical questions could be involved and adopt a consistent code of behavior. He or she should also explore the issue with upper management to be sure that this code does not conflict with that of the company.

ASQC's code of ethics can be used as a guide to develop a similar code for any individual or organization.

Code of Ethics

To uphold and advance the honor and dignity of the profession, and in keeping with high standards of ethical conduct I acknowledge that I:

Fundamental Principles

I. Will be honest and impartial, and will serve with devotion my employer, my clients and the public.

III. Will strive to increase the competence and prestige of the profession.

III. Will use my knowledge and skill for the advancement of human welfare, and in promoting the safety and reliability of products for public use.

IV. Will earnestly endeavor to aid the work of the Society.

Relations with the Public

1.1 Will do whatever I can to promote the reliability and safety of all products that come within my jurisdiction.

1.2 Will endeavor to extend public knowledge of the work of the Society and its members that relates to the public welfare.

1.3 Will be dignified and modest in explaining my work and merit.

1.4 Will preface any public statements that I may issue by clearly indicating on whose behalf they are made.

Relations with Employers and Clients

2.1 Will act in professional matters as a faithful agent or trustee for each employer or client.

2.2 Will inform each client or employer of any business connections, interests or affiliations which might influence my judgment or impair the equitable character of my services.

2.3 Will indicate to my employer or client the adverse consequences to be expected if my professional judgment is overruled.

2.4 Will not disclose information concerning the business affairs or technical processes of any present or former employer or client without his consent.

2.5 Will not accept compensation from more than one party for the same service without the consent of all parties. If employed, I will engage in supplementary employment of consulting practice only with the consent of my employer.

Relations with Peers

3.1 Will take care that credit for the work of others is given to those to whom it is due.

3.2 Will endeavor to aid the professional development and advancement of those in my employ or under my supervision.

3.3 Will not compete unfairly with others; will extend my friendship and confidence to all associates and those with whom I have business relations.

Other factors of importance to ethical conduct are confidentiality and conflict of interest. Confidentiality is of major importance regarding the business affairs and technical processes of employers and suppliers and confidences given to managers by employees. Information of this nature should not be disclosed without prior consent.

6.B. Quality Staffing Issues

The proper management of staffing is critical to the success of any organization and critical for organizations in transition to full implementation of TQ. Staffing needs have changed as dramatically as structure and management philosophy. Deming[3] wrote that managers for the new organization paradigm need *profound knowledge,* which may include a good understanding of all the subject matter in this book. He also advocated "more careful selection of people in the first place."

The new workplace involves newly evolved structures that emphasize process management by employee empowered teams. More flexibility and authority is given to initiate actions previously assigned to managers. In some advanced TQ organizations teams operate with a great deal of autonomy. They are given the schedule, tools, and materials, and they organize the tasks and assign responsibility for work completion. The capabilities demonstrated by these teams were not just randomly picked from the existing work force or easily found outside it.

Morgan and Smith[4] have done extensive research and consulting work on the new needs for staffing. They wrote

Assumptions that the work force can be trained to implement TQ are not always true. Many of the attributes needed are not available in the present work force and not easily trained for in practice. The new quality-focused organizations will require constant restaffing decisions as workers move from one location or project to another and in and out of the firm.

Organization staffing needs frequent reevaluation to identify changing skill needs.

There are identifiable key variables in staffing for TQ; failure to recognize and address them is a major factor in TQ implementation failure. This correlates with the ideas of the writers discussed in Chapter 1, that a mechanistic approach to TQ implementation won't work. In this case it cannot be assumed that worker training is all that is necessary to develop teams.

6.B.1. Selection

The new workplace requires the following:[5]

- A greater variety and complexity of skills (understand and apply QC tools).
- Flexibility and adaptability, openness, initiative.
- Ability to contribute. The ability to learn and apply knowledge varies among individuals.
- Skills and knowledge. Relatively few people are available who fit the new profile. Poor math and reading skills are common.

Other variables include

- Ineffective staffing is costly. It limits organization progress and raises training costs. Resulting termination is costly in terms of impact on the organization's efforts to build stability and trust.
- Putting people in leadership roles for which they are poorly prepared compounds the difficulty of developing the new organization.

Morgan and Smith also describe the mounting evidence suggesting that those firms making the greatest strides in the revision of their staffing practices report greater success with the TQ effort. For example, in a study of ASQC sustaining member organizations, the greater the extent to which the organization has incorporated TQ the more likely it is to include specific quality attributes in the staffing process. A recent survey of 245 human resource managers found that respondents from firms that had implemented more of these newer selection, promotion, and career development approaches describe their TQ outcomes more positively in terms of commitment and effectiveness.

A Systematic Approach. Human resource staffing needs must be closely aligned with strategic quality plans and initiatives. Following the establishment of those plans and their deployment throughout the organization, the specific job needs are be identified. Defining the new capability, skill, and knowledge needs is a critical step in planning. A comprehensive job analysis is required.

Staffing for quality improvement is managed as a process using the same process evaluation and development tools applied to other organization processes, with the same objective of continuous improvement. Like most processes, the decisions and actions taken at the beginning have the most impact on system effectiveness. The effects of other activities, such as restructuring and downsizing, must also be factored into staffing planning.

The staffing process can be expressed in terms of a sequence of design questions.[6]

- What is quality readiness? What specific attributes (knowledge, skills, aptitudes, and personal characteristics) must employees possess in a TQ setting? Which are most relevant to the organization? Which must new employees bring into the organization? Which can and should be developed through training?

- By what legal, professional, and technical standards is the staffing process measured and evaluated? How are these standards designed into the staffing process?

- What role does the staffing function play in the strategic plan of the organization? How can systematic staffing contribute to the quality initiative?

- What recruiting strategies and sources will generate quality-oriented applicants?

- What tools (interviews, written tests, performance tests, reference checks) will yield useful information about applicants? What are benchmarked companies doing now to build a staff for the challenges of the future?

- What should the organization do to foster continual development of its work force?

- How can quality-oriented leaders be identified, selected, and developed?
- What factors should be considered in staffing teams?
- What effect will the issues of downsizing and the use of contingent workers have on the quality effort?
- How should the staffing process be evaluated and improved?

Personnel Sources. A few colleges have course work to specifically train students in the skills and knowledge that contribute to TQ implementation (the appropriate personal characteristics would have to be evaluated before hiring). Another source of personnel is through ASQC certification programs, as well as initiatives such as partnerships between business and academia (Total Quality Business and Education Partnership).

The Baldrige Award criteria also include, under human resource planning, an evaluation element.

- Formation of partnerships with educational institutions to develop employees or to help ensure the future supply of well-prepared employees
- Establishment of partnerships with other companies or networks to share training or spread job opportunities
- Introduction of distance learning or other technology-based learning approaches

6.B.2. Performance Evaluation

The objective of performance appraisals is to provide improved performance, but many do not. Many managers don't like to do them, one reason being that they do not communicate ongoing performance evaluation with their subordinates. The appraisal event then becomes a confrontation. Appraisals are often performed superficially because managers are required to do them and quickly get the forms back to personnel. Some managers wait for the appraisal interview to unload all of their complaints and criticisms on employees. It is also not uncommon for a manager who can't handle confrontation simply to give everyone a good appraisal. Any of these situations will result in employee resentment or cynicism because the performance evaluation is distorted, adds little value, and results in little constructive change in behavior. Many books and articles have been written on the subject of appraisals, indicating that many managers are still looking for a more useful approach. It remains a subject of contention, but performance appraisals in team-managed organizations raise additional issues.

Appraisals are a management-directed process. In the opinion of many knowledgeable people, they are not compatible with team-structured organizations. They don't fit well with the role of manager as facilitator and coach. Performance appraisals are still widely used, and organizations are struggling to find something more compatible with empowered employees, team-driven cultures, and TQ philosophies.

Eckes[7] points out that there is still a prevailing attitude among many managers that their role is to control, organize and direct, and evaluate employees. Deming[8] also criticized performance appraisals. He and other quality leaders, such as Scholtes,[9] believe that there is a conflict between appraisals and TQ. The basis for the conflict is the contradiction between managers' view of their job and the empowerment of employees in teams to direct their own work.

The reasons why organizations continue to use appraisals, according to Eckes, are as follows:

- Appraisals provide feedback to employees.
- Appraisals are used to determine salary increases.
- Appraisals identify people for promotion.
- Appraisals are used to deal with human resource legalities.

Equally compelling but opposed to performance evaluations are the following reasons that highlight the conflict between TQ and appraisals. They also support Deming's opinion that appraisals are one of the seven deadly sins afflicting Western management.

- Appraisals nourish short-term performance and destroy long-term planning.
- Appraisals destroy teamwork.
- Appraisals foster mediocrity and are destructive to the individual being reviewed.
- Appraisals assume that people are responsible for all results.

- Appraisals contain subjectivity and immeasurables.

- Appraisals are detection oriented.

- Appraisals negate the concept of common-cause versus special-cause variation.

- Job descriptions are frequently obsolete, not reflecting the current job need. The appraisal then becomes more subjective.

- Appraisals usually don't identify future skills needed, or are derived from the strategic quality plans. The employee is not aware of the plans or given time to acquire identified skills.

There are as many variations of appraisal systems as there are organizations. What is needed is a process that matches the new order organizations. Eckes[10] offers two alternatives: customer-supplier appraisals and process appraisals.

Customer-supplier appraisals use customer satisfaction surveys to obtain performance evaluation information. As more organizations recognize internal as well as external customers, the logical next step is to examine how well the employees satisfy the customers. Five steps are suggested to incorporate such a change into the traditional appraisal process to take customer input into account.

1. Identify customers (internal and external).

2. Identify customer requirements (a few key ones).

3. Establish metrics for current performance (in one example, even subjective evaluation information was included by developing a 0-to-3 rating scale on satisfaction items).

4. Identify opportunities for improvement (low ratings in step 3 would require corrective action).

5. Form teams to develop improvement plans (teams are just to develop improvement plans for step 4.

Process appraisals deal with the components or traits that make a process successful rather than focusing on the output of the process. For example, if increased sales are the objective and the economy turns downward, the output may be beyond the control of the individual being appraised. But if the *components* of increasing sales (a better brochure, more frequent sales calls, better product knowledge) are the focus of the appraisal, the individual can work to improve, regardless of the forces beyond his or her control.

6.B.3. Professional Development

As a consequence of the continually changing organization structure, policies, and skills, professional development of employees is an increasingly important factor in modern management. Individuals have the responsibility for their own professional development, but management has the responsibility to provide employees with the opportunities that will allow them to develop, practice, and expand their professional knowledge and skills, and it must implement policies that encourage such development and give coaching and guidance during the process.

Proper job assignment is a key factor in successful development. Challenging job assignments paired with an individual's skills have proven to be a key factor in professional development and individual growth, progress, and self-confidence. Proper guidance and coaching are also important factors. Many managers guide subordinates to reflect their own image (management style and values). This may be harmful to the individual and the organization if it perpetuates a culture needing change. Professional individuals must therefore keep themselves informed of current management practices and trends. Upper management of organizations trying to change their culture may have to provide a coaching and guidance program separate from internal management.

Management can also improve professional development by selecting employees with high potential and offering opportunities for organization-sponsored special education. These can include special seminars and academic management training programs. Special nonprofessional training needs, identified by the strategic planning process output, can be accomplished with in-house training using internal or outside instructors, or by support for appropriate courses at outside educational institutions. This is discussed further in Chapter 7.

Professionals recognize that education is, more than ever, a never-ending process, and they need to increase and broaden their skills to be able to satisfy changing job requirements. Employees need multiple skills as organizations evolve to become more responsive and flexible to changing market conditions. Many professionals and other organization members entered their present jobs with qualifications narrowly fitting the job needs. One of the realities of organization restructuring, downsizing, reengineering, and team management is the need for members with broader and even multiple occupational skills. Many with narrow or obsolete skills are being classified as unqualified for the new jobs. These changing organization needs are expected to continue.

Toffler[11] states that displaced managers need new skills, but, most important, they need new cultural skills—how to operate in a different kind of organization culture. Juran[12] discusses the role of a corporate quality office in professional development as the collection and dissemination of information on quality methodology. Functional quality managers themselves must keep current with the latest trends and ideas in managing for quality and keep their managers informed of what new knowledge or skills will be required to meet objectives. New trends, ideas, and methodologies are disseminated through newsletters, bulletins, or training sessions. A major source for new ideas is through ASQC membership, seminars, other organization quality meetings, management and business publications, and the Internet.

6.B.4. Goals and Objectives

Chapter 3 discusses goals and objectives for the overall organization. Goals and objectives for quality function staffing flow from the organization's strategic and tactical plans, goals, and objectives for quality improvement. For example, if the organization's goals include specific process improvements and benchmarking, the quality manager could be responsible for determining the knowledge, skills, and time period required and the quality function role in meeting those objectives. The result of this analysis would be the quality staffing requirements: when, from where (source), how much, what kind, and the necessary resources.

Other goals would be the plans for developing existing quality function personnel to meet future needs. These requirements would identify all training needs, and they should be coordinated with the overall organization's training plans. Many organizations today plan the same kind of training, but related to teams and processes. Once planned, programs must be monitored, periodically reassessed, and action taken when any deviation appears. If, after initial planning, the tasks for staff training and development are significant, they should be managed as a project (see Chapter 8).

6.C. Quality Responsibilities in Job/Position Descriptions

An activity that frequently receives inadequate attention is the maintenance of job or position descriptions. This is particularly true during periods of organizational change. Unfortunately, that is when accurate descriptions are needed. Such changes usually result in new employees or employees in new positions with an unclear understanding of their responsibilities. If there are also changes in management the problem is compounded because the new managers have no accurate framework of expectations and scope of responsibility.

This deficiency needs the attention of every manager during the kinds of changes taking place in the modern organization; particularly where quality responsibilities are being shared by all members, these responsibilities must be clarified. For example, in industrial organizations the traditional quality function of inspection has been minimized or eliminated. It has been replaced with process control and inspection by the people doing the work. This not only requires new training for everyone in using quality improvement tools, but the redefinition of the responsibilities of many jobs. In addition, in many kinds of organizations a quality function never existed and the quality factor never appeared in positive descriptions New descriptions have to be developed systematically, like process improvement itself, so that the descriptions and processes match.

The ISO 9000 series does not specifically require job descriptions, but it does require documentation of the work and responsibilities of employees who manage, perform, or verify work affecting quality. In practical terms, such jobs would have to be described.

Approach. After an analysis of quality staff jobs for the short and long term, changes in quality manager and staff position descriptions include the following:

- Description of the role and relationship between quality staff and teams.
- Specific skills and knowledge requirements in every quality staff position description.

Quality responsibilities reflected in every level of job description should flow down from the top and include the following:

Top management

- Responsibility for maintaining the vision for the overall organization
- Leadership toward achieving world-class customer satisfaction
- Leadership in setting quality policies and goals for continuous improvement
- Setting quality goals and objectives using a management team approach
- Recognizing quality improvements

Other managers and professionals

- Planning for quality improvement
- Support and participation in teams and other quality improvement activities
- Acquisition and application of the skills and knowledge required to participate in team leadership and problem solving
- A focus on external and internal customer satisfaction
- Responsibility for obtaining assigned team resources

Employees

- Participation in and support of improvement teams
- Acquisition of the skills and knowledge required to participate in improvement teams
- A focus on internal and external customer satisfaction

6.D. Employee/Team Empowerment

A major principle in TQ is the empowerment of organization members to manage their work as members of process improvement teams. The definition of empowerment is giving employees the authority to decide and act on their own initiatives. Tompkins[13] defines empowerment as, "the leadership process of building, developing and increasing the power of an organization to perform through the synergistic evolution of teams."

Empowerment implies a significant degree of discretion and independence for those empowered, with some limitations. This means making decisions applying only to work or process improvements, that do not require capital expenditures or commit the company to any outside agents. Managers have always been empowered in their job scope and authority. Some of that now has to be shared with their subordinates.

Employee/team empowerment is a way to evaluate and manage change, but it is also very difficult to implement. In general, the larger the organization the more difficult it is to implement change.[14] To provide for a culture of empowerment, management style must be that of open team management (participative with a team structure). This requires managers who have the skills to support, coach, and develop people doing work in teams. They need to encourage employees to become more responsible for their own decisions and their own work-based learning. In-depth management development is required before employees can be empowered effectively, because empowerment requires a supportive, open style not commonly found in non-TQ organizations.

Empowerment differs from delegation. With delegation, an employee still has to consult with a supervisor before taking any significant action. But empowerment does not mean autonomy, where employees can act without limits. Since there is confusion about what empowerment does mean, organizations contemplating its use should establish and promulgate a clear definition of authority and boundaries.

Empowerment is of value because successful TQ organizations have found that it results in more effective and productive employees and significant, innovative process improvements. It permits decisions to be made quickly, based on an understanding of customer needs.

Applying the empowerment concept successfully requires the appropriate organization structure and management style. It is not effective in a hierarchical structure or under autocratic management because it requires management to surrender some of its power. Some degree of empowerment is necessary for effective management delayering and downsizing, but appropriate management training and development should precede those kinds of changes. Success in changing to a team-based, empowered organization requires gaining employees' trust and fostering a feeling of security. Suddenly announced reductions have the opposite effect, creating mistrust and anxiety.

The need for management preimplementation study can be critical. It is not uncommon for traditionally trained managers to underestimate the power shift that occurs when evolving to a climate of team empowerment. Later, when they recognize the shift and are not prepared to accept it, they may react autocratically and sabotage the TQ effort. Teams falter, and sometimes dissolve, and the team empowerment concept gets a bad name.

Features. Some features that highlight the differences between traditional and empowered organizations include

- Changes in decision-making rules. In a traditional organization, decisions are passed down through management. In an empowered organization, issues are handled by process employees. Teams solve operations problems and make decisions.

- Organization structures in traditional organizations are managed by functions with specialized members. Responsibilities are defined by the organization chart. In empowered organizations, the structures are broad and integrated, with teams managing at least the main work processes.

- Traditional, more vertical organizations have a narrow span of control. Decisions are management controlled. Using empowerment, authority is shared and organizations have fewer layers.

- Communication differences are significant. Traditionally, management controls information, and communication is mostly vertical. When empowered, organizations (teams) share information widely and in all directions, to where it is needed. There is open communication of all types.

Implementation. Converting a traditional organization to an empowered one takes time, careful planning, and continuous follow-up by management to give visible support and make adjustments as needed. It is an evolutionary process. The first step is to examine and understand all facets and ramifications of the concept, its organization implications, and management resource requirements to succeed. The basic long-term objective would be to develop an organization that is trained and motivated to make work management decisions, is customer focused, and needs little supervisory direction. Middle managers and employees are used to receiving direction. To make the transition to succeed, upper management must develop communication paths and methods that will constantly reinforce its new objectives. Management must earn employee trust. For example, mistakes or deficiencies must be treated as opportunities for improvement, not for blame and scapegoating. This can be very difficult, as it goes against many years of conditioning for managers to be the boss and give directions.

6.E. Team Formation and Evolution

Definition. Some the leaders in the quality movement have formulated their own description of what teams are. Juran says a team is a group of individuals, each with specific skills, knowledge, and interests, that enables members to contribute to the accomplishment of a common purpose. For Deming, a team is a group formed with an aim, a job, and a goal to improve the output of any stage. For Scholtes, it is a group of people pooling their skills, talents, and knowledge to improve quality and productivity. One could also say that a team is two or more people working together toward a common goal for which they hold themselves mutually accountable. There is obviously great similarity in all of these definitions.

A more fundamental look reveals that teams are the expression of employee empowerment and involvement. They become essential as an organization makes serious progress in becoming customer driven and process focused. Teams represent a basic and characteristic methodology in TQ organizations. Their proper formation and development are vital if they are to be effective. The guidelines and objectives in forming teams are as follows:

- Teams will evolve to manage the important organization processes.

- Teams should be trained to solve process problems and reduce variability. Training would begin as teams are formed and continue as new problem-solving skills are required.

- Continuous management support should be provided, as well as effective facilitation until teams mature.

- Teams must be given time to develop. The first teams to be formed need the most time and will set the example for those that follow.

- Each team should be allowed to evolve at their own rate, but team leaders or members should be replaced if needed to maintain effectiveness.

Stages of Team Formation and Evolution. This discussion is presented in some detail to indicate that team formation and management is not a simple activity. It is more than just identifying a group of people to work on a problem and turning them loose. To be successful, it involves a fundamental change in the way people relate to each other, to the organization, and to management. Top managers ought to consider the complexity and impact of these changes before implementing team management. Those who have not done so are frequently the ones who become impatient with the team process and decide it doesn't work.

A team changes over time. At inception it may have no clear sense of itself as an independent unit. Over time, however, it undergoes five stages of growth.[15]

Forming (How is this thing going to work?) While forming, members test the boundaries of acceptable behavior. This is a transition from individual to team member status, and of testing the leader's guidance. At this stage, the team focuses more on the task than on actual teamwork. They establish the team's structure, set goals and objectives, clarify issues of value, and develop the team's overall purpose. The manager's role at this stage is primarily to direct the initiative and to help team members reach consensus and a sense of commitment.

During this phase of team evolution, team members will develop a sense of pride and ownership in the assignment. They will identify with the team itself and have feelings of excitement and optimism as well as anxiety and fear about what lies ahead. Team member behavior fluctuates from trying to determine what acceptable group behavior is to complaining about the difficulties in accomplishing the assignment. Team leaders will try to instill trust and develop team members' interaction. Leadership by example is a priority at this stage.

Storming (Let's get on with it). This is a most difficult phase when enthusiasm gives way to frustration and anger. Members tend to rely on their own personal and professional experience and resist the need to work with other team members. The leader's role now includes both accomplishing the assignment and building relationships. Interpersonal skills, such as active listening, assertiveness, conflict management, and flexibility, need to be emphasized during this less-structured phase. The team completes tasks with sympathetic understanding, clarification, and belonging. The leader relies on authority as well as leadership skills to help the team survive this turbulent period of evolution.

The feelings evident during this stage include resistance to the task and fluctuations in attitude. Team members find themselves arguing about issues on which they agree, they start choosing sides, and they question the wisdom of those who selected the assignment and appointed the other team members. Other sources of tension are also prevalent during this stage. The team leader's role changes frequently, from participant to coach, to referee, all in an attempt not to upset the apple cart or violate trust.

Norming (Getting comfortable). During this stage, members come to grips with competing responsibilities and loyalty. They accept the team, team norms, their role in the team, and the individuality of other team members. They gradually resolve many difficulties and learn to focus on the assignment. The team-building process at this stage is more relationship based than task oriented. Recognition and esteem become important to the team members. The leader's role now relies more on communication, feedback, affirmation, humor, entrepreneurship, and networking. This group feels a real sense of involvement and support.

During the norming phase, team members exhibit an ability to express criticism constructively and express relief that things seem as though they are going to work out. Behavior is more friendly and there is a conscious effort to avoid conflict. The team leader increases the team's responsibility and authority during the norming stage and lends assistance in meeting challenges.

Performing (It works). The team begins performing—diagnosing and solving problems, and choosing and implementing changes. Team members have discovered and accepted each other's strengths and weaknesses and learned their roles. The team operates on its own. Managing the team is neither task nor relationship based. The reason for this, according to Dinsmore,[16] is that the team members are motivated by achievement and self-actualization. The team leader's role becomes one of mentor or coach. Individual team members focus on decision making and problem solving, relying on information and expertise to achieve their goals and objectives.

Feelings apparent during the performing phase include a better understanding of each other's strengths and weaknesses and satisfaction with the team's progress. Ability to work through or prevent group problems is the predominant behavior for team members. The team leader now steps back and lets the team demonstrate its capabilities.

Adjourning (Task complete). This is the wrap-up stage or point of closure. Although not commonly discussed, this fifth stage is sometimes used to describe team evolution. According to the *American Management Association Handbook,* management's focus at this point would be low task and high relationship oriented. The team leader's role includes evaluation, reviewing, and closure. Individual team members continue to be motivated by their feelings of accomplishment and self-actualization, and know when to disband the team.

6.E.1. Teams and Other Work Groups

Team has become the generic term for a variety of work groups, but there are basic differences in what they do and how they function.

Quality Circles. Quality circles are similar to process improvement teams in operating method but more limited in scope and authority. A quality circle is a group of people who work together, formed to identify and solve problems that affect their ability to be more productive and to improve the quality of their work. Usually their scope is limited to what directly affects their work. Quality circles were popular in the 1980s, but are less common today and weren't as effective as hoped. The reason relates to one of Deming's themes, that 85 percent of quality problems are systems problems that are management's job to correct. Quality circles were limited to the remaining 15 percent, and they usually didn't have a big impact. In comparison, process improvement teams, particularly those with multifunctional representation, work to improve processes and any factor or system that affects process output.

Problem-Solving Teams. It is common for management to use project or problem-solving teams (the names are often interchangeable). These teams are ad-hoc, frequently multifunctional, and organized to resolve specific problems identified by management. It is also common to have several operating at the same time. A weakness in using this approach as a standard operating method is that the teams tend to work on relieving symptoms rather than having a process improvement orientation to remove the systemic problem cause. Also, they typically don't operate long enough to reach the effectiveness level of process improvement teams.

Management Councils/Committees. These are problem-identification and sometimes problem-solving work groups composed of managers to address a variety of management and organization problems. They frequently assign problems to project teams. Management councils also operate to set process improvement objectives for process improvement teams and monitor progress. They can be effective in centralizing the direction of improvement efforts, and by tracking team needs and progress they have the power to provide resources and motivation.

Corrective Action Teams. These teams are usually assigned to react to deficiencies reported through a structured corrective action system. Too frequently their solutions are not permanent because they don't correct the processes generating the deficiencies.

Focus Groups. These groups are made up of members from both inside and outside an organization. They may include customers, community members, or suppliers to examine and report on specific problems that affect them and the organization.

Scholtes[17] developed a catalog description of seven different kinds of teams he identified from discussions with various people and a literature search.

- Natural work groups—people who work together

- Business teams—cross-functional with related work

- Management/executive teams—a group of managers (peers) who work together

- Management lynchpin groups—teams interrelated by common membership
- New product and service design teams—usually cross-functional
- Process or system redesign or reengineering teams
- Important project teams—typical cross-functional improvement teams

Tompkins[18] describes team types in a form that also reflects his idea of what the structure of his Genesis Enterprise (a team-based organization) would be, from the top down (see Table 6.1).

6.F. Team Management

Teams require some level of continuous management, as does any organization element. Teams also require a strong component of leadership.

Table 6.1. The types of teams in a team-based organization.

Type	Objective
Steering team	To establish, communicate, and maintain focus on the Model of Success, and to guide and support the Leadership Team.
Leadership team	To work toward Model of Success alignment; to define, charter, orient, encourage motivate, support, and accept accountability for teams; and to assure performance.
Communication team	To ensure that everyone in the organization has a clear understanding of the Model of Success, the status of teams, and the organization's status.
Design team	To design or redesign the company by using a blue-sky, clean-sheet, green-field process of innovation and creativity to bring about significant performance improvements.
Work team	To bring the process of continuous improvement to life. To unleash the power of the people in the organization.

Management involvement with team operation starts out high. The objective is to get teams to an operating level where management plays a secondary role and the teams become mostly self-managing.

The key factors in team management are as follows:

- Team roles and responsibilities. Each member plays a role. The team leader facilitates this identification for each member. Roles match individuals' capabilities. The workload is evenly distributed.

- Team leadership. This is probably the most important factor in team success. Leaders should be able to clarify issues and supply important information, resolve conflicts, and keep the team on track. Leaders are frequently the managers in the project area, so skill is required to avoid dominating meetings and to earn the trust of other members. The two roles are difficult to balance. The main characteristics of effective team leaders are described in Figure 6.1.

- Maintaining effective communication. This is very important in team leadership and operation.

- Team training. This is often the responsibility of the team leader. An important concept behind using teams is using members' collective experience, skills, and imagination—their creativity. A skill that few people have without training is problem solving, more specifically group problem solving. Most people have attended meetings, ostensibly to solve a problem, where the problem is never clarified and most participants want to talk about their solutions. Little is accomplished. To be effective, teams must be taught the tools of structured problem solving. These tools are discussed in Chapter 5.

- Project selection. This based on the project's importance and contribution to process improvement and customer satisfaction. Selection derives from the organization's strategic and tactical quality plans. Initially, projects are short term to give the team time to gain confidence.

- Facilitation. Meetings have a facilitator whose duties are to keep meetings orderly and focused on the problem, stimulate participation, provide training if necessary, and guide the team toward problem solution.

Effective leadership is essential to teamwork. Effective leaders can add enormous strength to the process and can have a positive effect on the teamwork climate. Effective team leaders:

- Understanding and accept their obligation to the team.

- Deal fairly and consistently with everyone.

- Believe that people want to do a good job.

- Are open, forthright, and consistently do what they say they will do. When they can't, they explain why not.

- Care about people and respect them as individuals.

- Believe that when their work groups do well, they themselves do well; they take pride in the groups' achievements and share credit for work the groups have done.

- Act as they expect others to act.

- Solicit ideas and listen carefully when ideas are offered.

- Are dedicated to improving people's work lives, to their safety, and to the efficient production of quality products and services.

- Seek out education, training, and development opportunities for team members, including themselves.

- Are willing to coach and advise and not rely solely on the authority of their positions.

- Keep themselves and members of their teams aware of the needs of other teams and those of internal and external customers.

- Meet regularly with their counterparts to openly exchange information and ideas.

- Support team efforts and get help for the team when it is needed.

- Strive for continuous improvement in themselves and in their relationships with people.

- Seek information that pertains to their work groups and regularly share it.

- Demonstrate their support for the groups and the individual members when things are not going smoothly.

- Conduct themselves as professional representatives of their respective organizations—with pride.

From "Team, We Are a Team," an information package from Ford Motor Co., 1988, p. 17.

Figure 6.1. Characteristics of effective team leaders.

- Performance evaluation. This has two aspects. First, a team should conduct an evaluation of its own performance as an ongoing methodology. For example, the final minutes of each meeting can be used to critique the meeting success. Simple checksheets can be developed to do this quickly. Second, when a final problem solution is reached the team should decide if the original objectives were met.

6.F.1. Facilitation Techniques[19]

Facilitation is of critical value to the proper development and operation of teams. The key duties of a facilitator are to keep meetings orderly and focused on the problem, to stimulate participation, and to guide the team to a solution. Some large organizations have full-time specialists to facilitate several teams who are also equipped to teach problem-solving tools and techniques. Another common approach is to rotate team members into the facilitator position to provide a development opportunity. This provides a different perspective on the team dynamics at work.

A facilitator must understand group (team) dynamics to keep teams on the problem-solving track, to resolve conflicts, and to teach teams problem-solving tools needed. Another important role for the facilitator is to provide guidance that develops trust, communication, and confidence between members.

Key facilitator techniques are

- Listening to what is really going on.

- Questioning, to allow members to identify problems and solutions, and sometimes to offer alternatives.

- Preventing domination by any member and soliciting input from all members.

- Providing a team memory to avoid repetition.

- Training in nonthreatening and consensus decision-making techniques like brainstorming or the Crawford Slip Method.[20]

- Counseling or coaching individual team members.

- Counseling or coaching a team leader on team leadership and management skills.

- Participating when difficult or controversial subjects are being discussed, to clarify issues.
- Ensuring that teams have adequate facilities and equipment.
- Providing feedback to teams on observed performance.

Potential Team Problems. Initiating teams, like any significant organization change, can cause operating problems. Most problems that fall outside those of typical team interaction are a result of management deficiencies of some kind. The facilitator should be aware that these problems can occur in any team and be prepared to deal with them. Some reasons for such problems include the following:

- Management initiates teams for the wrong reasons. It wants them because it has heard that they can save money, because competitors are using them, or because it is in crisis and looking for anything to help.
- Team management is sometimes started in one organization element by its manager. Regardless of that manager's sincerity, a team cannot be effective without top management support and other organizations' cooperation.
- Management doesn't understand the need to give teams time to mature. It is looking for some quick payback for the resources being consumed. It sees teams as an expense, not an investment.
- Changes in upper management may involve new executives that don't support the team concept. This is often the case when new management is brought in to cut costs and improve profits quickly.
- Management frequently overrides team recommendations or decisions. Teams will believe that they have wasted their time and management doesn't support them.
- Labor unions are not involved in the early discussions and planning for team introduction.

6.F.2. Performance Evaluation

The most important evaluation of team performance is conducted by the team itself, as an ongoing methodology. The final minutes in each meeting are devoted to a critique on the team functioning. Simple checksheets can speed up the process, with discussion following their completion. If a team decides it is not progressing toward a solution, it can make corrections to its activities. Periodic management council reviews should also be made to assess the effectiveness of each team and take the proper action to improve its effectiveness. The subject of performance evaluation is discussed more extensively in section 6B2.

6.F.3. Recognition and Reward

Recognition and reward, in some form, is valuable for motivating and sustaining the interest of teams. It is also a symbol of management's support for team activity and provides acknowledgment that what is being done is important to the success of the organization. Rewards reflect management values and reinforce their priorities.

The form and methodology of team recognition and reward must be given careful consideration before implementation. The following are some important considerations.

- Employees or their representatives should participate in the planning and execution of a reward program. It should also be fully explained to all employees.

- Recognition programs should not create winners and losers.

- Recognition should be given for serious efforts, not just goal attainment. Sometimes unforeseen factors limit goal achievement.

- Rewards are a reinforcement of Maslow's hierarchy of needs (belonging, esteem, self-actualization). (See Chapter 2F.)

- Recognition or rewards should be perceived as fair and be tied to accomplishment, not to management bias.

- Rewards should relate to management's vision, policies, and objectives.

- Rewards should not be tied to basic compensation, as this has proven to cause problems over time.

- Some common forms of recognition and rewards include public recognition of accomplishments, certificates, plaques, cash, merchandise, family outings, catered lunches, charitable gifts, and supplier or customer site visits.

Money as Motivation. Money has usually been considered the best motivator for high job performance and for attracting and retaining good employees. It is still important, but smart companies have had to rethink many of their basic employment practices in order to compete for a shrinking number of talented employees. These companies create an atmosphere in which workers believe they are not mere factors of production, but organic elements of an enterprise that respects them and will provide benefits that add to the quality of their life, beyond money.[21] They attend to Maslow's hierarchy of needs, providing such things as:

- Pay for alternative methods of medical care.
- Support for employees in community volunteer work.
- Laundry or cleaning service.
- Letting workers bring their dogs to work.
- Concierge service—house cleaning, picking up the car.
- Pay for exercise/gym time, babysitting, daycare, education.
- Flextime or work at home.
- Assistance to public schools of employees' children.
- Health insurance for unmarried partners.
- Birthday breakfasts with the chief executive officer.

Key Ideas—Chapter 6

1. The role of manager has changed to leading and facilitating change. In parallel, the role of the quality manager has also changed to one of leading and facilitating change through others, oftentimes a peer, and becoming a resource for quality management tools and training.

2. The TQ organization views problems as an opportunity to improve.

3. The transition from a traditional to TQ organization creates many opportunities for conflict, which must be recognized and managed for a successful transition.

4. New directions, change, and growth of an organization impose constantly changing staffing needs. The process requires management, training, and a flexible work force willing to grow and open to new ideas and continuing to learn.

5. Successful teams have a defined purpose and evolve through predictable stages of growth that must be managed appropriately.

References

1. Kotter, K. P. 1996. *Leading Change*. Boston, Mass.: Harvard Business School Press.

2. Buban, M. 1995. "Factoring Ethics Into the TQM Equation." *Quality Progress* (October).

3. Deming, W. E. 1986. *Out of the Crisis*. Cambridge, Mass.: Massachusetts Institute of Technology, Center for Advanced Engineering Study.

4. Morgan, R. B., and J. E. Smith. 1996. *Staffing the New Workplace: Selecting and Promoting for Quality Improvement*. Milwaukee, Wis.: ASQC Quality Press.

5. Deming. *Out of the Crisis*.

6. Ibid.

7. Eckes, G. 1994. "Practical Alternatives to Performance Appraisals." *Quality Progress* (November).

8. Deming. *Out of the Crisis*.

9. Scholtes, P. R. I 995. "Teams in the Age of Systems." *Quality Progress* (December).

10. Eckes. "Practical Alternatives to Performance Appraisals."

11. Toffler, A. 1996. "Riding the Waves" *Worth* (June).

12. Juran, J. M., and F. M. Gryna. 1988. *Juran's Quality Control Handbook*, 4th ed. New York, N.Y.: McGraw-Hill.

13. Tompkins, J. 1995. *The Genesis Enterprise*. New York, N.Y.: McGraw-Hill.

14. Hersey, P., and K. Blanchard. 1988. *Management of Organizational Behavior: Utilizing Human Resources.* Englewood Cliffs, N.J.: Prentice Hall.

15. Hersey and Blanchard. *Management of Organizational Behavior: Utilizing Human Resources.*

16. Dinsmore, P. C. 1993. *The AMA Handbook of Project Management.* New York, N.Y.: American Management Association.

17. Scholtes. "Teams in the Age of Systems."

18. Tompkins. *The Genesis Enterprise.*

19. Scholtes, P. R. 1988. *The Team Handbook.* Madison, Wis.: Joiner Associates.

20. Fiero, J. 1992. "The Crawford Slip Method." *Quality Progress* (May).

21. Dolan, K. A. 1996. "When Money Isn't Enough." *Forbes.* 18 November.

Related References

Beck, J. D. W., and N. M. Yeager. 1993. "How to Prevent Teams From Failing." *Quality Progress* (March).

Bennis, W. 1985. *The Strategy for Taking Charge.* New York, N.Y.: Harper and Row.

Claminiti, S. 1995. "What Team Leaders Need to Know." *Fortune.* 20 February.

Darnall, R. W. 1996. *The World's Greatest Project: One Project Team on the Path to Quality.* Upper Darby, Pa.: The Project Management Institute.

Denton, D. K. 1992. "Building a Team." *Quality Progress* (October).

Graber, J. M., and R. E. Breisch. 1992. "Performance Appraisals and Deming: A Misunderstanding." *Quality Progress* (June).

Hayes, B. E. 1994. "How to Measure Empowerment." *Quality Progress* (February).

Piczak, M. W., and R. Z. Hauser. 1996. "Self-Directed Work Teams: A Guide to Implementation." *Quality Progress* (May).

Raynor, S. R. 1996. *Team Traps: Survival Stories and Lessons From Team Disasters, Near-Misses, Mishaps, and Other Near-Death Experiences.* New York, N.Y.: Wiley.

The Team Memory Jogger: A Pocket Guide for Team Members. 1995. Methuen, Mass.: GOAL/QPC-Joiner.

Weaver, C. N. 1993. "How to Use Process Improvement Teams." *Quality Progress* (December).

Wuthrow, R. 1996. *Poor Richard 's Principle: Recovering the American Dream Through the Moral Dimension of Work Business, and Money.* Princeton, N.J.: Princeton University Press.

Chapter 7
Training and Education

Even a cursory review of all the factors involved in managing quality in the modern organization makes it obvious that it is a complex and dynamic arena. This also means that it requires new knowledge and skills for everyone in the organization. The very concept of TQ implies new and continual education and training. Quality management in the past meant the management of a functional organization responsible for the quality activities. TQ means the expansion of those and new activities to include the quality aspects of everyone in the overall organization, in addition to customers and suppliers. This requires new knowledge and skills, reeducation and training. With continued change, reeducation and training will never end.

Reeducation and training begins with management, shifting its emphasis away from individual competition to become skillful in collaboration, teamwork, and long-term customer-supplier alliances. These require high-level interpersonal interactions. An MBA, one of the previous requisites for success, is insufficient since it is typically finance rather than people oriented. This shift is not just a matter of changing style; it requires a basic understanding of behavior (including one's own), motivation, team management, and leadership. This requires skills different from those traditionally learned, and thinking differently about how to manage. As a demonstration of leadership, managers from the very top down should make a visible commitment to increasing their own learning. Much of the downsizing and restructuring that has taken place is the result of management awakening to the reality that the old ways of managing knowledge and skills won't keep an organization competitive today.

Juran[1] believes that training must be customized to fit an organization's needs and subsequently planned. Major issues to be considered are

1. Quality problems and challenges that face the organization.

2. Knowledge and skill level needed to solve identified problems and meet challenges.

3. Knowledge and skills actually possessed by the people within the organization. (A training needs analysis is discussed later in this chapter.)

4. Availability and appropriateness of training facilities available.

5. The current climate regarding training within the organization.

6. What is to be different from what is currently being done, at every level. (This should be determined after every organization change.)

Education and Training

It is useful to understand the difference between education and training because the approach to each is somewhat different in practice and techniques. The dictionary is not too helpful since it lumps the two terms together. The authors' purpose is not to present a treatise on education and training theory, but to indicate some basic differences that affect their application.

Education is the process of acquiring knowledge and information, usually in a formal manner. Some examples are the study and understanding of human behavior, team dynamics, and the principles of statistics.

Training is the process of acquiring proficiency in some skill or skills. Some examples are team leadership and facilitation, and the application of the seven quality control tools.

Juran and Gryna[2] do not differentiate between the two concepts, referring to everything as *quality training*. A key subject in their discussion is *instructional technology*, noting the methods and tools for training. But that field has also changed. The definition of instructional technology is now much more inclusive. It is the theory and practice of design, development, utilization, management, and evaluation of processes, products, and resources for learning.[3]

7.A. Importance of Top-Down Support and Strategic Planning for Quality Training

Change is a major theme in the business marketplace, as well as in government agencies. Creating rational change is the responsibility of management. There are two approaches being followed today. One is the result of chasing short-term financial gains. The other is based mainly on strategic planning. The press has reported both, but provided little information on their differences.

The first type of change, short term, is simple cost cutting to show improvements to investors or to improve top management bonuses. Sometimes it is the only option because management has allowed the enterprise to drift into a serious noncompetitive position and survival actions are required. Other actions, such as a 10 percent cut in personnel, that merely improve the financial picture, are a different matter. These leave organizations in turmoil and would seem to be short-sighted. They limit an organization's ability to change into what the future marketplace will require, because there is no trust between management and employees (or between managers). In the second category, however, are companies that base their changes (downsizing, privatizing, restructuring, reengineering, spin-offs) on the results of planning.

A critical element in organizational success is good planning, particularly strategic planning. The policies, structure, and identification of needed knowledge and skills evolve directly from this activity (see Chapter 3). Strategic plans are a look into the future and, based on where the organization is, deciding where the organization has to go, what it should be, and how it will get there. This provides a picture of what goods or services customers will expect and what competitors might do about it. This has traditionally been the limit of business planning. Now, the next critical step is to define what new knowledge and skills the organization will need, and then make plans for how and when they will be attained and the resources required.

For example, if the strategic plan sets a quality goal of 15 percent improvement in product quality, this must be followed by the identification of how that goal will be met; that is, what facilities, equipment, financing, skills, and other resources will have to be online by the plan time. Those that are well into becoming a TQ organization recognize the nature of the changes and the reeducation and training that is, and will continue to be, required. Just consider the potential effect on education and training needs of entering the global market—new languages, new cultures, and new business practices.

A new element in long-range planning is, rather than identifying how much bigger the organization will have to be, determining how best to meet those needs and stay flexible and ready to meet the unexpected. Many organizations are deciding that it isn't wise to accumulate more debt, facilities, or people, particularly for special skills. They have decided that they can be stronger by keeping and developing a core organization specifically related to their market, and using some form of outsourcing for other needs. New skills may be located in subcontractors, a now-common approach for filling a need for new skills that are different from what currently exists within the organization.

Up until about the 1980s, organizations mostly depended on the employment marketplace to find the skills they needed. The approach generally worked; skill needs changed slowly and the fluctuations in various business sectors provided a reasonable supply. But now, as reported in the business news, the employment markets are in turmoil. There has been considerable downsizing, and people are available. At the same time, management is complaining that it can't find new employees with the skills needed for the modern workplace, particularly in reading and math. As a result, more businesses are doing their own training and education. One example is the Motorola Corporation. It developed its own training center—Motorola University—and spends more than $150 million a year on a broad spectrum of training and education topics. The curriculum is relevant to the company, the individual, and the job. This is a clear demonstration of support for learning. Upper management support for quality training is based on how thoroughly it does strategic planning and how fully it evaluates and understands the implications of any new needs it identifies.

7.B. Training Subgroups and Topics

Effective training focuses on the following factors.[4]

- Examples and case studies are based on the business.
- Assessment of specific training needs is based on job categories and existing skill levels.
- Training is designed to fit existing tools, techniques, and methods (if effective).
- Training is designed to fit the existing learning culture.
- Material is designed to fit management's vision of improvement.
- Material is customized to fit the company.
- Implementation, the tracking system, and course evaluation are included in the design of the course schedule.
- Course prerequisites and specific skills needed are designed to make each module effective.
- Exercises are designed to contribute to the work situation.

The Baldrige Award criteria include the need for employee education, training, and development in what could be called the management quality principles. The criteria ask award applicants to describe how the company's education and training address company plans, including building company capabilities and contributing to employee motivation, progression, and development, and how they address the knowledge and skills that employees need to meet their work objectives. They suggest that this might include the following:

- Leadership skills
- Communications
- Teamwork
- Process analysis and problem solving

- Interpreting and using data
- Meeting customer requirements
- Process improvement
- Cycle time reduction
- Error proofing
- Priority setting based on cost and benefit data
- Training that effects employee effectiveness, efficiency, and safety

Considering America's diverse society, it might also include basic skills such as reading, writing, language, and arithmetic.

The subject list is comprehensive and far different from only a few years ago, when quality training was mostly in measurement, blueprint reading, work tools and procedures, and safety. In other words, only the minimum for employees to do their jobs was required. The Baldrige Award criteria go further, describing how education and training could be evaluated to address the following:

- Impact on work unit performance
- Cost effectiveness of education and training alternatives.

A continuous training process is required by ANSI/ISO/ASQC Q9004-1. It stipulates that training needs for all personnel be identified and documented. Particular attention should be given to the qualifications, selection, and training of new employees in their new assignments. It further describes the requirements for training quality executives, technical personnel, process supervisors, and operating personnel. It is a good training structure for any organization, except that it omits TQ training for upper management and the idea that training needs evolve from strategic quality planning.

The training element of ISO 9001 and 9002 (4.18) requires that

> The supplier shall establish and maintain documented procedures for identifying training needs and provide for the training of all personnel performing activities affecting quality. Personnel performing specific assigned tasks shall be qualified on the basis of appropriate education,

training, and/or experience, as required. Appropriate records of training shall be maintained.

In summary, the Baldrige Award and ISO 9000 training requirements reflect the increasing scope of training and education needs in modern organizations to improve quality and remain competitive.

Scope and Sources for Training and Education. The full scope of knowledge and the common sources of supply are given by category in the following lists. One respected source for all levels of quality training and education is ASQC. A partial list of its course offerings also indicates the scope of training needed by modern managers and quality professionals.

Analysis and Application of Customer Satisfaction Measurements

Baldrige Award Self-Assessment Training

Customer Satisfaction Measurement and Management

Customer-Supplier Partnerships

Design of Experiments

Increasing Customer Retention Through Improved Customer Service

Introduction to Quality Function Deployment

Introduction to Quality Management

ISO 9000 Internal Auditing

Preparing for ISO 9000 Registration

Principles of Quality Engineering

Quality Audits for Improved Performance

Reliability Engineering

Software Quality Engineering

Statistical Process Control

Statistics for Effective Decision Making

Strategic Quality Planning

Training for Service Organizations

Unlimited Innovation

No one can depend on obtaining his or her education in these subjects from his or her employer. Managers and professional employees supplement organization-sponsored training, which is usually task oriented, with subjects they think are appropriate to their own interests and what is or will be needed in their job market.

The scope of the subject matter of this book indicates a considerable breadth of knowledge is needed. One way to examine this is to review the following lists, which identify the minimum subject matter knowledge for different organization levels and common sources of information.

Upper management

Topic	*Sources of information*
Managing change	Readings
Process management	Seminars
Total quality concepts	Networking
Customer satisfaction	Information benchmarking
Employee empowerment	Consultants
Team building and management	Executive/management courses
Leadership and management	
Strategic quality planning	
ISO 9000 overview and implications	
Strategic supplier alliances	
Baldrige Award criteria	

Other management

Topic	*Sources of information*
Managing change	College courses
Total quality concepts	Seminars
Problem-solving methodologies	Consultants
Team management and leadership	Professional associations
Process performance measurement	Readings
Personal communications and interrela-tionship skills	Videos
ISO 9000 requirements	Internet—resource libraries and discussion groups
Quality planning and setting objectives	

Professional

Topic	*Sources of information*
Total quality principles	College courses
Quality planning and setting objectives	Seminars
Process measurement	Training sessions
Problem-solving methodologies	Professional associations
Interrelationship skills	Readings
Quality auditing	Video
Supplier partner management	Internet
Quality cost systems	
Team leadership and management	
Statistical thinking and techniques	
Principles of industrial engineering	
Principles of modern management	

Other employees

Topic	*Sources of information*
Language and arithmetic	Local schools and colleges
Total quality principles overview	In-house training
Team participation	Self-study/readings
Organization goals and objectives	Video courses
Quality work skills	Professional organizations
Standards and certification training	Refresher courses
Safety	

Teams

Several aspects of team training and subjects are mentioned in this chapter. But there is a core of knowledge and skills that every team member, and those who interact with teams, needs to learn.

Total quality principles overview	Continuous process improvement methods
Team operating rules	Quality costs
Process definition and analysis methods	ISO 9000 requirements, as appropriate
Problem solving tools	Setting quality objectives

7.B.1. Facilitator Training and Selection

Selection. Selecting people for the role of team facilitator should be carefully done. Facilitation is not a skill that most people have; it involves much more than may be assumed and only partially depends on technical knowledge. The type of facilitation needed for team problem solving, according to Schuman,[5] is very different from that used in training and informational meetings. In training situations, for example, the group has clear, predetermined goals and objectives, deals with a well-defined subject, and rarely encounters serious conflict. In contrast, problem-solving groups determine their own goals and objectives, define the nature and scope of the subject matter, and frequently encounter conflict, which, if not handled constructively, can lead to failure.

Four basic capabilities should be sought in a facilitator.

1. The capability to anticipate the complete problem solving and decision making process

2. The use of procedures that support both the group social and cognitive processes

3. The ability to remain neutral regarding content issues and values

4. Respect for the group's need to understand and learn from the problem solving process

The Training Question. Training the facilitators of groups engaged in problem solving and other improvement initiatives is key to their success. Facilitator training grew in application with the advent of quality circles because companies recognized the need to improve the skills of people performing these roles. This is even more necessary with the use of teams, which have a broader scope of initiatives and authority.

Training and Education. Before initiating team management, it is necessary to plan how the teams will operate and define the role and qualifications for team facilitation. There is no serves-all model for a facilitator. Management must define the selection, training, and education process.

Education. Facilitator education is required, particularly for those involved with the complexities of multifunctional teams. Such facilitators should understand and be able to apply

- The various theories of learning and how and where they are effective[6]

- The theory and practice of instructional technology[7]

- Fundamentals of quality control statistics[8]

Training

- Group/team facilitator skills[9]

- Group dynamics, motivation, problem-solving tools, listening, conflict resolution, negotiating, influencing

Training in group dynamics is essential because the decision-making process of the group focuses more on consensus than majority vote. Training in group motivation, and stimulating motivation from within the individual, is emphasized along with communication skills. Problem-solving tools must be mastered, as they are essential in the work of teams and facilitators. Listening, conflict resolution, negotiating, and influencing are other essential abilities.

The role of the facilitator is to provide guidance, be the team consultant, and teach the team the tools for problem solving, when appropriate.

Unless there is no alternative the facilitator should not assume a permanent leadership role or get involved in the specifics of a problem. The facilitator should be coach, teacher, mentor, mediator, and resource. In smaller organizations, where facilitators are not full time, and where leader, manager, and facilitator may be the same person, proper training is critical to wear all of these hats successfully. Because they are not a mix of roles for the traditional manager, they may at times conflict.

Issues. When teams get bogged down there is a tendency for facilitators to get involved in the problem resolution rather than remain focused on the group process. Intervention should be made when a group stops progressing, but only to the extent of getting it to move forward. Some intervention techniques that can be used effectively include

- Asking questions to stimulate discussion—to help the group understand the idea or problem it is addressing.

- Summarizing the positions being taken regarding the idea or problem—to describe and clarify opposing views.

- Restating the idea so that everyone listens to what is said. Also, restating it so that the originator hears how it was expressed.

- Suggesting an alternative technique that fits the current needs of the group.

As teams gain experience and improve their skills, the need for a full-time facilitator decreases. When this point is reached a leader should have been established. Sometimes the role of facilitator is rotated among members. This also contributes to their development.

The timeliness of training is another issue organizations have to resolve; namely, how much and when. One common practice for organizations beginning the TQ implementation is to start with a massive training program, teaching all or most of the subject matter to most of the employees. This may satisfy the curiosity of employees as to what management is up to, but the intent of the training should be to make teams effective. Mass training early in implementation has several drawbacks.

- It may be perceived as another management program, something everyone is required to attend.

- It oversimplifies the issue of training in the subjects required. Many of the skills and techniques require some abstract thought that is likely best stimulated by tackling a real work problem. Also, a skill is not really understood and mastered until it is practiced in the work situation.

Training teams in the use of quality improvement tools with the objective of continuous process improvement is better achieved using what is referred to as *just-in-time training*. The facilitator or leader trains the team in the use of the various tools as an application presents itself in the course of team functioning. Learning is then immediately reinforced by a real-time application, making the tool much more likely to be remembered. Also, not all teams need to use all the tools. An office process team may not need to know variables control charts. Conversely, a concurrent engineering team may need to know that and more.

7.C. Training Needs Analysis

Training is expensive and important to the success of the organization. Modern organizations' education and training needs are greater and more comprehensive than pre-TQ management has experienced. More significantly, trained personnel can support change and improvements the organization must make to succeed or survive.

Small businesses have other problems with training and education. They typically operate in a small market area. Their main interest is satisfying the immediate needs of their customers, most of which are larger business. They may not be aware of the magnitude of the changes occurring in their customers' markets that will affect them.

In most cases they cannot afford significant training. Most of these small companies rely on their customers to tell them what is needed; however, their relationship has traditionally been almost adversarial (see purchasing policies, Chapter 4F), and there is little likelihood of forward-looking information exchanges. The supplier-customer partnership concept can offer small companies the opportunity to find out what new skills are needed and even obtain customer assistance in providing training.

Training and education should be managed, like any other important investment, beginning with planning. Training needs should be derived from the overall and functional strategic and tactical quality plans. The following steps provide a measure of the gap between what exists and what the plans identify as future needs.

1. Prepare an inventory of the present organization skills and who has them. Managers and employees should also identify what they think they need.

2. Analyze the strategic and tactical plans and objectives for quality improvement.

3. Identify the skills required to meet those objectives.

4. Compare those results with the present inventory to identify new needs, or an essential increase in the quantity of present skills.

5. Prepare a plan for when the skills are needed, when and how the training will be provided, who will receive it, and what resources will be required. This plan should also be the basis for deciding if and when recruitment will be necessary and a schedule for any new job or position descriptions. This plan may highlight the magnitude of the training problem so that management can decide whether future outsourcing or an acquisition is a better alternative.

6. These plans should be coordinated with the overall organization to prepare a master plan for training.

Figure 7.1 is one possible outcome of the training needs planning activity. It provides a basis for scheduling and planning specific training to fill different employee needs.

Training for Standards. A training needs analysis is required by the ANSI/ISO/ASQC Q9000 series of quality management standards. Two documents, in final draft status, are particularly helpful.

- ISO 10015, which provides details of the overall training process

- ANSI/ASQC Z1.11-1996, *Guidance for the Application of ANSI/ ISO/ASQC Q9001-1994 or Q9002-1994 to Education and Training Institutions,* which provides considerable information on how such organizations can become qualified to the ISO standards and what quality system they must maintain (a large number of European

Students	Consultant	Total quality seminar	Team leader training	Facilitator	Leadership/people skills	Advanced problem solving	Process control methods	Introduction to design of experiments	Design of experiments	Data gathering	Implementation
Team leader	●	●	●	▲	▲	■	▲	■	■	■	●
Team member	■	■	■	■	◆	■	■	■	■	■	▲
Facilitator	●	●	●	●	▲	■	▲	▲	■	▲	▲
Statistician	●	●	●	●	▲	■	●	●	●	■	●
Improvement manager	●	●	●	●	●	●	●	●	●	▲	●
Nonmanagement	■	■	■	■	◆	■	■	■	■	■	■
Other key members	■	■	■	▲	▲	▲	▲	▲	▲	▲	■
Manufacturing	■	■	■	■	▲	■	■	■	■	■	■
Engineering	■	■	■	■	▲	▲	▲	▲	▲	■	▲
Office/administrative	■	■	■	■	▲	■	■	■	■	■	▲
Management	●	●	●	▲	●	▲	▲	▲	■	■	●

● Required   ▲ Recommended   ■ Optional   ◆ Not required

Figure 7.1. Quality improvement education and training plan.

242

institutions are already qualified). It is a useful document for quality managers and auditors to understand training requirements and a system of delivery. Figure 7.2 is a guideline map of the acceptable practices for education and training.

As programs or training units are developed and implemented, an ongoing evaluation process is a part of the training system.

Training Alternatives. One of Deming's basic teachings was that 85 percent of organization problems are system problems. This can also apply to training systems. Sometimes what appears to be a need for training is a problem caused by the operating system, or what appears to be inadequate training is a training system deficiency, such as poor instruction or wrong methodology. Rossett[10] stated that training is often perceived as the instant cure for many quality problems when some other organizational

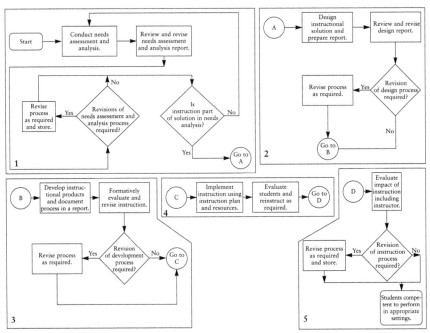

Note: Numbers within each box relate to the appropriate section of the guideline. *Source:* ANSI/ASQC Z1.11-1996.

Figure 7.2. Design of instruction within a quality system.

intervention may be more appropriate. This is because the cause and the solution are not appropriately linked. For example, the following list illustrates situations where training is only one option among several.

Causes	*Solutions*
Skill and knowledge discrepancies	Training
	Coaching
	Job aids
Flawed incentives	New policies
	New contracts
	Training for supervision
Flawed environment	Work redesign
	New and better tools
	Better match between person and job
Lack of motivation	Training so workers can see benefits
	Better processes or tools
	Training that provides early, tangible success to build confidence

7.D. Post-Training Evaluation and Reinforcement

When making fundamental changes in an organization, training is critical to a successful transition. But training is expensive. It needs to be evaluated for effectiveness. After an employee completes a training session or a course, he or she should complete an evaluation of its usefulness and benefits. This can most easily be accomplished using a questionnaire or interview, with such questions as the following:

- Did the course/session meet your expectations? Briefly explain.

- Was the content adequate and complete?

- Was the subject matter applicable to your work? Describe briefly.

- What facts, techniques, skills, or attitudes did you understand and retain?

- Did the instructor seem to know the material? Was the presentation well done?
- Was the training material clear and complete?
- What suggestions do you have for improvement?

The collected data should be analyzed to provide continuous training program improvement.

Workplace Follow-up Evaluation.

1. Did the instructional product change the learner's behavior in a way that impacts on-the-job performance? (This requires measuring how well skills have been transferred to the job.)

2. Did the training program have an impact beyond the individual learner? (This requires measuring whether instruction/job aids have been effective in achieving the kind of organization change intended.)

Training Issues. Training program problems or failures can have many causes. According to Juran and Gryna,[11] these problems can be caused by the following:

- Cultural resistance by line managers
- Doubt as to the usefulness of the training
- Lack of participation by the line managers
- Technique versus problem orientation
- Inadequacies of leaders
- Mixing of levels of participants (this wouldn't be a big problem in an open, nontraditional organization)
- Lack of application during the course
- Language that is too complex
- Lack of participation by the training function (where applicable)
- Operational and logistic deficiencies

7.E. Training Tools

The tools of training and education make up the delivery system used to provide the learning opportunity to the participants. They include the method and means of making the information exchange between the provider and trainee. The best systems invariably use several tools during the delivery. Things to consider when designing a training program would be the training objectives, the nature of the subject matter, materials to be used, and the knowledge or education level of the intended audience.

Self-development is also an important means for providing training on a continuous basis. Key points for the individual to consider are the following:

- Identify strategies that worked for others.
- Seek honest feedback.
- Analyze and learn from mistakes.
- Never stop seeking to learn.
- Avoid being defensive to suggestions.
- Seek opportunities to work on new and difficult problems.
- Use role models. Be careful to identify who is leading change (the model).
- Evaluate your strengths and weaknesses.
- Have a long-term personal growth plan.
- Monitor progress.

7.E.1. Lectures, Workbooks, Case Studies, On-the-Job Training

The tools used in education and training have increased in scope and effectiveness, with many new innovations available. One of the results of this growth has been the better integration of various tools with content. Training programs must be carefully designed, integrating the proper learning theories, methodologies, and tools. This requires special expertise; just an expert level of knowledge in the subject will not make the teaching effective.

Lectures provide a one-dimensional form of training. In conjunction with other tools, they are the most used technique and can put large amounts of information into short time frames. Given by seasoned experts, they can provide listeners with top-quality information. The full effectiveness of lectures can only be realized when combined with workshops and student self-study of the subject matter.

Roundtable discussions are open forum debates on pertinent subjects. They give participants a chance to present their views, opinions, and ideas in a candid and unrestricted environment. They are frequently used in college seminar-type courses. Somewhat similar are panel discussions by specialists or experienced individuals. The participants interact with each other on specified subjects. These exchanges can stimulate thinking in all present.

Seminars or workshops combine the informational content of a lecture with the opportunities for participation offered by a roundtable discussion. Information is dispensed in smaller doses and supplemented with group discussion and debate. Workshops can provide a simulated application of the subject to a real work project, reinforcing what was discussed.

Case studies following lectures and study are effective in illustrating applications of the subject matter. They can demonstrate that different approaches can be used in applying knowledge to problem solving. They can also stimulate vigorous discussion and idea exchange.

On-the-job training is one of the oldest and most widely used training techniques. It varies widely in effectiveness. It can be done one-on-one or conducted in groups and can be formal or informal. The informal approach is what most new employees receive after a formal indoctrination on organization policies, procedures, and so on. This training is usually directed by the supervisor or work group leader. Teams are often involved in this kind of training when they are taught new problem-solving tools or how to solve different kinds of problems.

7.E.2. Use of Technology in Training (Videos, Computer-Delivered Instruction, and Others)

Computer-based training provides some unique advantages to enhance the learning experience for individuals as well as groups. It offers a systematic approach to training and testing personnel for the purpose of instruction or certification. Computers can be used with great effectiveness in training for complex jobs by using simulation, with the student involved and functioning as he or she would on the job. Pilot flight simulators are one of the oldest applications. The military is also a prolific user of computer-based training to teach operation and maintenance of complex weapons systems.

Computer training is becoming more common and acceptable as computers become an integral part of many job functions and even family life. Innovations and new techniques such as virtual reality are keeping this technology in the forefront of training methods. Used with such aids as workbooks, computer-based training provides repeatable expertise economically. With the proliferation of PCs in the workplace it also provides greater flexibility in training location and conforms to the pace of the individual. A disadvantage is that when customized training is needed program preparation can be expensive and take considerable time to complete. So-called off-the-shelf programs should be carefully evaluated before selection, as they are not easily or cheaply modified.

User-prepared or purchased video training modules can be cost-effective. Even if limited to lectures, a common practice in universities, they can convey concepts, knowledge, or skills by giving a greater scope and reality to the subject, and the benefit of professionally prepared scripts and materials. They can be effective in teaching skills because the student can replay them as needed. Videos can also be effectively used for self-development in home studies. Video presentations to managers, by recognized experts, can give new ideas authenticity and gain acceptance by wide audiences. Video conferences are useful for promulgating specific management decisions throughout the organization, particularly when the organization is large and geographically dispersed. Computer and video training is also cost-effective for smaller organizations or those that do not have easy access to other educational resources. The explosive growth of subject matter available through the Internet promises also to become useful in organization training and individual development.

Key Ideas—Chapter 7

1. Education is the acquisition of knowledge. Training is the use of knowledge and development of specific skills.

2. A continuously changing organization drives the need for a continuously learning staff to keep pace with and support change.

3. Training should be managed as any other long-term investment, with directions originating from management strategic plans and objectives, and beginning with a training needs assessment (gap analysis).

4. There are many sources of continuing professional development, and employees should not be solely dependent on the organization to assess and provide for their training needs.

5. Facilitator skills are different from leadership skills. A facilitator is concerned with the process, a leader with achieving the vision.

References

1. Juran, J. M., and F. M. Gryna. 1988. *Juran's Quality Control Handbook,* 4th ed. New York, N.Y.: McGraw-Hill.

2. Ibid.

3. Seels, B. B., and R. C. Richey. 1992. *Instructional Technology: Definitions.* Washington, D.C.: Association for Education, Communication and Technology.

4. Miller, J. A. 1992. "Training Requirements to Support Total Quality Management." *CMA Magazine* (November).

5. Schuman, S. P. 1996. "What to Look for in a Group Facilitator." *Quality Progress* (June).

6. Seels, B. B. 1995. *Instructional Design Fundamentals: A Reconsideration.* Englewood Cliffs, N.J.: Educational Technology Publications.

7. Ibid.

8. Duncan, A. J. 1974. *Quality Control and Industrial Statistics.* Homewood, Ill.: Richard D. Irwin.

9. Doyle, M., and D. Straus. 1976. *How to Make Meetings Work: The New Interaction Method.* New York, N.Y.: Jove Books.

10. Rossett, A. 1987. *Training Needs Assessment: Techniques in Training and Performance Development Series.* Englewood Cliffs, N.J.: Educational Technology Publications.

11. Juran and Gryna. *Juran's Quality Control Handbook.*

Related References

Hawthorne, E. M. 1987. *Evaluating Employee Training Programs.* Westport, Conn.: Greenwood Press.

Kaufman, R., and A. M. Rojas. 1993. *Needs Assessment: A Users Guide.* Englewood Cliffs, N.J.: Educational Technology Publications.

Kirkpatrick, D. L. 1975. *Evaluating Training Programs.* American Society for Training and Development.

Chapter 8
Project Management

Project management (PM) is, as Kerzner[1] describes it, "a system approach to planning, scheduling, and controlling. It is a methodology to provide greater assurance that objectives are met in an efficient manner. Its techniques and principles can be followed in organizationwide initiatives, single organization elements, and short- or long-term projects. It is of special interest in quality management because it is being adopted in a variety of organizations to improve quality, productivity, and competitiveness. It is an effective way to manage product development, production, and internal organizations during significant change; namely, implementing TQ. These structural changes (downsizing, restructuring, management reduction, reengineering) are driven by world competition and customer expectations, particularly for higher quality. Even after TQ implementation has reached maturity, PM is still valuable to manage the changes resulting from continuous improvement.

This chapter discusses the key elements of PM and, to a limited degree, its applications. Special emphasis is placed on quality management applications. PM is also discussed in Chapter 2 in relation to different organization structures.

PM is appropriate for managing any significant quality improvement. It provides structure and techniques for planning and monitoring. (Managing an ongoing project in a modern organization also requires an understanding and application of the other management principles and techniques discussed in previous chapters.)

General Discussion

The term *project* is used to describe any series of activities and tasks that have the following:

- A specific objective with specific requirements to be met
- A schedule that must be met (a beginning and an end)
- Usually, cost objectives and constraints
- Resources requirements (financial and physical)

Projects can be short or long term. They can be used to complete one event, such as constructing a building, or they can be ongoing, such as developing a housing project, a customer service organization, or a new quality supplier base. Internal projects can have an objective of, say, introducing a new software program or organizing a team to improve a specific process, with a schedule and objectives. Managing such projects requires planning, implementing, operating, and controlling the activities that will satisfy the project requirements.

Another view describes the applications of PM as

- Project scope management
- Quality management
- Time management
- Cost management
- Human resources management
- Procurement management
- Communication and information management
- Customer interface management[2]

Structure. When used to manage major events, PM is an overlay of the management function across the functional organization. In a sense it acts as the representative of executive management to ensure the functional organizations meet specific project objectives. Larger projects are frequently organized as a project office, with functional managers reporting to a peer or senior executive. This serves to make their authority visible. This office is also usually staffed with a team of functional organization representatives led by the project manager. Each team member acts as the communicator to and from his or her home function. Each is responsible for his or her function, meeting the project requirements, schedule, and cost allocations.

Project and Process Management

The description of what a project is and its function in an organization sounds very similar to the description of process management discussed throughout this book. The two are similar in that PM is structured to get specific work accomplished across and through the functional organizations. Process management objectives are similar but more fundamental. A basic difference is that a project is task oriented to get specific work done in a specified time. Process management is a method of managing the organization all the time and may include completing specific tasks. It is a change from functional organization autonomy to managing how most work actually gets done; that is, horizontally, across and through functions. These work flows are the processes. In addition, to be most successful in process management, organizations are using process improvement team management.[3]

Darnall[4] describes the uniqueness of PM.

> A PM transforms someone's dream into a reality. She transforms a raw concept into a deliverable, builds an organization and structure to produce that deliverable, and then decommissions that organization. It is the temporary nature of this organization that gives rise to the special character of a project, a character that is very different from that of an ongoing organization. The character of a project organization defines the skills, the knowledge and the management approach that is needed to be successful.

To summarize, PM is task oriented, with a beginning and an end. Process management is a specific management method, combined with a policy of continuous improvement, which has no planned end but can be made up of many tasks as projects.

Whether or not an organization uses PM to manage a product or contract, *project* is often the term applied to the goals of a team. The project manager is the team leader. The following paragraphs identify and discuss the main elements of PM and how they fit together.

8.A. Planning and Monitoring

Two critical activities of PM involve project planning and project monitoring. *Planning* is the continuous process of

- Defining organization objectives for the project: become more competitive, develop expertise, enter new markets, initiate organizationwide process improvements.

- Defining project/customer requirements and translating these into work requirements.

- Defining responsibilities, quality, and quantity of work.

- Defining the type, quantity, and timing of resources needed.

- Establishing the incremental milestones and completion schedule.

- Operating with and within organization elements.

- Identifying constraints and limitations on success and making plans to overcome them.

Monitoring includes

- Tracking progress

- Comparing actual status to predicted and required outcomes

- Analyzing the impact of deviation from plans, and defining corrective action or selecting alternatives

- Making adjustments for changes in customer requirements, technical problems, resource problems, supplier problems, cost overruns, and so on

Output of the Planning Process. In addition to the schedules and resources, the planning process output provides a *statement of work* (SOW). This is usually in narrative form and identifies the design criteria, specifications, requirements, constraints, the basis for the costs, and other factors.

From the SOW, a *work breakdown structure* (WBS) is prepared by, or in conjunction with, the organization that will do the work. The WBS is the final delineation of all work tasks to be done. It is structured according to the way work will be done and how the ongoing status will be reported. The combination of the project plan, SOW, and WBS should provide a complete work package containing the what, when, and how; the costs and work elements; and the objectives of the project.

Project Performance. A project is successful when it meets its planned objectives. Measuring success would be easy if organization life were simple and unchanging, but the reality is far different.

PM itself is a complicating factor. It is a management system to cross functional boundaries and get those organizations to satisfy the project's requirements. People doing the work (staff in particular) now have two bosses. There are even greater complications when there is more than one project.

This can create all kinds of interface problems related to communication, priorities, direction, control. Conditions in an organization are never static. There can be structure changes, personnel changes, process and equipment changes, product changes, changes in financial conditions, and policy changes. All of these have an impact on PM. The longer the project time line, the more frequently a project manager will have to change plans and schedules. Project performance measurements in long-term and complex projects in particular are often difficult to evaluate and compare to the initial plan because many factors change from initial planning to completion. For this reason alone, project managers must maintain firm control over the initial, and all subsequent, planning.

Problems in Managing Projects. Every project, of any size, encounters problems, any of which can seriously affect the project success. Common problems include the following:

- Interpersonal problems anywhere people have to work together. Such problems can reach the point where they can sabotage the project.
- Initiating a project beyond the capability of the manager, or one or all of the key functional organizations.

- Inadequate project monitoring; failure to recognize poor performance and take corrective action.

- Conflicts. Conflict management is a normal part of a project manager's job. There are conflicts between people and organizations over priorities, over funding, over mistakes, and over abilities. (Conflict management is discussed in Chapter 6.)

- Dependence on firefighting rather than true problem cause removal.

- Failure to reprioritize as problems change with project progress.

- Sacrificing requirements to schedule or cost limitations. This can create a difficult management decision when a project is late and the customer demands delivery.

- Project management without authority to get functional organizations to meet project requirements. Related to this is the failure of upper management to support the project manager.

- Weak functional management that accepts unrealistic direction for the project. This will ensure some objectives are missed if the problem is not detected and corrected.

The Importance of Project Selection. Project selection is a critical management responsibility because

- It is an allocation of finite organization resources to meet an objective.

- It is a reflection to the organization of management priorities.

- It directly affects the health and vitality of the overall organization.

The basis for project selection includes

- Importance to the organization's future, to the customer, to the product, to service, or to the team.

- Competitive factors; cost control; or reduction in any of the steps of development, manufacture, materials, delivery, distribution, or sales.

- Market/customer-related issues, such as quality, reliability, function, service, or repair.

- Strategic or tactical organization and quality improvement initiatives.

- The need to properly manage the production and introduction of a new product or service, or improve those that already exist.

8.A.1 Integrated Quality Initiatives

Integrated quality improvement initiatives are those affecting several or all functional units. With such scope and complexity, PM is the most common tool to achieve success. Initiatives are broad in scope and are formulated in general terms. They originate in the overall strategic planning process. Quality projects are the separate elements of the initiatives that are planned, implemented, and monitored to meet the broad objectives.

Basic Requirements. Every organization dedicated to becoming best in class must have systems (appropriate to the size and nature of the organization) that incorporate common quality management concepts, including the following (these are discussed in Chapters 2 and 3):

- Quality policies

- Quality objectives

- Quality assurance

- Quality control

- Quality audits

- Quality plans (as a part of project plans)

These concepts must exist as realities—policies, procedures, organizations, and people—throughout the organization if quality projects are to be successfully integrated into the organization units. Some examples of quality initiatives include

- Planned strategic and tactical quality improvement objectives (such as, initiate TQ in the organization).

- Developing a quality supplier base.

- Seeking a quality award or ISO registration.

- Meeting new government regulations.

- Implementing QFD planning at the inception of a new product or service.

Quality Projects. Quality projects can be derived from breaking down the quality initiatives into manageable elements, or they can be quality improvement projects of organization units that are integral to their own planned improvements. They may be short or long term. Some examples of quality improvements are

- Projects initiated for the organization to become registered to ISO 9000 or begin Baldrige Award preparation
- Specific process improvements in all units
- Developing a quality cost measurement and reporting system
- Implementing the QFD matrix for a product identified in the quality initiatives
- Planning the implementation of process control and performance measures with the teams involved
- Identifying a product for a DOE application
- Improving the customer service system

Integrating quality initiatives into new or existing projects requires careful planning to avoid disruptions or excessive costs. These factors should be considered when quality initiatives are developed.

8.A.2. Short- and Long-Term Quality Plans and Objectives

One of the common themes in business and government agencies is becoming more competitive by delivering high-quality goods and/or services at lower cost in a shorter time. A key to surviving in this environment is to become proactive; that is, to aggressively search and plan for breakthrough improvements. The key word is *plan*.

Significant improvements won't materialize unless they are clearly identified and aggressively pursued. This process can't be left to good intentions. Objectives must be identified, quantified, scheduled, assigned, and continuously monitored. That is the strength and function of PM.

Short-term quality planning is the tactical planning stage, while long-term quality planning is the strategic planning stage. Strategic initiatives are planned for three to five years out, while tactical efforts are planned for intervals of one to three years. Typically, tactical planning considers only the current year or less. Short-term planning includes recovery planning, when a work-around plan is needed to solve an unanticipated problem.

Strategic quality planning efforts focus on the fundamental questions: What's the nature of our business? Are we correct in staying in each part of the business? What long-term trends are likely to affect our customers? What/how do we change to maintain or improve our competitive position? What must we do to prepare?

Tactical planning and objectives focus on many of the same issues: What skills do our personnel need to compete in the new environment? What must we do now so that they will be ready? and so on. A shorter view, or what is sometimes referred to as operational planning, focuses on what needs to be done day to day and week to week. Tactical planning objectives are relatively easy to establish and meet because the variables are more visible, better known, and understood. Strategic planning has more unknowns, more unpredictables, and more risks. Tactical and strategic planning are also discussed in Chapter 3.

Projects are started with definite objectives in mind. Project objectives, including quality, should be

- Specific, not general
- Important to the future of the organization
- As simple as possible
- Measurable, tangible, and verifiable
- Difficult but realistic and obtainable
- Established within the resources that are available or anticipated
- Consistent with organizational plans, policies, and procedures

Some reasons for setting objectives of any kind include the following:

- If there are no objectives, the organization does not have any idea of what is important, or where to apply resources.
- Without objectives it is difficult to measure results against prior achievements. The organization has no sense of progress or achievement.

Some organizations use management by objectives (MBO) methodologies for setting objectives for both PM and the functional managers. Using MBO has become less common in recent years because MBO rewards individuals, not teams. This tends to generate competition for rewards such as bonuses and merit increases, and objectives are achieved at the expense of other functions. Individual MBOs are not always in the long-term best interests of the overall organization, customer, or development of strong teams.

8.A.3. Feedback Loops

Information feedback from functional units on a project is basic for good project management. The project manager has to keep current with what is going on—are plans being met, are problems affecting the project in any way, and so on.

The adequacy of information provided by the project staff or manager to functional units completes the feedback loop. The information from the functions, required by the project office or manager, should be complete and timely to take any corrective actions necessary.

Much of the information in large or midsized organizations should come from the basic management information system, such as material and labor costs, earned value (when that system is used), budgets, and milestone status. Reports special to each project are needed to summarize and report total status. Effective program managers develop their own supplemental communications links to stay on top of the key activities in their projects.

Other Communication Factors. Communications are essential to the success of project management, and methodologies must be established in the planning phase. Communication can be formal or informal, written or oral, but one should not assume that the communications are received and understood. An effective communication system is necessary not only to communicate project information to the individual, but to provides motivational information as well. Formal feedback procedures are specified by the PM or organization procedures. Some of these include

- Regular meetings with project leader.

- Regular status reporting (meeting reports).

- Regular meetings with customers.

The problem then becomes how to communicate such information. Six steps are suggested.[5]

1. Think what you wish to accomplish.

2. Determine the way you will communicate.

3. Appeal to the interest of those affected.

4. Give feedback on ways others communicate to you.

5. Get feedback on what you communicate.

6. Test the effectiveness of communications through reliance on others to carry out your instructions.

Techniques for improving communications include the following:

- Obtaining feedback

- Establishing multiple communication channels

- Using face-to-face communications when possible

- Determining how sensitive the receiver is to your communication

- Being aware of symbolic meanings (body language)

- Communicating at the proper time

- Reinforcing words with actions

- Using redundancy wherever possible (expressing a thought in more than one way, such as following up verbal messages with written confirmation or letters of understanding)

When setting up a continuous monitoring activity for a project, it is important to keep in mind that there are numerous barriers to effective communication.

- People starting with different and uncommunicated assumptions

- People hearing what they want to hear

- Different perceptions between the people doing the communicating

- Evaluating the source before accepting the communication

- Ignoring conflicting information
- Words meaning different things to different people
- Recipient or sender being emotionally upset

Since quality activities exist in all functions of a TQ organization, the quality manager in particular has a complex and critical leadership role in maintaining effective feedback loops with all elements. He or she should periodically assess his or her own effectiveness and set personal objectives to continuously improve.

8.A.4. Performance Measures and Timelines

Measuring PM performance has two components.

1. Personnel. The project manager and individuals with functional responsibility for project management; that is, the people assigned to a project office.

2. Project. The ongoing measure of the status and progress of a project in meeting objectives.

Personnel. Everyone is concerned with receiving a fair evaluation of his or her performance. Within functional organizations there is usually a close tie between manager and employee, and the employee can be directly observed. When a functional employee is assigned to a project team, however, the primary management interfaces change, and the employee takes most direction from the project manager.

Organizations successfully using PM will implement a reliable two-way evaluation system (project manager–functional manager) for PM personal performance evaluation or there will be little motivation for a member to perform for the best interests of the project. Functional managers usually retain salary control of their employees working on a project. The appraisal system will include some formal methodology for a project manager's input to the appraisal of assigned team members.

Project. Project performance measures are straightforward, but they must be structured to go beyond just measuring whether objectives are met. When objectives are not met, there should be some provision to determine such things as whether the cause was beyond a project manager's control (such as a change in the market) as well as an assessment of the manager's awareness and reaction to problems.

Some key project performance issues include

- Are objectives met or exceeded? (cost, schedule, customer satisfaction)

- Is risk management performed effectively and on appropriate problems?

- If objectives are not met, is the cause known?

- Are potential problems detected early enough to take corrective action?

- Are problems solved effectively?

- Is status reporting timely and accurate?

- Does the project manager or leader demonstrate effective leadership?

- Are objectives maintained in spite of problems?

- Is the customer relationship satisfactory?

Product and process measurements are also meaningful to track, particularly when they are product requirements or process improvement objectives. The pricing on long-term projects is often based on expected improvements in material costs, even though it isn't clear how the reductions will be achieved (labor improvements are often based on learning curves). Organizations emphasizing process management forecast costs based on planned, quantified process improvements.

Some measured factors in project performance are

- Labor and material costs versus planned reductions.

- Cycle times.

- Reliability mean time between failures (MTBF) demonstration.

- Budget controls.

- Reject/rework rates.

- Scrap costs.

- Planned process capability improvements.

- Quality costs.

- Milestone achievements, including quality.

Project performance measurement is also a measurement of the effectiveness of the project manager. The measurement also reflects whether the managers of project managers show consistent interest and support for the project and its objectives.

8.A.4.a. Resources. Project resources include manpower, procurement costs, facilities, and equipment. Their quantities are finite and are budgeted during the planning process. It is a common procedure to set aside a resource budget for contingencies, particularly for projects running more than a year or of high risk and complexity. Ten percent of a budget is a common quantity. The initial project resources are established by the project manager, team, and functional manager and reviewed and approved by upper management as previously discussed. Accurate resource planning and allocation begins with complete and accurate statements of work and the subsequent work breakdown structure and through milestone planning. Project planning also must incorporate the various support requirements, such as financial operation and software systems.

Resource control issues will arise periodically and require continued communication and negotiation between project and functional management. The more limited the project management authority, the more likely the conflicts. Labor requirements are the most frequent source of resource conflicts. Some reasons include the following:

- Functional management has to support more than one project.

- Project needs for labor fluctuate.

- Different projects may require the same resource at the same time.

8.A.4.b. Methodologies. Methodologies for measuring project performance vary with the complexity and length of a project. A specific process improvement team manager may only need to periodically report status, verbally or in writing, to upper management.

As projects get larger, longer, involve several functional organizations, and are higher risk, additional methods and tools are used for plan monitoring and control. The simplest method should be chosen that will provide adequate control. The greater the complexity, the more expensive it will be. Whatever method is used, the choice is made in the early planning stages and becomes the basis of the plan.

Three methods (PERT, CPM, and Gantt, discussed later in this section) are commonly used to manage projects. They can be administered manually or by using computer programs. Some key advantages in using computer analysis are

- Simplified calculation of critical paths, slack time, resource usage, and schedules in PERT and CPM.

- Quicker visibility of variances to plan.

- Simulation capability to evaluate the effects of different decisions or alternatives.

- Easy publication of reports in different formats.

- Most practical way to accumulate and report complex and multiple-source data.

Some disadvantages include

- Generally higher costs (for data formulation and entry, computer time).

- Software capability and options not matching needs.

The three most common project management methods, or tools, are the program evaluation and review technique (PERT), Gantt chart, and critical path method (CPM).[6]

A *PERT chart* is a graphical representation (networks) of task relationships, a road map of the project. It has many significant advantages over the other methods, particularly for large and long-running projects. It

- Assists management in planning for the best use of resources

- Provides a method for management to evaluate the effect of changes in plans

- Shows the critical path in project activities; that is, the longest and controlling path in the project

- Allows for the determination of the probability of meeting schedule dates by developing alternate plans

- Provides the ability to evaluate the effect of proposed changes in resource allocation
- Shows interdependencies between events and activities

In charting a network, the basic rules are as follows:

- Events are shown as circles and represent specific accomplishments.
- An event is the starting or ending point for a group of activities.
- Activities are shown as arrows. They are the work required to proceed from one event or point in time to another. The length and direction of the arrows have no meaning. The number over each arrow specifies the time needed.

The objective in using PERT is to determine project completion time.[7] Therefore, time is the basic scale against which to measure factors that directly affect success, such as time, cost, and performance.

The first step is to identify whether each event is the start or completion of an activity. Event completions are generally used. The second step is to define the sequence of events, as shown in Table 8.1.

Table 8.1. Sequence of events.

Activity	Title	Immediate predecessor	Activity time (weeks)
1-2	A	—	1
2-3	B	A	4
2-4	C	A	2
3-5	D	B	3
3-7	E	B	2
4-5	F	C	2
4-8	G	C	3
5-6	H	D, F	2
6-7	I	H	3
7-8	J	E, I	3
8-9	K	G, J	3

The sequence of events is converted into a network, as shown in Figures 8.1 and 8.2. The critical path shown in Figure 8.1 is 1, 2, 3, 5, 6, 7, 8, 9. This shows that there is no slack time in the path. Any slippage in the sequence will result in a slippage in the final date. The critical path shows which events have to be managed closely (or improved).

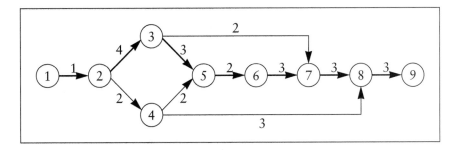

Figure 8.1. The data as a network.

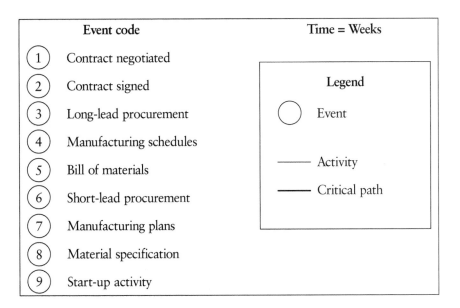

Figure 8.2. A simplified PERT network.

PERT identifies the earliest possible date an event can be expected to occur, or an activity to start or end. A few networks may be too simple for a computer, but when there is a large number of events, their interaction can only be evaluated with a computer program.

The second technique in management and control of projects is the *critical path method* (CPM). It is similar to PERT in structure, but with some differences.

- PERT is event rather than activity oriented and is most useful in research and development projects, where calculating percent complete is usually impossible.

- CPM is activity oriented; percent complete can be calculated. Projects are well defined, with few uncertainties, such as in construction.

- CPM is, like PERT, a mathematical model. It involves time and cost estimates for each activity.

- In CPM, only those activities on the critical path are considered.

Further details on CPM can be found in the references.

A *Gantt* or *bar chart* shows the timeline activity of tasks (the base can also be dollars). The beginning of the bar in a Gantt chart depicts the starting date for tasks, and the end of the bar is the planned or actual completion date. The length of each bar is the task time. In use, the bar is blocked in to show the status or percent of completion of a task. Gantt charts are often used in conjunction with PERT or CPM. Figure 8.3 shows an example of a Gantt chart for the steps and times in preparing and delivering a job bid. It is basically a bar chart with tasks or events plotted with respect to time.

Advantages to a Gantt chart include the following:

- It is easy to prepare, understand, and maintain.

- It requires simple data.

- It provides a quick picture of status.

Its disadvantages include

- It does not depict how an entire project stands.

- It doesn't show the interdependent relationships between activities.

ID	Task name	Duration	Start	Finish
1	Bid process	1.8w	6/19/96	7/1/96
2	Receive bid	1d	6/19/96	6/19/96
3	Distribute bid for review	1d	6/20/96	6/20/96
4	Review bid	5d	6/21/96	6/27/96
5	Team review	1d	6/27/96	6/27/96
6	Comments and pricing out	2d	6/28/96	7/1/96
7	Bid due to customer	1d	6/28/96	6/28/96

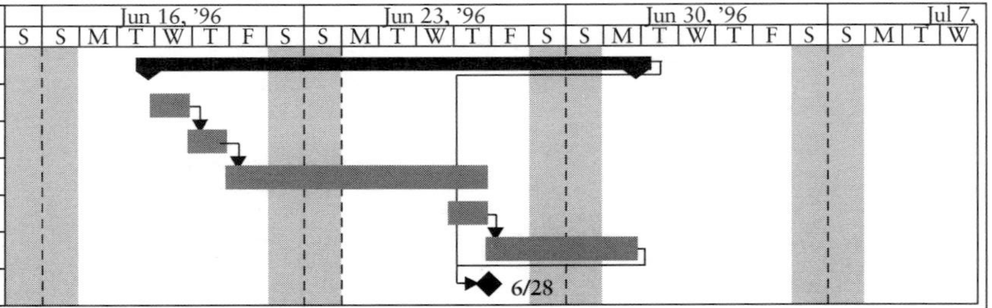

Project: Bid review
Date: 6/24/96

Task
Progress
Milestone

Summary
Rolled up task
Rolled up milestone

Rolled up progress

Page 1

Figure 8.3. The bid process Gantt chart showing key milestones.

- Since relationships are not shown, Gantt charts have little predictive capability.

- The effects of a late start to an activity are not shown.

A simple technique for controlling smaller projects is a *line of balance* methodology. Details can be found in a text on production control.

8.A.5. Relevant Stakeholders

The relevant stakeholders in projects are the entities and individuals with a vested interest in the project's success, such as the stockholders of the company, management, employees, and the company's suppliers and customers. Benefits of successful projects are realized at all of these levels. Stockholders benefit when earnings for the company rise as a result of a successful venture. Management and employees have an acute interest in a project's success to continue in their ability to do the things that provide their livelihoods and keep the business healthy in general. This implies that stakeholders have a right to determine what happens within an organization and projects. This particularly applies to organizations that are using self-directed teams or developing partnership agreements with their customers.

8.A.6. Benchmarking

Benchmarking is a comparative analytical tool that organizations can use to improve their products and processes. It can be defined as comparing products, internal processes, and methods with the best practices found in outside organizations and adapting or adopting them as quality improvement projects. It is most effective when conducted by a trained team using a project management approach. Benchmarking is an important competitive tool, and when properly applied it provides significant, frequently breakthrough, improvements in all sizes and types of organizations. It has been valuable in

- Setting strategies and tactical organizational goals and objectives. Setting goals based on improvements found in the benchmarking process often results in achievable goals much tougher than would have been set using internal ideas. Even though challenging, they are accepted because they are obviously attainable.

- Setting project goals and objectives.

- Making breakthrough quality improvements
- Motivating teams and employees to think beyond just in-house improvement ideas.
- Reducing destructive internal competition (because the focus is external).
- Achieving a high rating in or winning the Baldrige or other quality awards. (Examiners look for successful use of benchmarking.)

The first step in using benchmarking is to educate upper management in the benchmarking concept, practices, resources, and time required to do an effective job. Benchmarking can fail if management thinks it is a cheap, quick fix to gain some competitive advantage.

The second step is to select a small team of knowledgeable people and train them in the principles and practices of benchmarking. The team then selects the methodology to be used.

Benchmarking can be conducted as a routine activity in organization management to achieve continuous improvement. The basic steps in benchmarking can be depicted as a sequence or process, in a manner analogous to the plan-do-check-act problem-solving methodology. This process is shown in Figure 8.4.

Important factors for successful benchmarking are as follows:

- Management support and sponsorship of teams.
- Beginning with short-term projects.
- Having something to trade with organizations that have been targeted as benchmarks. That means first getting your own house in order. Get processes under control and determine the organization's capabilities. (Benchmarking is not one of the first things to do when implementing TQ, except that it is useful to talk to other, similar kinds of organizations to share their experiences.)
- Selecting team members carefully. They have to know their process intimately and be good listeners and communicators. They are representatives of the organization to outside benchmarking targets.
- Focusing on the process, not the process metrics. Better methods are the goal.

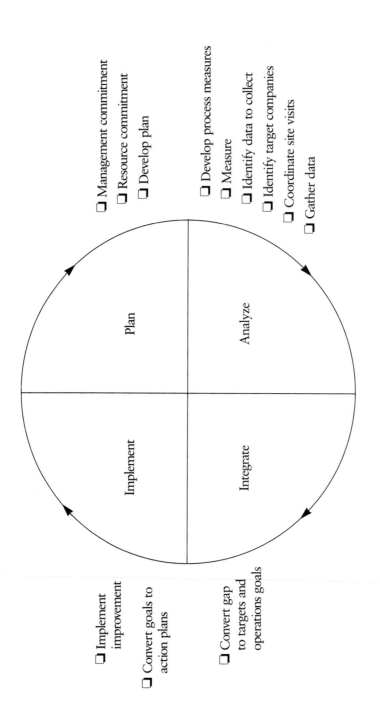

Figure 8.4. The plan-do-check-act methodology applied to the benchmarking process.

Plan
- ❏ Management commitment
- ❏ Resource commitment
- ❏ Develop plan

Analyze
- ❏ Develop process measures
- ❏ Measure
- ❏ Identify data to collect
- ❏ Identify target companies
- ❏ Coordinate site visits
- ❏ Gather data

Implement
- ❏ Implement improvement
- ❏ Convert goals to action plans

Integrate
- ❏ Convert gap to targets and operations goals

- Selecting off-site visits carefully, using them sparingly, and being prepared.

8.A.7. Budgeting

The project budget is the plan for the allocation and distribution and expenditure of resources throughout the life of the project. It is one of the results of the planning cycle. Budgets must be reasonable, attainable, and, when appropriate, based on contractually negotiated costs and the SOW. Budgets should also be prepared for smaller in-house projects, like a benchmarking program. If small projects are not carefully budgeted, their cost can threaten the larger project or impact other project costs (a negative effect on overhead for example).

The budget is the standard, the basis, for project cost performance measurement. There are always variances to this standard as a project progresses. These can be tracked and reported as such, or the project budget can be replanned. Usually on larger projects replanning is only done when there is a significant change in the scope of work.

The basis for a project budget is historical cost, best estimates, or industrial engineering labor standards. Expected subcontracted and material costs are also included. It must identify the planned labor requirements, allocated funds from all sources, and a management reserve for contingencies. Other cost elements that can affect project success are such things as equipment costs or leases, overhead cost allocations and projections, and projected material and labor cost increases.

Budgets play important roles in accomplishing business objectives.

- Planning. Budgets provide a detailed financial plan of what the company intends to accomplish. This would be true for implementing a TQ program or completing a complex customer contract over a period of time.

- Motivation. Using a budget and holding managers accountable for performance to meet the company's objectives provides a disciplined approach to accomplish that end, especially when compensation and advancement are linked to budget performance.

- Direction. Budgets provide for the quantification of management's goals and objectives, from which it can direct its actions.

- Evaluation. Budgets provide a suitable standard that can be used in comparison with a project's or manager's results.

- Coordination. Diverse activities can be coordinated by consolidating the plan of action through the use of a budget.

- Education. Companies should implement training programs to instruct employees on the budget's role in meeting goals and objectives.

Quality Project Budgets. Establishing project budgets for quality program requirements or initiatives is no different except that the quality activities usually involve several, if not all, the functions of the enterprise. This makes planning and estimating more complex. In budgeting for government contracts, care must be taken to be consistent in labor and material practices.

The key factors in quality budget preparation and management are as follows:

1. Identify and analyze quality requirements in the proposal.

2. Identify and analyze new requirements to determine scope and compatibility (for example, ISO requirements).

3. Describe the impact of any new requirements in terms of cost, new skills, labor, or equipment.

4. Discuss results with the proposal or project manager.

5. Prepare a statement of work for quality activities and obtain project management approval.

6. Prepare work breakdown structures for every work element.

7. Estimate element costs, with rationale to support the numbers.

8. Negotiate final budget with the project manager. It is also imperative that authorities and responsibilities be established for all work elements. This is important to avoid future organizational conflicts.

9. Performance to established budgets is a quality management responsibility. The quality project representative usually is responsible for cost tracking, variance analysis, and reporting. The quality manager must constantly be aware of any anticipated budget variances to cost or schedule for quality activities to take corrective action and keep the project staff informed.

8.A.8. Cost-Benefit Analysis (CBA)

CBA is a method of evaluating a project to assess whether it will provide a satisfactory financial benefit to justify the proposed expenditure. It is used prior to project approval.

Deming frequently wrote that quality improvements should be economically justifiable. It is not enough to make improvements that might satisfy the customer without some financial basis. Unless there is market value or a higher return their value is suspect, if not zero.

The difficulty is in determining the benefits. CBA can be a complex exercise in larger projects and where many risk factors exist. It is usually performed by the financial function, using computer models with numerous inputs, such as standard cost data, estimated labor, material, subcontracts, overhead, inventory projections, facilities, equipment, cost of money over the period, warranty costs, and customer service. In other words, all the costs that would or could be incurred if the project was approved are included. CBA is also used to evaluate and justify expenditures for tools or equipment, software programs, product/service quality improvements, process improvements, training, or consultants. It can also be used for making in-house or purchase decisions, comparing the benefits of competing products, and for simulation (comparing the benefits and risks of alternatives in project management).

Some analyses are based on estimates of benefits when factors are intangible or unknown. Cost and benefit, in purely financial terms, are not the only basis of management decisions, although CBA is a valuable financial tool in evaluating different options and plans. The quality manager should play an active role in all cost-benefit analyses involving quality initiatives and improvements. (Johnson and Melicher[8] explain the different methodologies in detail.)

8.B. Implementation

Once the initial budget plans have been established, they are implemented and managed. The plan is the road map. But it is rarely that simple. The operating world is dynamic; budget estimates prove to be unattainable or suppliers get in trouble. Managing a project means constantly solving problems.

8.B.1. Management Support and Organization Roadblocks

Management support is necessary to achieve anything significant in an organization. But PM, by its very nature (a management structure overlay on functional organizations with a narrow focus), requires more than ordinary management support and commitment at all levels. Functional organizations tend to want to do their own thing: design, build, count money, or audit. They are also more comfortable with the vertical chain of command. Adding a second boss, the project manager, complicates the environment and work of functional organizations. These are the conditions that all managers must accept when the organization uses PM. The middle managers can be a special problem: They are assigned work and objectives by their functional managers, frequently have little contact with the projects, and have difficulty in accepting project priorities or the impact of supporting a project when it means changing functional commitments.

Management Support. If projects are to succeed—avoid or get out of trouble—they must have visible, continuous upper management support. The following are a few things upper management can do.

- Be consistent and fair in accepting project plans. Make it clear (and act accordingly) that the functions have no authority to overspend or miss schedules. Reinforce the project leader's authority when problems arise; the functions must work it out with the project manager.

- Stay well informed on project progress, risks, and important problems.

- Regularly attend project meetings, particularly any where the customer is present.

- Be available when conflicts threaten the project.

- Do not meddle in ongoing project management. This will weaken the manager's authority.

Roadblocks occur in every kind of organization. Some are caused by human factors, some by inadequate planning, some by operating systems. Common roadblocks include

- Differing outlooks, priorities, and interests. Serious roadblocks exist when team members or functional groups hold views, interests, and priorities different from the project's objectives.

- Unclear project objectives or outcomes. Unclear project objectives frequently lead to conflict, ambiguities, and power struggles. It becomes difficult, if not impossible, to define roles and responsibilities clearly.

- Dynamic project environments. When the project team has to operate in an environment of continual change, such as when management keeps changing the scope of work or when outside influences such as regulatory agencies or the customers want changes, the team can become demoralized.

- Competition over team leadership. Difficulties of this type usually occur early in the project or when the project team runs into severe problems.

- Lack of team definition and structure. Teamwork is seriously impaired when there is a lack of a clearly defined task responsibilities and reporting structures

- Project team personnel selection. This barrier develops when personnel feel unfairly treated or threatened during staffing of a project.

- Credibility of project team leader. Efforts are hampered when team members or other managers lack confidence in the project leader. In cases where credibility is an issue, the team members are reluctant to commit to the project or the leader.

- Lack of team member commitment. There can be numerous reasons for this problem, from the project leader suffering from credibility problems to team members having professional interests elsewhere.

- Communication problems. Poor communication is a major roadblock to effective development and project management.

Project managers who perform well in their role not only recognize these organizational roadblocks, but also know when they are likely to occur during the life cycle of the project. They take corrective action and foster an environment conducive to effective project and team management. Effective project managers develop or find mutual goals to encourage functional support, creating a win-win for those involved or affected.

8.B.2. Short-Term (Tactical) Plans

Planning, including short-term (tactical) planning, is discussed in Chapter 3. The subject is also related to short-term quality plans and objectives discussed earlier in this chapter. Preparing short-term plans, to reach a short-term objective or resolve a current problem, has not been a common practice in traditional management, except in well-managed projects. Most commonly, when management wanted something changed or a problem solved, it assigned the task to a subordinate. At best, the order included a completion date. The subordinate was left to his or her own devices. Usually something got done, but without the tie-in to a prepared plan, no one really knew how well it was done. Without a plan the who, what, when, and how much were never defined.

Every activity absorbs resources and may affect meeting some objectives. Therefore, when any change in objectives or new problem is to be worked on, the first response should be to prepare a short-term correction plan for review and approval. Without this discipline the normal accumulation of changes and problems will result in a loss of control of the project. Also, there would be no record of the project performance history, which makes performance reviews subjective.

Quality improvement project teams are the doers in a TQ organization. Their world is dynamic; it is a series of problems, changes and actions. The project or team leader is responsible for maintaining control, relying first on the initial planning. Changes and their impact must be continually reviewed and, with approval, plans changed to meet current needs. Short-term planning is not an end in itself, but is used to keep the team on track and as a road map for the team to follow. The plan doesn't have to be formalized, but a team needs to have some record of what it has accomplished, of the project status, and, in longer projects, of the learning curve to avoid repeating past actions that were not productive.

8.B.3. Cross-Functional Collaboration

Collaboration between functional elements in meeting objectives is valuable in any organization, and one of the most difficult management tasks. The difficulty in doing it effectively led to the development and wide use of PM. The need becomes more acute as organizations move into team-based management. As discussed in the preface and several of the preceding chapters, the leading TQ organizations are drastically changing the role of functional units, to make them a resource for teams. In the many traditional organizations that still exist, PM is a major tool to obtain cross-functional collaboration. It is by definition cross-functional management, giving PM the authority to cross functional boundaries to get the project work done.

Small projects, like a specific process quality improvement, that involve the suppliers and customers of the process in a cooperative effort may have a more difficult time because they lack the authority of a large project. One effective method for supporting small projects is to assign reporting responsibility and accountability to a functional manager. It is then this manager's responsibility to assist project teams in getting the cross-functional collaboration they need. Multifunctional teams, by definition, are composed of multifunctional representatives. Part of their initial assignment is the responsibility to obtain the support of their home functions. The leader should emphasize collaborative efforts and shared team rewards.

Concurrent engineering is a device to obtain the collaboration of key functions in the design, development, and production of new products as parallel activities. It provides the structure for functional collaboration. The leader must be capable of managing a group of diverse technical specialists to achieve a collaborative effort, a complex management task. The quality manager is usually in a position to play a key role in facilitating cross-functional collaboration because he or she manages the quality system, which typically involves all functional organizations, external customers, and suppliers. In monitoring the status of quality improvement activities he or she communicates directly with the functional managers.

8.B.4. Continuous Review and Enhancement of Quality Process

Too often in the organization of a quality system, the system is documented, proceduralized, and then allowed to become out-of-date. Because of the dynamics of the workplace, the operating quality systems change, often in a haphazard manner. Procedures are changed ad hoc and never documented.

There are two major exceptions. Businesses working on government contracts are required to document and maintain an effective quality system. Customer inspectors check periodically to see that those requirements are met. The second exception is those organizations with

ISO 9000 series registration. They are required to designate an executive to be responsible for defining and documenting a quality plan, including quality objectives and quality commitment. ISO 9001 requires that, "responsibility, authority, and the interaction of personnel who manage, perform, and verify work affecting quality shall be defined and documented."

The quality system must also provide that internal personnel have the organizational freedom and responsibility to do the following:

- Initiate corrective actions to prevent process or product nonconformances.

- Identify and record quality system, process, and product deficiencies.

- Initiate and recommend solutions to problems through approved channels.

- Verify implementation of the solutions so the deficiency doesn't recur.

- Control processing and delivery to ensure deficiencies are root-cause corrected.

These requirements form the basis for the continuous quality system review process and are a good model for any organization.

Methodology. There three basic information sources for reviewing and enhancing the quality process (system).

1. The reviews required by ISO registration and other contractual documents. These reviews should be led by the quality manager, and findings should be developed into corrective actions to improve or update the quality system and documentation, as well as resolve problems and conflicts affecting quality and customer satisfaction.

2. Valuable information on the health of the quality system, processes, products, and services is provided by quality system/product audits, those required by ISO 9001 or a customer contract, or the audits that should be routinely conducted by every quality-oriented organization.

3. Project reviews, formal or informal, special or routine, can be a source of information for the improvement and enhancement of the quality process. The quality manager should assign the project or team quality representative the responsibility for identifying and reporting any quality system or process needs or opportunities for enhancement or improvement.

8.B.5. Documentation and Procedures

Quality documentation and procedures for project use have several sources. First are the overall organization quality policies and procedures. These describe the quality policies and objectives of the enterprise, assign organization and management responsibilities for implementation, and define the procedures to be followed.

In medium or small companies or those with one main product or service, the documentation can be easily integrated into operations. For organizations using projects and team-based process management, the situation is more complex. Projects defined by direct customer contracts have to find a way to meet contract quality requirements whether or not the organization's basic quality system requires them. To do this, project quality procedures are often prepared. The project and quality managers are mutually responsible for assuring that all contract quality requirements are met.

Internal projects and teams are again different. Some work well within the existing quality system. Others, particularly multifunctional, that are trying to lead radical changes in organization structure and operation can encounter difficulties with existing quality documentation. Such teams are charged with the objective to be innovative and take risks while at the same time meeting contract requirements. This can lead to serious conflicts. In organizations with these kinds of teams the quality manager and team must evaluate such conflicts and prepare interim, team-oriented quality procedures that allow the team to progress and still provide evidence that quality is not reduced.

8.C. Project Closure[9]

The activities just preceding and at the time of project completion should be identified and planned. The degree of planning is dependent on the project size and complexity. Project closure has its own special needs. The main activities to be considered are as follows:

1. Project requirements and objectives. Determine what has to be done to complete the project. The result may be a new work breakdown structure and budget, or the closure may take the form of a new project.

2. Administrative tasks, which include the following:

   • Personnel needs/changes

   • Completion of all documentation requirements

   • Disposition of inventory and equipment

   • Written project history, achievements, lessons learned, recommendations

   • Final audit

   • Schedule

Key Ideas—Chapter 8

1. Process and project management differ in focus, metrics, and as a result in constraints. Process management has as its objective the long-term management and improvement of a process. The objective of project management is to complete a specific task with schedule, cost, and personnel considerations.

2. Schedules and budgets can be monitored with several tools, such as PERT, Gantt, and CPM charts.

3. The project team is often cross-functional and the successful project leader must manage multiple priorities, conflicts, and communication as closely as time or money.

References

1. Kerzner, H. 1995. *Project Management: A Systems Approach to Planning, ,Scheduling, and Controlling.* New York, N.Y.: Van Nostrand Reinhold.

2. Leavett, J. S., and P. C. Nunn. 1994. *Total Quality Through Project Management.* New York, N.Y.: McGraw-Hill.

3. Tompkins, J. 1994. *The Genesis Enterprise: Creating Peak-to-Peak Performance.* New York, N.Y.: McGraw-Hill.

4. Darnall, R. W. 1996. *The World's Greatest Project: One Project Team on the Path to Quality.* Upper Darby, Pa.: Project Management Institute.

5. Kerzner. *Project Management: A Systems Approach to Planning, Scheduling, and Controlling.*

6. Ibid.

7. Ibid.

8. Johnson, R. B., and R. W. Melicher. 1982. *Financial Management,* 8th ed. Allyn and Bacon.

9. Darnall. *The World's Greatest Project.*

Related References

Archibald, R. D., and R. L. Villoria. 1967. *Network-Based Management Systems (PERT/CPM).* New York, N.Y.: John Wiley.

Camp, R. C. 1989. *Benchmarking: The Search for Industry Best Practices That Lead to Superior Performance.* Milwaukee, Wis.: ASQC Quality Press.

———. 1995. *Business Process Benchmarking: Finding and Implementing Best Practices.* Milwaukee, Wis.: ASQC Quality Press.

Micklewright, M. J. 1993. "Competitive Benchmarking: Large Gains for Small Companies." *Quality Progress* (June).

Parker, G. M. 1994. "Cross-Functional Collaboration." *Training and Development* (October).

Swanson, R. 1993. "Quality Benchmark Deployment." *Quality Progress* (December).

Appendix A
Control Chart Test Patterns and Control Limit Formulae

Tables of constants for variables control charts

$\bar{X}$ and R Control Charts				$\bar{X}$ and S Control Charts				
n	A_2	D_3	D_4	d_2	n	A_3	B_3	B_4	C_4
2	1.880	0	3.265	1.128	10	0.975	0.284	1.716	.9727
3	1.023	0	2.574	1.693	11	0.927	0.321	1.679	.9754
4	0.729	0	2.282	2.059	12	0.886	0.354	1.646	.9776
5	0.577	0	2.114	2.326	13	0.850	0.382	1.618	.9794
6	0.483	0	2.004	2.534	14	0.817	0.406	1.594	.9810
7	0.419	0.076	1.924	2.704	15	0.789	0.428	1.572	.9823
8	0.373	0.136	1.864	2.847	16	0.763	0.448	1.552	.9835
9	0.337	0.184	1.816	2.970	17	0.739	0.466	1.534	.9845
10	0.308	0.223	1.777	3.078	18	0.718	0.482	1.518	.9854
11	0.285	0.256	1.744	3.173	19	0.698	0.497	1.503	.9662
12	0.266	0.283	1.717	3.258	20	0.680	0.510	1.490	.9869
					21	0.663	0.523	1.477	.9876
					22	0.647	0.534	1.466	.9882
					23	0.633	0.545	1.455	.9887
					24	0.619	0.555	1.445	.9892
					25	0.606	0.565	1.435	.9896

Tests for Special Causes

1. These tests are applicable to $\bar{X}$ charts and to individuals (X) charts. A normal distribution is assumed. Tests 1, 2, 5, and 6 are to be applied to the upper and lower halves of the chart separately. Tests 3 and 4 are to be applied to the whole chart.

2. The upper control limit and the lower control limit are set at 3σ above the center line and 3σ below the center line. For the purpose of applying the tests, the control chart is equally divided into six zones, each zone being 1σ wide. The upper half of the chart is referred to as A (outer third), B (middle third), and C (inner third). The lower half is taken as the mirror image.

3. The presence of a cross indicates that the process is not in statistical control. It means that the point is the last one of a sequence of points (a single point in Test 1) that is very unlikely to occur if the process is in statistical control.

4. Although this can be taken as a basic set of tests, analysts should be alert to any patterns of points that might indicate the influence of special causes in their process.

Formulae for upper and lower control limits

Type of data	Control chart	Sample size n	What is to be controlled	Central line	Control limits		Process standard deviation
Variables	$\bar{X} - R$ control chart	Small normally < 10 usually 3 or 5	$\bar{X}$ – Variation of sample means	$\bar{\bar{X}}$	$UCL_{\bar{X}} = \bar{\bar{X}} + A_2\bar{R}$	$LCL_{\bar{X}} = \bar{\bar{X}} - A_2\bar{R}$	$\hat{\sigma} = \bar{R}/d_2$
			R – Variation of sample ranges	$\bar{R}$	$UCL_R = D_4\bar{R}$	$LCL_R = D_3\bar{R}$	
	$\bar{X} - S$ control chart	Large usually >10	$\bar{X}$ – Variation of sample means	$\bar{\bar{X}}$	$UCL_{\bar{X}} = \bar{\bar{X}} + A_3\bar{S}$	$LCL_{\bar{X}} = \bar{\bar{X}} - A_3\bar{S}$	$\hat{\sigma} = \bar{S}/c_4$
			S – Variation of sample standard deviation	$\bar{S}$	$UCL_S = B_4\bar{S}$	$LCL_S = B_3\bar{S}$	
	X control chart (individuals with moving range)	1	X – Variation of individuals	$\bar{X}$	$UCL_X = \bar{X} + 3\bar{R}/d_2$	$LCL_X = \bar{X} - 3\bar{R}/d_2$	$\hat{\sigma} = \bar{R}/d_2$
		When rational subgroups are impossible	R – Variation between individuals	$\bar{R}$	$UCL_R = D_4\bar{R}$	$LCL_R = D_3\bar{R}$	
Attributes	p control chart	Large changeable	p: Fraction defective	$\bar{p}$	$UCL_p = \bar{p} + 3\sqrt{\bar{p}(1-\bar{p})/n}$	$LCL_p = \bar{p} - 3\sqrt{\bar{p}(1-\bar{p})/n}$	$\sqrt{\dfrac{\bar{p}(1-\bar{p})}{n}}$
	np control chart	Large constant	np: Number of defects	$n\bar{p}$	$UCL_{np} = n\bar{p} + 3\sqrt{n\bar{p}(1-\bar{p})}$	$LCL_{np} = n\bar{p} - 3\sqrt{n\bar{p}(1-\bar{p})}$	$\sqrt{n\bar{p}(1-\bar{p})}$
	c control chart	Constant unit	c: Number of defects per unit	$\bar{c}$	$UCL_c = \bar{c} + 3\sqrt{\bar{c}}$	$LCL_c = \bar{c} - 3\sqrt{\bar{c}}$	$\sqrt{\bar{c}}$
	u control chart	Changeable unit	$u = \dfrac{c}{n}$: Average defects per unit	$\bar{u}$	$UCL_u = \bar{u} + 3\sqrt{\bar{u}/n}$	$LCL_u = \bar{u} - 3\sqrt{\bar{u}/n}$	$\sqrt{\bar{u}/n}$

Test 1
One point beyond Zone A

Test 2
Eight points in a row in Zone C or beyond

Test 3
Six points in a row steadily increasing or decreasing

Test 4
Fourteen points in a row alternating up and down

Test 5
Two out of 3 points in a row in Zone A or beyond

Test 6
Four out of 5 points in a row in Zone B or beyond

Appendix B
Certified Quality Manager Body of Knowledge

The following is an outline of the topics that constitute the Body of Knowledge for Quality Manager.

I. **QUALITY STANDARDS (8 questions)**
    A. Total Quality Management (TQM)
    B. Continuous Process Improvement
    C. Cycle Time Reduction
    D. Supplier Management
    E. Customer Service
    F. Quality Award/Quality Standards Criteria (e g., Baldrige, ISO 9000)

II. **ORGANIZATIONS AND THEIR FUNCTIONS (12 questions)**
    A. Organizational Assessment
    B. Organizational Structures (e.g., matrix, hierarchical)
    C. Quality Functions Within the Organization
    D. Communication Within the Organization
    E. Change Agents and Their Effects on Organizations
    F. Management Styles (e.g., by facts and data, by coaching/other leadership styles)
    G. Business Functions
       1. External: safety, legal and regulatory, product liability, environment, technology process

2. Internal: human resources, engineering, sales and marketing, finance, R& D, purchasing

III.   **QUALITY NEEDS AND OVERALL STRATEGIC PLANS (18 questions)**
   A. Linkage Between Quality Function Needs and Overall Strategic Plan
   B. Linkage Between Strategic Plan and Quality Plan
   C. Theory of Variation (common and special causes)
   D. Quality Function Mission
   E. Priority of Quality Function Within the Organization
   F. Metrics and Goals That Drive Organizational Performance
   G. Formulation of Quality Principles and Policies
   H. Resource Requirements to Manage the Quality Function

IV.   **CUSTOMER SATISFACTION AND FOCUS (30 questions)**
   A. Types of Customers (e.g., internal, external, end-user)
   B. Elements of Customer-driven Organizations
   C. Customer Expectations, Priorities, Needs, and "Voice"
   D. Customer Relationship Management and Commitment (e.g., complaints, feedback, guarantees, corrective actions)
   E. Customer Identification and Segmentation
   F. Partnership and Alliances Between Customers and Suppliers
   G. Communication Techniques (e.g., surveys focus groups, satisfaction/complaint cards)
   H. Multiple-customer Management and Conflict Resolution
   I. Customer Retention/Loyalty

V.   **PROJECT MANAGEMENT (30 questions)**
   A. Planning
      1. Integrated quality initiatives
      2. Short- and long-term quality plans and objectives
      3. Feedback loops
      4. Performance measures
         a. Timelines
         b. Resources
         c. Methodology

  5. Relevant stakeholders
  6. Benchmarking
  7. Budgeting
  8. Benefit-cost analysis
 B. Implementation
  1. Management support and organizational roadblocks
  2. Short-term (tactical) plans
  3. Cross-functional collaboration
  4. Continuous review and enhancement of quality process
  5. Documentation and procedures

VI. **CONTINUOUS IMPROVEMENT (22 questions)**
 A. Tools
  1. Quality control tools (charts and diagrams)
  2. Quality management tools (diagrams and matrices)
  3. PDCA (plan, do, check, act)
 B. Cost of Quality
 C. Process Improvement
 D. Trend Analysis
 E. Measurement Issues
  1. Reliability and validity
  2. Sampling plans and other statistical analysis
  3. Specifications, calibration, and process capability
 F. Concurrent Engineering and Process Mapping

VII. **HUMAN RESOURCE MANAGEMENT (15 questions)**
 A. Leadership Roles and Responsibilities
  1. Conflict resolution
  2. Professional ethics
 B. Quality Staffing Issues
  1. Selection
  2. Performance evaluation
  3. Professional development
  4. Goals and objectives
 C. Quality Responsibilities in Job/Position Descriptions
 D. Post-training Evaluation and Reinforcement

E. Team Formation and Evolution
1. Process improvement teams
2. Work groups
3. Other self-managed teams
F. Team Management
1. Facilitation techniques
2. Member roles and responsibilities
3. Performance evaluation
4. Recognition and reward

VIII. TRAINING AND EDUCATION (15 questions)
A. Importance of Top-down Support and Strategic Planning for Quality Training
B. Training Subgroups and Topics
1. Management training—general quality principles
2. Employee training—implementation of quality plans
3. Facilitator training
C. Training Needs Analysis
D. Post-training Evaluation and Reinforcement
E. Tools
1. Lectures, workbooks, case studies, on-the-job training
2. Use of technology in training (videos, computer-delivered instruction, etc.)

Appendix C
ASQC Glossary of Terms

acceptable quality level (AQL): when a continuing series of lots is considered, a quality level that, for the purposes of sampling inspection, is the limit of a satisfactory process average.

acceptance sampling: inspection of a sample from a lot to decide whether to accept or not accept that lot. There are two types: attributes sampling and variables sampling. In attributes sampling, the presence or absence of a characteristic is noted in each of the units inspected. In variables sampling, the numerical magnitude of a characteristic is measured and recorded for each inspected unit; this involves reference to a continuous scale of some kind.

acceptance sampling plan: a specific plan that indicates the sampling sizes and the associated acceptance or nonacceptance criteria to be used. In attributes sampling, for example, there are single, double, multiple, sequential, chain, and skip-lot sampling plans. In variables sampling, there are single, double, and sequential sampling plans. (For detailed descriptions of these plans, see the standard ANSI/ISO/ASQC A35342, *Statistics—Vocabulary and Symbols—Statistical Quality Control*.)

accreditation: certification by a duly recognized body of the facilities, capability, objectivity, competence, and integrity of an agency, service, or operational group or individual to provide the specific service or operation needed. For example, the Registrar Accreditation Board accredits those organizations that register companies to the ISO 9000 series standards.

ACSI: The American Customer Satisfaction Index, released for the first time in October 1994, is a new economic indicator, a cross-industry measure of the satisfaction of U.S. household customers with the quality of the goods and services available to them—both those goods and services produced within the United States and those provided as imports from foreign firms that have substantial market shares or dollar sales. The ACSI is co-sponsored by the University of Michigan Business School and ASQC.

analysis of means (ANOM): a statistical procedure for troubleshooting industrial processes and analyzing the results of experimental designs with factors at fixed levels. It provides a graphical display of data. Ellis R. Ott developed the procedure in 1967 because he obsened that nonstatisticians had difficulty understanding analysis of variance. Analysis of means is easier for quality practitioners to use because it is an extension of the control chart. In 1973, Edward G. Schilling further extended the concept, enabling analysis of means to be used with nonnormal distributions and attributes data where the normal approximation to the binomial distribution does not apply. This is referred to as analysis of means for treatment effects.

analysis of variance (ANOVA): a basic statistical technique for analyzing experimental data. It subdivides the total variation of a data set into meaningful component parts associated with specific sources of variation in order to test a hypothesis on the parameters of the model or to estimate variance components. There are three models: fixed, random, and mixed.

ANSI: American National Standards Institute

AOQ: average outgoing quality

AOQL: average outgoing quality limit

AQL: acceptable quality level

AQP: Association for Quality and Participation

ASME: American Society of Mechanical Engineers

ASQC: a society of individual and organizational members dedicated to the ongoing development, advancement, and promotion of quality concepts, principles, and technologies. The Society serves more than 130,000 individuals and 1000 corporate members in the United States and 63 other countries.

ASTD: American Society for Training and Development

ASTM: American Society for Testing and Materials

attribute data: go/no-go information. The control charts based on attribute data include percent chart, number of affected units chart, count chart, count-per-unit chart, quality score chart, and demerit chart.

availability: the ability of a product to be in a state to perform its designated function under stated conditions at a given time. Availability can be expressed by the ratio:

$$\frac{\text{uptime}}{\text{uptime} + \text{downtime}}$$

uptime being when the product is operative (in active use and in standby state) and downtime being when the product is inoperative (while under repair, awaiting spare parts, and so on).

average chart: a control chart in which the subgroup average, $\bar{X}$, is used to evaluate the stability of the process level.

average outgoing quality (AOQ): the expected average quality level of outgoing product for a given value of incoming product quality.

average outgoing quality limit (AOQL): the maximum average outgoing quality over all possible levels of incoming quality for a given acceptance sampling plan and disposal specification.

benchmarking: an improvement process in which a company measures its performance against that of best-in-class companies, determines how those companies achieved their performance levels, and uses the information to improve its own performance. The subjects that can be benchmarked include strategies, operations, processes, and procedures.

big Q, little Q: a term used to contrast the difference between managing for quality in all business processes and products (big Q) and managing for quality in a limited capacity—traditionally in only factory products and processes (little q).

blemish: an imperfection that is severe enough to be noticed but should not cause any real impairment with respect to intended normal or reasonably foreseeable use (see also "defect," imperfection," and "nonconformity).

block diagram: a diagram that shows the operation, interrelationships, and interdependencies of components in a system. Boxes, or blocks (hence the name), represent the components; connecting lines between the blocks represent interfaces. There are two types of block diagrams: a functional block diagram, which shows a system's subsystems and lower-level products, their interrelationships, and interfaces with other systems; and a reliability block diagram, which is similar to the functional block diagram except that it is modified to emphasize those aspects influencing reliability.

brainstorming: a technique that teams use to generate ideas on a particular subject. Each person in the team is asked to think creatively and write down as many ideas as possible. The ideas are not discussed or reviewed until after the brainstorming session.

Brumbaugh, Martin A. (deceased): the founder and first editor of *Industrial Quality Control* magazine. A former professor of statistics at the University of Buffalo, Brumbaugh's writings on applied statistics were regularly published. Brumbaugh was instrumental in getting two separate quality organizations—the Federated Societies and the Society for Quality Control—merged into one national organization: ASQC. Brumbaugh is an ASQC Honorary member.

BSI: British Standards Institute

c chart: count chart

calibration: the comparison of a measurement instrument or system of unverified accuracy to a measurement instrument or system of a known accuracy to detect any variation from the required performance specification.

cause-and-effect diagram: a tool for analyzing process dispersion. It is also referred to as the Ishikawa diagram, because Kaoru Ishikawa developed it, and the fishbone diagram, because the complete diagram resembles a fish skeleton. The diagram illustrates the main causes and subcauses leading to an effect (symptom). The cause-and-effect diagram is one of the seven tools of quality.

CEO: chief executive officer.

check sheet: a simple data-recording device. The check sheet is custom-designed by the user, which allows him or her to readily interpret the results. The check sheet is one of the seven tools of quality. Check sheets are often confused with data sheets and checklists (see individual entries).

checklist: a tool used to ensure that all important steps or actions in an operation have been taken. Checklists contain items that are important or relevant to an issue or situation. Checklists are often confused with check sheets and data sheets (see individual entries).

CMI: certified mechanical inspector (ASQC)

Collier, Simon (deceased): an ASQC president who led the Society during a critical growth period in 1952-53. His term was marked by numerous milestone events, including a membership increase of 22% and the formation of 11 new sections and the first divisions. Collier, an ASQC Honorary member, was a chemist who began his career at the National Bureau of Standards (now the National Institute of Standards and Technology). Later he worked at Johns-Manville Corporation, where he produced a quality training film used by more than 300 companies.

common causes: causes of variation that are inherent in a process over time. They affect every outcome of the process and everyone working in the process (see also "special causes").

company culture: a system of values, beliefs, and behaviors inherent in a company. To optimize business performance, top management must define and create the necessary culture.

conformance: an affirmative indication or judgment that a product or service has met the requirements of a relevant specification, contract, or regulation.

continuous improvement: the ongoing improvement of products, services, or processes through incremental and breakthrough improvements.

control chart: a chart with upper and lower control limits on which values of some statistical measure for a series of samples or subgroups are plotted. The chart frequently shows a central line to help detect a trend of plotted values toward either control limit.

corrective action: the implementation of solutions resulting in the reduction or elimination of an identified problem.

cost of poor quality: the costs associated with providing poor-quality products or services. There are four categories of costs: internal failure costs (costs associated with defects found before the customer receives the product or service); external failure costs (costs associated with defects found after the customer receives the product or service); appraisal costs (costs incurred to determine the degree of conformance to quality requirements); and prevention costs (costs incurred to keep failure and appraisal costs to a minimum).

cost of quality (COQ): a term coined by Philip Crosby referring to the cost of poor quality.

count chart: a control chart for evaluating the stability of a process in terms of the count of events of a given classification occurring in a sample.

count-per-unit chart: a control chart for evaluating the stability of a process in terms of the average count of events of a given classification per unit occurring in a sample.

C_p: a widely used process capability index. It is expressed as

$$C_p = \frac{\text{upper control limit} - \text{lower control limit}}{6\sigma}$$

C_{pk}: a widely used process capability index. It is expressed as

$$C_{pk} = \text{the lesser of } \frac{USL - \mu}{3\sigma} \text{ or } \frac{\mu - USL}{3\sigma}$$

CQA: certified quality auditor (ASQC)

CQE: certified quality engineer (ASQC)

CQI: continuous quality improvement (ASQC)

CQT: certified quality technician (ASQC)

CRE: certified reliability engineer (ASQC)

Crosby, Philip: the founder and chairman of the board of Career IV, an executive management consulting firm. Crosby also founded Philip Crosby Associates, Inc. and the Quality College. He has written many books, including *Quality Is Free, Quality Without Tears, Let's Talk Quality,* and *Leading: The Art of Becoming an Executive.* Crosby, who originated the zero defects concept, is an ASQC senior member and past president.

cross pilot: see "scatter diagram"

cumulative sum control chart: a control chart on which the plotted value is the cumulative sum of deviations of successive samples from a target value. The ordinate of each plotted point represents the algebraic sum of the previous ordinate and the most recent deviations from the target.

customer: see "external customer" and "internal customer"

customer delight: the result of delivering a product or service that exceeds customer expectations.

customer satisfaction: the result of delivering a product or service that meets customer requirements.

customer supplier partnership: a long-term relationship between a buyer and supplier characterized by teamwork and mutual confidence. The supplier is considered an extension of the buyer's organization. The partnership is based on several commitments. The buyer provides long-term contracts and uses fewer suppliers. The supplier implements quality assurance processes so that incoming inspection can be minimized. The supplier also helps the buyer reduce costs and improve product and process designs.

d chart: demerit chart

decision matrix: a matrix used by teams to evaluate problems or possible solutions. After a matrix is drawn to evaluate possible solutions, for example, the team lists them in the far-left vertical column. Next, the team selects criteria to rate the possible solutions, writing them across the top row. Third, each possible solution is rated on a scale of 1 to 5 for each criterion and the rating recorded in the corresponding grid. Finally, the ratings of all the criteria for each possible solution are added to determine its total score. The total score is then used to help decide which solution deserves the most attention.

defect: a product's or service's nonfulfillment of an intended requirement or reasonable expectation for use, including safety considerations. There are four classes of defects: Class 1, Very Serious, leads directly to severe injury or catastrophic economic loss; Class 2, Serious, leads directly to significant injury or significant economic loss; Class 3, Major, is related to major problems with respect to intended normal or reasonably foreseeable use; and Class 4, Minor, is related to minor problems with respect to intended normal or reasonably foreseeable use (see also "blemish," "imperfection," and "nonconformity").

demerit chart: a control chart for evaluating a process in terms of a demerit (or quality score), i.e., a weighted sum of counts of various classified nonconformities.

Deming Cycle: see "plan-do-check-act cycle"

Deming Prize: award given annually to organizations that, according to the award guidelines, have successfully applied companywide quality control based on statistical quality control and will keep up with it in the future. Although the award is named in honor of W. Edwards Deming, its criteria are not specifically related to Deming's teachings. There are three separate divisions for the award: the Deming Application Prize, the Deming Prize for Individuals, and the Deming Prize for Overseas Companies. The award process is overseen by the Deming Prize Committee of the Union of Japanese Scientists and Engineers in Tokyo.

Deming, W. Edwards (deceased): a prominent consultant, teacher, and author on the subject of quality. After he had shared his expertise in statistical quality control to help the U.S. war effort during World War II, the War Department sent Deming to Japan in 1946 to help that nation recover from its wartime losses. Deming has published more than 200 works, including the well-known books *Quality, Productivity, and Competitive Position* and *Out of the Crisis.* Deming, who developed the 14 points for managing, is an ASQC Honorary member.

dependability: the degree to which a product is operable and capable of performing its required function at any randomly chosen time during its specified operating time, provided that the product is available at the start of that period. (Nonoperation-related influences are not included.) Dependability can be expressed by the ratio

$$\frac{\text{time available}}{\text{time available} + \text{time required}}$$

design of experiments (DOE): a branch of applied statistics dealing with planning, conducting, analyzing, and interpreting controlled tests to evaluate the factors that control the value of a parameter or group of parameters.

designing in quality vs. inspecting in quality: see "prevention vs. detection"

diagnostic journey and remedial journey: a two-phase investigation used by teams to solve chronic quality problems. In the first phase, the diagnostic journey, the team journeys from the symptom of a JOURNEY chronic problem to its cause. In the second phase, the remedial journey, the team journeys from the cause to its remedy.

Dodge, Harold F. (deceased): an ASQC founder and Honorary member. His work with acceptance sampling plans scientifically standardized inspection operations and provided controllable risks. Although he usually is remembered for the Dodge-Romig sampling plans he developed with Harry G. Romig, Dodge also helped develop other basic acceptance sampling concepts (e.g., consumer's risk, producer's risk, average outgoing quality level), and several acceptance sampling schemes.

Dodge-Romig sampling plans: plans for acceptance sampling developed by Harold F. Dodge and Harry G. Romig. Four sets of tables were published in 1940: single-sampling lot tolerance tables, double-sampling lot tolerance tables, single-sampling average outgoing quality limit tables, and double-sampling average outgoing quality limit tables.

Edwards, George D. (deceased): first president of ASQC. Edwards was noted for his administrative skills in forming and preserving the Society. He was the head of the inspection engineering department and the director of quality assurance at Bell Telephone Laboratories. He also served as a consultant to the Army Ordnance Department and the War Production Board during World War II. Edwards is an ASQC Honorary member.

80-20: a term referring to the Pareto principle, which was first defined by J. M. Juran in 1950. The principle suggests that most effects come from relatively few causes, that is, 80% of the effects come from 20% of the possible causes.

employee involvement: a practice within an organization whereby employees regularly participate in making decisions on how their work areas operate, including making suggestions for improvement, planning, goal setting, and monitoring performance.

empowerment: a condition whereby employees have the authority to make decisions and take action in their work areas without prior approval. For example, an operator can stop a production process upon detecting a problem or a customer service representative can send out a replacement product if a customer calls with a problem.

experimental design: a formal plan that details the specifics for conducting an experiment, such as which responses, factors, levels, blocks, treatments, and tools are to be used.

external customer: a person or organization who receives a product, a service, or information but is not part of the organization supplying it (see also "internal customer").

failure mode analysis (FMA): a procedure to determine which malfunction symptoms appear immediately before or after a failure of a critical parameter in a system. After all the possible causes are listed for each symptom, the product is designed to eliminate the problems.

failure mode effects analysis (FMEA): a procedure in which each potential failure mode in every sub-item of an item is analyzed to determine its effect on other sub-items and on the required function of the item.

failure mode effects and criticality analysis (FMECA): a procedure that is performed after a failure mode effects analysis to classify each potential failure effect according to its severity and probability of occurrence

Feigenbaum, Armand V.: the founder and president of General Systems Co., an international engineering company that designs and implements total quality systems. Feigenbaum originated the concept of total quality control in his book, *Total Quality Control*, which was published in 1951. The book has been translated into many languages, including Japanese, Chinese, French, and Spanish. Feigenbaum is an ASQC Honorary member and served as ASQC president for two consecutive terms.

fishbone diagram: see "cause-and-effect diagram"

fitness for use: a term used to indicate that a product or service fits the customer's defined purpose for that product or service.

flowchart: a graphical representation of the steps in a process. Flowcharts are drawn to better understand processes. The flowchart is one of the seven tools of quality.

FMA: failure mode analysis

FMEA: failure mode effects analysis

FMECA: failure mode effects and criticality analysis

force field analysis: a technique for analyzing the forces that aid or hinder an organization in reaching an objective. An arrow pointing to an objective is drawn down the middle of a piece of paper. The factors that will aid the objective's achievement, called the driving forces, are listed on the left side of the arrow. The factors that will hinder its achievement, called the restraining forces, are listed on the right side of the arrow.

14 points: W. Edward Deming's 14 management practices to help companies increase their quality and productivity: (1) create constancy of purpose for improving products and services, (2) adopt the new philosophy, (3) cease dependence on inspection to achieve quality, (4) end the practice of awarding business on price alone; instead, minimize total cost by working with a single supplier, (5) improve constantly and forever every process for planning, production, and service, (6) institute training on the job, (7) adopt and institute leadership, (8) drive out fear, (9) break down barriers between staff areas, (10) eliminate slogans, exhortations, and targets for the work force, (11) eliminate numerical quotas for the work force and numerical goals for management, (12) remove barriers that rob people of pride of workmanship and eliminate the annual rating or merit system, (13) institute a vigorous program of education and self-improvement for everyone, and (14) put everybody in the company to work to accomplish the transformation.

funnel experiment: an experiment that demonstrates the effects of tampering. Marbles are dropped through a funnel in an attempt to hit a flat-surfaced target below. The experiment shows that adjusting a stable process to compensate for an undesirable result or an extraordinarily good result will produce output that is worse than if the process had been left alone.

Gantt chart: a type of bar chart used in process planning and control to display planned work and finished work in relation to time.

gauge repeatability and reproducibility (GR&R): the evaluation of a gauging instrument's accuracy by determining whether the measurements taken with it are repeatable (i.e., there is close agreement among a number of consecutive measurements of the output for the same value of the input under the same operating conditions) and reproducible (i.e., there is close agreement among repeated measurements of the output for the same value of input made under the same operating conditions over a period of time).

geometric dimensioning and tolerancing (GDT): a method to minimize production costs by showing the dimension and tolerancing on a drawing while considering the functions or relationships of part features.

George M. Low Trophy: the trophy presented by NASA to those NASA aerospace industry contractors, subcontractors, and suppliers that consistently maintain and improve the quality of their products and services. The award, which was formerly called the NASA Excellence Award for Quality and Productivity, is given in two categories: small business and large business. George M. Low was the NASA administrator for nearly three decades.

go/no-go: state of a unit or product. Two parameters are possible: go—conforms to specifications, and no-go—does not conform to specifications.

Grant, Eugene L.: professor emeritus of economics engineering at Stanford University and an ASQC Honorary member. Grant was part of a small team of professors assigned during World War II to introduce statistical quality control concepts to improve manufacturing production. He has written many textbooks, including *Principles of Engineering Economy and Statistical Quality Control,* editions of which he coauthored with W. Grant Ireson and Richard S. Leavenworth.

histogram: a graphic summary of variation in a set of data. The pictorial nature of the histogram lets people see patterns that are difficult to see in a simple table of numbers. The histogram is one of the seven tools of quality.

hoshin planning: breakthrough planning. A Japanese strategic planning process in which a company develops up to four vision statements that indicate where the company should be in the next five years. Company goals and work plans are developed based on the vision statements. Periodic audits are then conducted to monitor progress.

IEEE: Institute of Electrical and Electronics Engineers

imperfection: a quality characteristic's departure from its intended level or state without any association to conformance to specification requirements or to the usability of a product or service (see also "blemish," "defect," and "nonconformity").

in-control process: a process in which the statistical measure being evaluated is in a state of statistical control, i.e., the variations among the observed sampling results can be attributed to a constant system of chance causes (see also "out-of-control process").

inspection: measuring, examining, testing, and gauging one or more characteristics of a product or service and comparing the results with specified requirements to determine whether conformity is achieved for each characteristic.

instant pudding: a term used to illustrate an obstacle to achieving quality: the supposition that quality and productivity improvement is achieved quickly through an affirmation of faith rather than through sufficient effort and education. W. Edwards Deming used this term, which was initially coined by James Bakken of Ford Motor Co., in his book *Out of the Crisis.*

internal customer: the recipient, person or department, of another person's or department's output (product, service, or information) within an organization (see also "external customer").

IQA: Institute of Quality Assurance

Ishikawa diagram: see "cause-and-effect diagram"

Ishikawa, Kaoru (deceased): a pioneer in quality control activities in Japan. In 1943, he developed the cause-and-effect diagram. Ishikawa, an ASQC Honorary member, published many works, including *What Is Total Quality Control? The Japanese Way, Quality Control Circles at Work,* and *Guide to Quality Control.* He was a member of the quality control research group of the Union of Japanese Scientists and Engineers while also working as an assistant professor at the University of Tokyo.

ISO: International Organization for Standardization

ISO 9000 series standards: a set of five individual but related international standards on quality management and quality assurance developed to help companies effectively document the quality system elements to be implemented to maintain an efficient quality system. The standards, initially published in 1987, are not specific to any particular industry, product, or service. The standards were developed by the International Organization for Standardization (ISO), a specialized international agency for standardization composed of the national standards bodies of 91 countries.

Juran, Joseph M.: the chairman emeritus of the Juran Institute and an ASQC Honorary member. Since 1924, Juran has pursued a varied career in management as an engineer, executive, government administrator, university professor, labor arbitrator, corporate director, and consultant. Specializing in managing for quality, he has authored hundreds of papers and 12 books, including *Juran's Quality Control Handbook, Quality Planning and Analysis* (with F. M. Gryna), and *Juran on Leadership for Quality.*

JUSE: Union of Japanese Scientists and Engineers

just-in-time manufacturing (JIT): an optimal material requirement planning system for a manufacturing process in which there is little or no manufacturing material inventory on hand at the manufacturing site and little or no incoming inspection.

kaizen: a Japanese term that means gradual unending improvement by doing little things better and setting and achieving increasingly higher standards. The term was made famous by Masaaki Imai in his book, *Kaizen: The Key to Japan's Competitive Success.*

KK: Koalaty Kid (ASQC)

leadership: an essential part of a quality improvement effort. Organization leaders must establish a vision, communicate that vision to those in the organization, and provide the tools and knowledge necessary to accomplish the vision.

lot: a defined quantity of product accumulated under conditions that are considered uniform for sampling purposes.

lower control limit (LCL): control limit for points below the central line in a control chart.

maintainability: the probability that a given maintenance action for an item under given usage conditions can be performed within a stated time interval when the maintenance is performed under stated conditions using stated procedures and resources. Maintainability has two categories: serviceability, the ease of conducting scheduled inspections and servicing, and repairability, the ease of restoring service after a failure.

Malcolm Baldrige National Quality Award (MBNQA): an award established by Congress in 1987 to raise awareness of quality management and to recognize U.S. companies that have implemented successful quality management systems. Two awards may be given annually in each of three categories: manufacturing company, service company, and small business. The award is named after the late Secretary of Commerce Malcolm Baldrige, a proponent of quality management. The U.S. Commerce Department's National Institute of Standards and Technology manages the award, and ASQC administers it.

mean time between failures (MTBF): the average time interval between failures for repairable product for a defined unit of measure, for example, operating hours, cycles, miles.

MIL-STD: military standard

MIL-Q-9858A: a military standard that describes quality program requirements.

MIL-STD-105E: a military standard that describes the sampling procedures and tables for inspection by attributes.

MIL-STD-45662A: a military standard that describes the requirements for creating and maintaining a calibration system for measurement and test equipment.

multivariate control chart: a control chart for evaluating the stability or a process in terms of the levels of two or more variables or characteristics.

n: sample size (the number of units in a sample)

NDE: nondestructive evaluation (see "nondestructive testing and evaluation")

NIST: National Institute of Standards and Technology

nominal group technique: a technique similar to brainstorming, used by teams to generate ideas on a particular subject. Team members are asked to silently come up with as many ideas as possible, writing them down. Each member is then asked to share one idea, which is recorded. After all the ideas are recorded, they are discussed and prioritized by the group.

nonconformity: the nonfulfillment of a specified requirement (see also "blemish," "defect," and "imperfection").

nondestructive testing and evaluation (NDT): testing and evaluation methods that do not damage or destroy the product being tested.

NQM: National Quality Month

number of affected units chart (np chart): a control chart for evaluating the stability of a process in terms of the total number of units in a sample in which an event of a given classification occurs.

operating characteristic curve (OC curve): a graph used to determine the probability of accepting lots as a function of the lots' or processes' quality level when using various sampling plans. Three are three types: Type A curves, which give the probability of acceptance for an individual lot coming from finite production (will not continue in the future); Type B curves, which give the probability of acceptance for lots coming from a continuous process; and Type C curves, which, for a continuous sampling plan, give the long-run percentage of product accepted during the sampling phase.

Ott, Ellis R. (deceased): an educator who devoted his career to providing U.S. industry with statistical quality control professionals. In 1946, Ott became the chairman of the mathematics department at Rutgers University's University College with one condition: that he could also consult on and teach quality control. His influence led the university to establish the Rutgers Statistics Center. Ott, an ASQC Honorary member, developed the analysis of means procedure and published many papers.

out-of-control process: a process in which the statistical measure being evaluated is not in a state of statistical control, i.e., the variations among the observed sampling results can be attributed to a constant system of chance causes (see also "in-control process").

out of spec: a term used to indicate that a unit does not meet a given specification.

p chart: percent chart

Pareto chart: a graphical tool for ranking causes from most significant to least significant. It is based on the Pareto principle, which was first defined by J. M. Juran in 1950. The principle, named after 19th-century economist Vilfredo Pareto, suggests that most effects come from relatively few causes; that is, 80% of the effects come from 20% of the possible causes. The Pareto chart is one of the seven tools of quality.

PDCA cycle: plan-do-check-act cycle

PE: professional engineer

percent chart: a control chart for evaluating the stability of a process in terms of the percent of the total number of units in a sample in which an event of a given classification occurs. The percent chart is also referred to as a proportion chart.

plan-do-check-act cycle: a four-step process for quality improvement. In the first step (plan), a plan to effect improvement is developed. In the second step (do), the plan is carried out, preferably on a small scale. In the third step (check), the effects of the plan are observed. In the last step (act), the results are studied to determine what was learned and what can be predicted. The plan-do-check-act cycle is sometimes referred to as the Shewhart cycle because Walter A. Shewhart discussed the concept in his book *Statistical Method From the Viewpoint of Quality Control* and as the Deming cycle because W. Edwards Deming introduced the concept in Japan. The Japanese subsequently called it the Deming cycle.

prevention vs. detection: a term used to contrast two types of quality activities. Prevention refers to those activities designed to prevent nonconformances in products and services. Detection refers to those activities designed to detect nonconformances already in products and services. Another term used to describe this distinction is "designing in quality vs. inspecting in quality."

process capability: a statistical measure of the inherent process variability for a given characteristic. The most widely accepted formula for process capability is 6σ.

process capability index: the value of the tolerance specified for the characteristic divided by the process capability. There are several types of process capability indexes, including the widely used C_{pk} and C_p.

product or service liability: the obligation of a company to make restitution for loss related to personal injury, property damage, or other harm caused by its product or service.

Q-Q: quantile-quantile

QA: quality assurance

QC: quality control

Q9000 series: refers to ANSI/ISO/ASQC Q9000 series standards, which is the Americanized version of the 1994 edition of the ISO 9000 series standards. The United States adopted the ISO 9000 series standards as the ANSI/ISO/ASQC Q9000 series.

QEIT: quality engineer in training (ASQC)

QIC: Quality Information Center

QMJ: *Quality Management Journal*

QP: *Quality Progress*

quality: a subjective term for which each person has his or her own definition. In technical usage, quality can have two meanings: (1) the characteristics of a product or service that bear on its ability to satisfy stated or implied needs and (2) a product or service free of deficiencies.

quality assurance/quality control: two terms that have many interpretations because of the multiple definitions for the words "assurance" and "control." For example, "assurance" can mean the act of giving confidence, the state of being certain, or the act of making certain; "control" can mean an evaluation to indicate needed corrective responses, the act of guiding, or the state of a process in which the variability is attributable to a constant system of chance causes. (For a detailed discussion on the multiple definitions, see ANSI/ISO/ASQC A35342, *Statistics—Vocabulary and Symbols—Statistical Quality Control.*) One definition of quality assurance is: all the planned and systematic activities implemented within the quality system that can be demonstrated to provide confidence that a product or service will fulfill requirements for quality. One definition for quality control is: the operational techniques and activities used to fulfill requirements for quality. Often, however, "quality assurance" and "quality control" are used interchangeably, referring to the actions performed to ensure the quality of a product, service, or process.

quality audit: a systematic, independent examination and review to determine whether quality activities and related results comply with planned arrangements and whether these arrangements are implemented effectively and are suitable to achieve the objectives.

quality circles: quality improvement or self-improvement study groups composed of a small number of employees—10 or fewer—and their supervisor. Quality circles originated in Japan, where they are called quality control circles.

quality control (QC): see "quality assurance/quality control"

quality costs: see "cost of poor quality"

quality engineering: the analysis of a manufacturing system at all stages to maximize the quality of the process itself and the products it produces.

quality function deployment (QFD): a structured method in which customer requirements are translated into appropriate technical requirements for each stage of product development and production. The QFD process is often referred to as listening to the voice of the customer.

quality loss function: a parabolic approximation of the quality loss that occurs when a quality characteristic deviates from its target value. The quality loss function is expressed in monetary units: the cost of deviating from the target increases quadratically the farther the quality characteristic moves from the target. The formula used to compute the quality loss function depends on the type of quality characteristic being used. The quality loss function was first introduced in this form by Genichi Taguchi.

quality score chart (Q chart): a control chart for evaluating the stability of a process in terms of a quality score. The quality score is the weighted sum of the count of events of various classifications where each classification is assigned a weight.

quality trilogy: a three-pronged approach to managing for quality. The three legs are quality planning (developing the products and processes required to meet customer needs), quality control (meeting product and process goals), and quality improvement (achieving unprecedented levels of performance).

quincunx: a tool that creates frequency distributions. Beads tumble over numerous horizontal rows of pins, which force the beads to the right or left. After a random journey, the beads are dropped into vertical slots. After many beads are dropped, a frequency distribution results. In the classroom, quincunxes are often used to simulate a manufacturing process. The quincunx was invented by English scientist Francis Galton in the 1890s.

RAM: reliability/availability/maintainability (see individual entries).

random sampling: a commonly used sampling technique in which sample units are selected in such a manner that all combinations of n units under consideration have an equal chance of being selected as the sample.

range chart (R chart): a control chart in which the subgroup range, R, is used to evaluate the stability of the variability within a process.

red bead experiment: an experiment developed by W. Edwards Deming to illustrate that it is impossible to put employees in rank order of performance for the coming year based on their performance during the past year because performance differences must be attributed to the system, not to employees. Four thousand red and white beads, 20% red, in a jar and six people are needed for the experiment. The participants' goal is to produce white beads, because the customer will not accept red beads. One person begins by stirring the beads and then, blindfolded, selects a sample of 50 beads. That person hands the jar to the next person, who repeats the process, and so on. When everyone has his or her sample, the number of red beads for each is counted. The limits of variation between employees that can be attributed to the system are calculated. Everyone will fall within the calculated limits of variation that could arise from the system. The calculations will show that there is no evidence one person will be a better performer than another in the future. The experiment shows that it would be a waste of management's time to try to find out why, say, John produced four red beads and Jane produced 15; instead, management should improve the system, making it possible for everyone to produce more white beads.

Registrar Accreditation Board (RAB): a board that evaluates the competency and reliability of registrars (organizations that assess and register companies to the appropriate ISO 9000 series standards). The Registrar Accreditation Board, formed in 1989 by ASQC, is governed by a board of directors from industry, academia, and quality management consulting firms.

registration to standards: a process in which an accredited, independent third-party organization conducts an on-site audit of a company's operations against the requirements of the standard to which the company wants to be registered. Upon successful completion of the audit, the company receives a certificate indicating that it has met the standard requirements.

regression analysis: a statistical technique for determining the best mathematical expression describing the functional relationship between one response and one or more independent variables.

reliability: the probability of a product performing its intended function under stated conditions without failure for a given period of time.

right the first time: a term used to convey the concept that it is beneficial and more cost-effective to take the necessary steps up front to ensure a product or service meets its requirements than to provide a product or service that will need rework or not meet customers' needs. In other words, an organization should engage in defect prevention rather than defect detection.

robustness: the condition of a product or process design that remains relatively stable with a minimum of variation even though factors that influence operations or usage, such as environment and wear, are constantly changing.

Romig, Harry G. (deceased): an Honorary member and founder of ASQC who was most widely known for his contributions in sampling. At AT&T Bell Laboratories, Romig and Harold F. Dodge developed the Dodge-Romig sampling tables, operating characteristics for sampling plans, and other fundamentals. Romig alone developed the first sampling plans using variables data and the concept of average outgoing quality limit. Later in his life, Romig was a consultant and taught quality-related courses at several universities.

sample standard deviation chart (s chart): a control chart in which the subgroup standard deviation, s, is used to evaluate the stability of the variability within a process.

scatter diagram: a graphical technique to analyze the relationship between two variables. Two sets of data are plotted on a graph, with the y axis being used for the variable to be predicted and the x axis being used for the variable to make the prediction. The graph will show possible relationships (although two variables might appear to be related, they might not be: those who know most about the variables must make that evaluation). The scatter diagram is one of the seven tools of quality.

seven tools of quality: tools that help organizations understand their processes in order to improve them. The tools are the cause-and-effect diagram, check sheet, control chart, flowchart, histogram, Pareto chart, and scatter diagram (see individual entries).

Shewhart cycle: see "plan-do-check-act cycle"

Shewhart, Walter A. (deceased): referred to as the father of statistical quality control because he brought together the discipline of statistics, engineering, and economics. He described the basic principles of this new discipline in his book *Economic Control of Quality of Manufactured Product*. Shewhart, ASQC's first Honorary member, was best known for creating the control chart. Shewhart worked for Western Electric and AT&T Bell Telephone Laboratories in addition to lecturing and consulting on quality control.

signal-to-noise ratio (S/N ratio): a mathematical equation that indicates the magnitude of an experimental effect above the effect of experimental error due to chance fluctuations.

six-sigma quality: a term used generally to indicate that a process is well controlled, i.e., process limits ±3 sigma from the centerline in a control chart and requirements/tolerance limits ±6 sigma from the centerline. The term was initiated by Motorola.

special causes: causes of variation that arise because of special circumstances. They are not an inherent part of a process. Special causes are also referred to as assignable causes (see also "common causes").

specification: a document that states the requirements to which a given product or service must conform.

statistical process control (SPC): the application of statistical techniques to control a process. Often the term "statistical quality control" is used interchangeably with "statistical process control"

statistical quality control (SQC): the application of statistical techniques to control quality. Often the term "statistical process control" is used interchangeably with "statistical quality control" although statistical quality control includes acceptance sampling as well as statistical process control.

structural variation: variation caused by regular, systematic changes in output, such as seasonal patterns and long-term trends.

supplier quality assurance: confidence that a supplier's product or service will fulfill its customers' needs. This confidence is achieved by creating a relationship between the customer and supplier that ensures the product will be fit for use with minimal corrective action and inspection. According to J. M. Juran, there are nine primary activities needed: (1) define product and program quality requirements, (2) evaluate alterative suppliers, (3) select suppliers, (4) conduct joint quality planning, (5) cooperate with the supplier during the execution of the contract, (6) obtain proof of conformance to requirements, (7) certify qualified suppliers, (8) conduct quality improvement programs as required, and (9) create and use supplier quality ratings.

Taguchi, Genichi: the executive director of the American Supplier Institute, the director of the Japan Industrial Technology Institute, and an honorary professor at Nanjing Institute of Technology in China. Taguchi is well-known for developing a methodology to improve quality and reduce costs, which, in the United States, is referred to as the Taguchi methods. He also developed the quality loss function.

Taguchi methods: the American Supplier Institute's trademarked term for the quality engineering methodology developed by Genichi Taguchi. In this engineering approach to quality control, Taguchi calls for off-line quality control, on-line quality control, and a system of experimental design to improve quality and reduce costs.

tampering: action taken to compensate for variation within the control limits of a stable system. Tampering increases rather than decreases variation, as evidenced in the funnel experiment.

top-management commitment: participation of the highest-level officials in their organization's quality improvement efforts. Their participation includes establishing and serving on a quality committee, establishing quality policies and goals, deploying those goals to lower levels of the organization, providing the resources and training that the lower levels need to achieve the goals, participating in quality improvement teams, reviewing progress organizationwide; recognizing those who have performed well, and revising the current reward system to reflect the importance of achieving the quality goals.

total quality management (TQM): a term initially coined by the Naval Air Systems Command to describe its Japanese-style management approach to quality improvement. Since then, total quality management (TQM) has taken on many meanings. Simply put, TQM is a management approach to long-term success through customer satisfaction. TQM is based on the participation of all members of an organization in improving processes, products, services, and the culture they work in. TQM benefits all organization members and society. The methods for implementing this approach are found in the teachings of such quality leaders as Philip B. Crosby, W. Edwards Deming, Armand V. Feigenbaum, Kaoru Ishikawa, and J. M. Juran.

trend control chart: a control chart in which the deviation of the subgroup average, X-bar, from an expected trend in the process level is used to evaluate the stability of a process.

type I error: an incorrect decision to reject something (such as a statistical hypothesis or a lot of products) when it is acceptable.

type II error: an incorrect decision to accept something when it is unacceptable.

u chart: count per unit chart

upper control limit (UCL): control limit for points above the central line in a control chart.

value-adding process: those activities that transform an input into a customer-usable output. The customer can be internal or external to the organization.

variables data: measurement information. Control charts based on variables data include average ($\bar{X}$) chart, range (R) chart, and sample standard deviation (s) chart.

variation: a change in data, a characteristic, or a function that is caused by one of four factors: special causes, common causes, tampering, or structural variation (see individual entries).

vital few, useful many: a term used by J. M. Juran to describe his use of the Pareto principle, which he first defined in 1950. (The principal was used much earlier in economics and inventory control methodologies.) The principal suggests that most effects come from relatively few causes; that is, 80% of the effects come from 20% of the possible causes. The 20% of the possible causes are referred to as the "vital few"; the remaining causes are referred to as the "useful many." When Juran first defined this principle, he referred to the remaining causes as the "trivial many," but realizing that no problems are trivial in quality assurance, he changed it to "useful many."

Wescott, Mason E.: ASQC founder and Honorary member. A professor emeritus at the Rochester Institute of Technology (RIT), Wescott has been teaching mathematics and statistics since 1925. He has taught at Northwestern University, Rutgers University, and RIT, where the Wescott Statistics Laboratory was dedicated in his honor in 1984. Wescott succeeded Martin A. Brumbaugh as the editor of *Industrial Quality Control* in 1947, a position he held until 1961.

world-class quality: a term used to indicate a standard of excellence: best of the best.

$\bar{X}$ chart: average chart

zero defects: a performance standard developed by Philip B. Crosby to address a dual attitude in the workplace: people are willing to accept imperfection in some areas, while, in other areas, they expect the number of defects to be zero. This dual attitude had developed because of the conditioning that people are human and humans make mistakes. However, the zero defects methodology states that, if people commit themselves to watching details and avoiding errors, they can move closer to the goal of zero.

Index

A

acceptable quality level (AQL), 168, 293

acceptance sampling, 170, 293
plans, 293

accreditation, 293–94

ACSI (American Customer Satisfaction Index), 294

activity network diagrams, 145

affinity diagrams, 144

alpha, 169

American Customer Satisfaction Index (ACSI), 294

analysis of means (ANOM), 294

analysis of variance (ANOVA), 294

ANOM (analysis of means), 294

ANOVA (analysis of variance), 294

ANSI (American National Standards Institute). *See* ISO 9000 standards

AOQ (average outgoing quality), 295

AOQL (average outgoing quality limit), 295

appraisals
customer-supplier, 207
process, 207–8

of product quality, 150, 151
project, 255, 262–70
staff performance, 205–8
team performance, 222, 223–24, 262
of training, 244–45

AQL (acceptable quality level), 168, 293

arrow diagrams, 145

ASQC, 295
Certified Quality Manager Body of Knowledge, 289–92
code of ethics, 200–202
courses, 235
standards, 28–29, 234–35, 241–43, 311

assessments
by outside agencies, 42
culture gap analysis, 41–42
definition, 40
self-, 42–45
structures, 43–45
uses, 41

AT&T, 42–43

attributes data
control charts, 140–42, 295

attributes data—*continued*
   go/no-go information, 295
   over time, 162–63
audits, quality, 40, 45, 91, 280, 311
autocratic managers, 65, 66–67, 68
automobile industry
   customer satisfaction, 107
   QS-9000 standards, 32–33
   TE-9000 standards, 33
availability, of products, 295
average outgoing quality (AOQ), 295
average outgoing quality limit
   (AOQL), 295
averages
   moving, 163
   process, 138
   sample, 138
averages charts, 295
awards. *See* quality awards

B
Baldrige Award. *See* Malcolm
   Baldrige National Quality
   Award (MBNQA)
bar charts, 268–70
benchmarking, 270–73
   definition, 295
   goals based on, 95
   improvements resulting from, 160
   steps, 271
   value of, 270–71
beta, 169
big Q, 8, 296
blemishes, 296
block diagrams, 296
Body of Knowledge, Certified
   Quality Manager, 289–92
Boeing, 94
brainstorming, 124, 296
Brandon, J., 159
breakthrough improvements, 6,
   89–90, 95, 160

Brumbaugh, Martin A., 296
Buban, M., 199
budgets, project, 273–74
business climate, 71
business plans, 83

C
C_p, 181, 298
C_{pk}, 181, 182, 298
C_{pm}, 182
calibration, 178, 296
capability index (C_p), 181
cause-and-effect diagrams, 129, 131,
   297
CBA (cost-benefit analysis), 275
c charts, 142
CE (concurrent engineering), 147,
   183–86, 279
Certified Quality Manager Body of
   Knowledge, 289–92
Champy, J., 159
change
   climate for, 58–63
   errors in efforts for, 195–96
   in organizations, 4–5
   short term, 231
   technological, 72–73
   types needed, 62–63
change agents, 58, 59. *See also*
   leaders
Charm, Joel, 32
checklists, 297
checksheets, 132, 297
Chrysler, 32, 33, 107
CI. *See* continuous improvement
coaching, 70–71, 208
Cognitive Communications, 54
Collier, Simon, 297
common causes, of variation, 10, 297
communication
   barriers to, 261–62
   by leaders, 53–54

communication—*continued*
  by quality function, 55–56, 262
  with customers, 57, 109–10
  effective, 57–58
  in empowered organizations, 213
  model of, 54–55
  in project management, 56,
    260–62
  with suppliers, 57
  value of, 57
  within teams, 56–57
complaints, customer, 109–10, 116
compliance, 40–41
computers
  information systems, 54
  networks, 54
  use in project tracking, 265
  use in training, 247–48
concurrent engineering (CE), 147,
    183–86, 279
conflicts
  with customers, 118–20
  resolving, 196–99
  in teams, 197–98
conformance, 297
consensus
  benefits of, 198
  techniques for reaching, 126
continuous improvement (CI), 5–6
  Body of Knowledge topics, 291
  costs reduced by, 151
  definition, 298
  tools, 123
continuous process improvement
    (CPI), 11–14
  approach, 155–58
  breakthrough improvements, 6,
    89–90, 160
  continuous review, 279–81
  implementation of, 12
  implications for purchased materi-
    als, 19, 20

objectives, 153–55
  reducing cycle times, 17
  systems approach, 14–15
  tools, 126–34
  use in United States, 2
control
  activities, 89
  by management, 199
  span of, 213
control charts, 137–39, 298
  applications, 142, 143, 178
  interpreting, 142
  limitations, 142
  test patterns, 286
  types, 140–42
control limits, 137, 138
  lower, 287, 307
  upper, 287, 317
COQ. *See* cost of quality
corrective actions, 298
corrective action teams, 218
cost-benefit analysis (CBA), 275
cost of quality (COQ), 149–53, 298
  economic model, 150–51
  managing, 151–52
  in service businesses, 151
costs
  effect of reduced cycle times, 16
  effect of reduced variation, 11
  life cycle, 153
  of poor quality, 298
  project, 273–74
count charts, 298
count-per-unit charts, 298
CPI. *See* continuous process improve-
    ment
CPM (critical path method), 268
Crawford slip method, 125
critical path method. *See* CPM
Crosby, Philip, 299
cross pilot. *See* scatter diagrams
culture gap analysis, 41–42

cultures, of companies, 297
cumulative sum control charts, 299
customer councils, 116
customers
    businesses, 107, 112, 114–15
    communication with, 57, 115–17
    conflict resolution, 118–20
    databases, 118
    delight, 299
    expectations, needs, and priorities,
        106–9, 120
    external, 23, 104, 105–6, 302
    feedback from, 109–10, 115–16
    identification, 111, 118
    intermediate, 104
    internal, 23, 104, 106, 107–8,
        117, 306
    loyalty, 120
    partnerships with, 113–15, 299
    relationship management, 106,
        109–11
    retention, 120–21
    segmentation, 111–13
    surveys, 115–16, 117, 207
    targeting, 111
    voice of, 108
customer satisfaction, 22
    of Baldrige Award winners,
        165–66
    Body of Knowledge topics, 290
    complaints, 109–10, 116
    definition, 299
    guarantees, 110–11
    importance of, 63, 103–4
    measuring, 166–67
    setting goals for, 92–93
    surveys, 115–16, 117, 207
customer service, 22–23
customer-supplier appraisals, 207
cycle times
    definition, 16
    reducing, 15–17, 147, 155

D
Danaher, P. J., 22
Darnall, R. W., 253
data
    decision-making based on, 68–69
    gathering, 69
d charts. *See* demerit charts
decision-making
    by managers, 68–70
    by teams, 123–24, 197–99
    in empowered organizations, 213
    tools, 123–24, 143–45
decision matrices, 299–300
Deevy, E., 3, 4–5
defects, 300
    control charts, 140, 142
    preventing, 149, 151
defense contractors, 51
delegation, 212
Delphi method, 126
demerit charts, 300
Deming cycle, 145–46, 310
Deming Prize, 24, 30, 300
Deming, W. Edwards, 2, 18, 202,
        206, 214, 275, 300–301,
        303–4
Department of Defense. *See*
        U.S. Department of Defense
        (DOD)
dependability, 301
design of experiments (DOE),
        172–74, 301
design tolerances, 137, 175–77
diagnostic journey, 301
Dinsmore, P. C., 217
DOD (Department of Defense). *See*
        U.S. Department of Defense
        (DOD)
Dodge, Harold F., 301
Dodge-Romig sampling plans, 301
DOE. *See* design of experiments
DuPont Corporation, 29, 34

E

Eckes, G., 206, 207
economic models, of quality cost, 150–51
education. *See also* training
    compared to training, 230–31
    of facilitators, 238
Edwards, George D., 302
effectiveness, assessments of, 41
80-20 principle, 302
employee involvement, 302
employees. *See* staff
empowerment, 54, 211–14, 302
engineering, 74
    concurrent, 147, 183–86, 279
    quality, 91, 99, 312
    reliability, 52, 91, 100
environmental management stan-
        dards (ISO 14000), 31–32
environmental regulations, 71, 73
equipment, maintenance of, 186
errors
    of measurement, 164, 166–67
    preventing, 149
    type I, 317
    type II, 317
ethics codes, 199–202
European Quality Award, 27
evaluations. *See* appraisals
events, in PERT charts, 266–68
experimental design, 302
experiments
    design of (DOE), 172–74, 177,
        301
    funnel, 304
    red bead, 313
external customers, 23, 104, 105–6,
        302

F

facilitators, 220, 222–23
    roles, 238–39

selecting, 237–38
team leaders as, 198
training, 238
failure mode analysis (FMA), 302
failure mode effects analysis
        (FMEA), 302
failure mode effects and criticality
        analysis (FMECA), 303
failures
    external, 150
    internal, 150
FDA. *See* Food and Drug
        Administration
Feigenbaum, Armand V., 2, 40, 303
finance function, 74
fishbone diagrams. *See* cause-and-
        effect diagrams
Fisher, Sir Ronald, 172
fitness for use, 303
Florida Power and Light, 24
flowcharts, 126–27, 303
FMA (failure mode analysis), 302
FMEA (failure mode effects analy-
        sis), 302
FMECA (failure mode effects and
        criticality analysis), 303
focus groups, 116, 218
Food and Drug Administration
        (FDA), 29
force field analysis, 303
Ford Motor Company, 32, 33, 107
14 points (Deming), 303–4
functions. *See also* quality function
    definition, 39
    external, 71–73
    internal, 73–74
funnel experiments, 304

G

Gantt charts, 268–70, 304
gauge repeatability and reproducibil-
        ity (GR&R), 304

GDT (geometric dimensioning and tolerancing), 304
General Electric (GE), 59, 186
General Motors (GM), 32, 33
    Cadillac Division, 165–66
genesis enterprises, 4–5, 219
geometric dimensioning and tolerancing (GDT), 304
George M. Low Trophy, 304
GMP (Good Manufacturing Practices), 29
goals. *See also* objectives
    basis of, 94
    breakthrough, 95
    incremental, 95
    operating, 92
    quality, 84, 92
    setting, 92–93, 94
    strategic, 92
    tactical, 92
    types, 95
go/no-go states, 305
Good Manufacturing Practices (GMP), 29
government regulations
    environmental, 71, 73
    safety, 71–72
GR&R (gauge repeatability and reproducibility), 304
Grant, Eugene L., 305
Gray, J., 151
Gryna, F. M., 230, 245
guarantees, 110–11

H
Hammer, M., 159
Harrington, H. J., 159
Hart, C. W. L., 110
Hayes, B., 167
Herzberg, F., 65
hierarchical organizations, 47, 48–49, 59

Hierarchy of Needs (Maslow), 64, 225
hiring. *See* staff
histograms, 132–34, 305
hoshin planning, 305
human resources management, 193. *See also* management; staff
    activities, 73
    Body of Knowledge topics, 291–92
hygienic factors, 65

I
imperfections, 305
improvements. *See also* continuous improvement (CI); continuous process improvement (CPI)
    breakthrough, 6, 89–90, 95, 160
    incremental, 6, 95
in-control processes, 305
information. *See* communication; data
information systems. *See* computers
innovation, encouraging, 58–63
inspection
    activities, 52, 91
    costs, 150
    definition, 305
    staff, 99
instant pudding, 305–6
Institute of Electrical and Electronics Engineers (IEEE), 94
instructional technology. *See* training
intermediate customers, 104
internal customers, 23, 104, 106, 107–8, 117, 306
International Organization for Standardization (ISO), 27. *See also* ISO 9000
interrelationship digraphs, 144
intranets, 54

Ishikawa diagrams. *See* cause-and-effect diagrams
Ishikawa, Kaoru, 306
ISO 9000 standards, 27–29, 30, 31, 35, 306
   registration, 29, 34, 280
   training requirements, 234–35, 241–43
ISO 14000 standards, 31–32

J

Japan
   Deming Prize, 24, 30, 300
   quality circles, 2
   quality management in, 2
   total productive maintenance (TPM), 186
   use of design of experiments (DOE), 175
JIT. *See* just-in-time
Juran, Joseph M., 2, 39, 40, 209, 214, 306
   on training, 230–31, 245
Juran Trilogy, 6, 88–90, 160
just-in-time (JIT) agreements, 115
just-in-time (JIT) manufacturing, 307
just-in-time training, 240

K

kaizen, 307
Kerzner, H., 251
Kinni, T. B., 3
Koselka, R., 174
Kotter, K. P., 195

L

La Torre, Jim, 19
LCL (lower control limits), 287, 307
leaders
   communication skills, 53–54, 55
   compared to managers, 195
   definition, 307

   ethics of, 200
   motivation by, 63–65
   roles, 194–95
learning organizations, 5
legal issues, 72
life cycle costs, 153
line of balance methodology, 270
little Q, 8, 296
lots, 307
lot tolerance percent defective (LTPD), 169
lower control limits (LCL), 287, 307
Low, George M., 304
LTPD. *See* lot tolerance percent defective

M

maintainability, 307
maintenance, total productive (TPM), 186
Malcolm Baldrige National Quality Award (MBNQA), 24–27, 30, 307
   criteria, 24, 25, 26, 42, 233–34
   customer satisfaction and, 165–66
   stock performance of winners, 9
management. *See also* leaders
   attitudes toward change, 58–61
   by objectives (MBO), 260
   by walking around, 67
   changes in roles in TQ organizations, 46–47
   coaching, 70–71, 208
   commitment needed for TQM, 8–9, 317
   committees, 85–86, 87, 218
   common mistakes, 195–96
   control factor, 199
   decision-making styles, 68–70
   delegation, 212
   employee empowerment and, 212, 213–14

management—*continued*
  need for profound knowledge, 202
  performance evaluations by, 205–6
  of quality function, 194, 196,
    200, 209, 210, 262
  in quality organizations, 100, 193,
    211, 229–30
  responsibilities, 63
  skills needed, 229–30
  span of control, 213
  styles, 63, 65–69, 212
  support for projects, 276
  training, 229–30, 236
marketing function, 74, 111–13
market research, 107, 111–12
Martin, Tripp, 32, 33
Maslow, Abraham, 64, 225
matrix charts, 145
matrix organizations, 47–48, 49–50
MBNQA. *See* Malcolm Baldrige
  National Quality Award
MBO (management by objectives),
  260
McGregor, Douglas, 65
mean time between failures (MTBF),
  165, 308
measurement
  accuracy, 164–65, 178
  calibration, 178, 296
  of customer satisfaction, 166–67
  instruments, 164–65
  precision, 165, 178
  of processes, 96–97
  reliability, 164–65, 166–67
  reproducibility, 165
  standards for, 91
  systems, 178–79
  validity, 164
  variation in, 164–65
medical devices, quality standards, 29
metrics. *See* measurement
metric system, 179

metrology, 91
military, specifications for contractors,
  51, 308
Mintzberg, H. I., 81
missions, 79
  of quality functions, 87–88, 194
monitoring projects, 254
Morgan, D. M., 47
Morgan, R. B., 202, 203
Morris, D., 159
motivation
  money as, 225
  of teams, 224–25
  theory, 63–65
Motorola Corporation, 232
moving averages, 163
MTBF (mean time between failures),
  165, 308
multiple-customer management, 118
multivariate control charts, 308
multi-vari charts, 174–75
multivoting, 124–25

N
National Institute for Standards and
  Technology (NIST), 9, 178
NDT (nondestructive testing and
  evaluation), 100, 308
NIST. *See* National Institute for
  Standards and Technology
nominal group technique, 125–26,
  308
nonconformity, 308
nondestructive testing and evaluation
  (NDT), 100, 308
nonprofit organizations, 63
normal distribution, 139
Northrop Grumman Corporation,
  117
np charts, 140, 308
number of affected units charts. *See*
  np charts

O

objectives, 79. *See also* goals
   project, 259–60, 277
OC curves. *See* operating characteristic curves
operating characteristic curves (OC curves), 169, 309
operational planning, 259
organizational structures
   in empowered organizations, 213
   hierarchical, 47, 48–49, 59
   matrix, 47–48, 49–50
   matrix/team, 48, 50
   quality function in, 51–53
   reorganizing, 158–59
   in small companies, 51
   trends in, 46–47
organizations
   Body of Knowledge topics, 289
   change in, 4–5
   customer-driven, 105–6
   functional separation, 11–12
   learning, 5
   nonprofit, 63
   TQ, 6–7, 46–47
Ott, Ellis R., 309
out-of-control processes, 309
outsourcing, of quality activities, 101
out of spec units, 309

P

Pareto diagrams, 134, 309
participative management, 65, 66
partnerships
   with customers, 113–15, 299
   internal, 115
   with suppliers, 19–21, 113–15,
      299
parts, tolerances of, 177–78
p charts, 140, 310
PDCA. *See* plan-do-check-act cycle
percent charts. *See p* charts

performance evaluations, 205–8
   criticisms of, 206–7
   customer-supplier, 207
   of projects, 255, 262–70
   of teams, 222, 223–24
personnel. *See* staff
PERT (program evaluation and review technique) charts, 265–68
Peters, T., 22
plan-do-check-act (PDCA) cycle,
      145–46, 310
planning. *See also* strategic planning
   activities, 81, 88–89
   business plans, 83
   goal-setting, 92–93, 94
   importance of, 79–80
   operational, 259
   projects, 254–55, 258–59, 278
   quality plans, 83–85, 86–87,
      258–59
   tactical, 80, 258–59, 278
   tools, 86, 143–45
PM. *See* project management; project managers
policies, quality, 85–86, 97–98, 281
positioning, 111
precision, of measurement, 165, 178
prevention
   costs, 149, 151
   vs. detection, 310
prioritization matrices, 145
problem-solving
   culture of, 59–60
   teams, 218, 220
   tools, 123–26
process appraisals, 207–8
process averages, 138
process capability, 179–83
   definition, 8, 139, 310
   design tolerances and, 175–77
   indexes, 181–83, 310
   six-sigma goal, 139, 183, 315

process decision program charts, 145

processes. *See also* continuous process improvement (CPI)
  classification, 129, 132
  control charts, 137–42
  cycle times, 15–17
  definition, 7, 13
  gathering data on, 69
  in-control, 305
  macro, 14, 128
  mean time between failures (MTBF), 165, 308
  metrics, 96–97
  micro, 14, 128
  modules, 14–15
  out-of-control, 309
  in statistical control, 11, 139, 165, 179
  validating, 165
  value-adding, 317

process management, compared to project management, 253

process maps, 128–29, 130

procurement. *See* suppliers

production, variation in, 9–10

product liability, 72, 310

products
  availability, 295
  concurrent engineering of, 147, 183–86
  dependability, 301
  design tolerances, 175–77
  return policies, 110
  specifications, 175–77
  warranties, 72, 110

professional development, 208–9. *See also* training

profound knowledge, 202

program evaluation and review technique charts. *See* PERT

program management, 48

project management (PM). *See also* projects
  applications, 252
  Body of Knowledge topics, 290–91
  communication, 260–62
  compared to process management, 253
  cross-functional collaboration, 278–79
  definition, 251
  management support, 276
  monitoring, 254
  organizational roadblocks, 276–77
  performance evaluation, 262–70
  planning, 254–55, 258–59, 278
  potential problems, 255–56, 276–77
  structure, 252–53
  value, 251–52

project managers
  effective, 277
  information needs, 56
  team leaders as, 48

project offices, 252–53

projects. *See also* project management (PM); teams
  budgets, 273–74
  closure, 281–82
  definition, 252
  documentation, 281
  feedback, 260–62
  objectives, 259–60, 277
  performance, 255, 262–70
  quality, 257–58, 274
  resources, 264, 273–74
  reviews, 281
  selecting, 256–57
  small, 279
  staffing, 264
  stakeholders, 270

projects—*continued*
    statement of work (SOW), 254, 255
    time to completion, 266–68
    work breakdown structure
        (WBS), 255
purchasing function, 74. *See also*
    suppliers

Q
Q9000 standards, 311
QA. *See* quality assurance
QC. *See* quality control
Q charts, 312
QFD. *See* quality function deployment
QS-9000 requirements, 32–33
quality
    definition, 311
    in service businesses, 22–23, 63
    Taguchi on, 153–55
    world-class, 318
quality assurance (QA), 52, 91, 99,
    311
quality audits. *See* audits
quality awards, 29–30, 35. *See also*
        Malcolm Baldrige National
        Quality Award
    Deming Prize, 24, 30, 300
    European, 27
    internal, 24, 42–43
    U.S. Senate Award, 27, 35
quality circles, 2, 217–18, 312
quality control (QC), 90, 311
    history, 1–2
    tools, 123–43
    work elements, 52
quality councils, 85–86, 87
Quality Digest, 27
quality engineering, 91, 99, 312
quality function
    activities, 90–91
    Body of Knowledge topics, 289,
        290

communication by, 55–56, 262
conflicts with other parts of orga-
    nization, 196
definitions, 8, 39
link with strategic plan, 82–83,
    84–85
managers of, 194, 196, 200, 209,
    210, 262
mission, 87–88, 194
outside resources, 101
place within organization, 51
resources needed, 98–101
responsibilities in job descriptions,
    210–11
as responsibility of entire organiza-
    tion, 39, 46, 53, 91–92, 101
as separate organization, 40, 46,
    51–53, 87–88, 90–91, 92,
    101
in service businesses, 53
staffing, 99–100, 209, 210
training, 100, 209
quality function deployment (QFD),
    146–48, 312
    voice of customer and, 108–9
quality loss function, 312
quality management. *See also* total
        quality management (TQM)
    history, 1–2
    of suppliers, 17–21, 91, 316
    tools, 143–45
quality managers. *See* quality func-
    tion, managers of
quality plans, 83–85, 86–87, 258–59
quality policies, 85–86, 97–98, 281
quality projects, 257–58, 274
quality score charts, 312
quality training. *See* training
Quality Trilogy, 88–90, 312
questionnaires. *See also* surveys
    reliability of, 166
quincunx, 312–13

R

RAB (Registrar Accreditation Board),
　313–14
random sampling, 313
range control charts, 140, 313
ranges, 138, 174–75
R charts. *See* range control charts
red bead experiment, 313
reengineering, 158–62
Registrar Accreditation Board (RAB),
　313–14
registration
　to ISO 9000, 29, 34, 280
　to standards, 314
regression analysis, 314
regulatory agencies, 71–72, 73
relationship diagrams, 144
reliability, 314
　of measurement, 164–65, 166–67
　of processes, 165
reliability assurance, 91
reliability engineering, 52, 91, 100
remedial journey, 301
reorganizations, 158–59
repeatability, of measurement, 165
reproducibility, of measurement, 165
research and development, 74
right the first time concept, 314
robustness, 314
Romig, Harry G., 314
Rossett, A., 243
run charts, 135–37, 162
Rust, R. T., 22

S

safety, 71–72, 74
sales function, 74
sample averages, 138
sample standard deviation charts, 314
sampling, 167–68
　acceptance, 170, 293
　double, 170

multiple, 171
plans, 168, 170
random, 313
single, 170
terminology, 168–70
scatter diagrams, 134–35, 315
s charts, 314
scheduling tools, 145, 265–70
Scholtes, P. R., 206, 214, 218
Schuman, S. P., 237
scientific management, 63–64
self-directed work groups, 46–47.
　See also teams
Senate Award. *See* U.S. Senate Award
Senge, P., 5
service businesses
　cost of quality in, 151
　measurement of variation in, 10
　quality functions in, 53
　quality in, 22–23, 63
service liability, 310
Shewhart cycle. *See* plan-do-check-
　act (PDCA) cycle
Shewhart, Walter A., 1, 145, 315
signal-to-noise ratio (S/N ratio), 315
Silverman, M., 65
simultaneous engineering. *See* con-
　current engineering (CE)
SI system, 179
six-sigma capability, 139, 183, 315
skills. *See also* training
　communication, 53–54, 55
　of managers, 229–30
　staff, 203, 208
small businesses
　organizational structures, 51
　training and education, 240
Smith, J. E., 202, 203
SOW. *See* statement of work
SPC. *See* statistical process control
special causes, 10, 315
specification limits, 137

specifications, 315
  product, 175–77
Spectrum, 94
staff. *See also* training
  assignments, 208
  attributes needed, 202–3, 204–5
  benefits, 225
  empowerment, 54, 211–14
  motivating, 224–25
  performance evaluations, 205–8
  professional development, 208–9
  for quality audits, 45
  for quality function, 99–100, 209,
    210
  quality responsibilities, 211
  selecting, 203–5
  skills of, 203, 208
stakeholders, in projects, 270
standard deviation, 138
standards, 29–30. *See also* ISO 9000
  in automobile industry, 32–33
  Body of Knowledge topics, 289
  environmental management
    (ISO 14000), 31–32
  Good Manufacturing Practices
    (GMP), 29
  military, 51, 308
  QS-9000, 32–33
  registration to, 314
  TE-9000, 33
statement of work (SOW), 254,
  255
statistical control, 11, 139
statistical methods
  in quality control, 1–2
  reducing variation with, 171
  trend analysis, 163
statistical process control (SPC),
  142–43, 316
statistical quality control (SQC), 316
steering committees, 85–86, 87
Stewart, Potter, 199

strategic alliances. *See also* partnerships
  with suppliers, 19–21, 115
strategic planning, 79, 80, 258
  Body of Knowledge topics, 290
  implications for training, 231–33,
    241
  link with quality function, 82–83,
    84–85
  link with quality plan, 83–85, 259
  process, 81
strategies, 79, 81
structural variation, 10, 316
suppliers
  in automobile industry, 32–33
  certification of, 20
  communication with, 57
  competition among, 18
  partnerships with, 19–21,
    113–15, 299
  quality management of, 17–21,
    91, 316
  selecting, 114
surveys, 40
  customer, 115–16, 117, 207
  sampling for, 167–68

T
tactical planning, 80, 258–59, 278
Taguchi, Genichi, 153–55, 175, 177,
  316
Taguchi methods, 316
tampering, 10, 316
targeting, 111
Taylor, Frederick, 63–64
TE-9000 standards, 33
team leaders
  as facilitators, 198
  managers as, 66, 67, 193, 215,
    219–22
  as project managers, 48
  responsibilities, 57
  roles, 216, 217

teams. *See also* projects
  coaching, 70–71
  communication within, 56–57
  conflicts in, 197–98
  corrective action, 218
  decision-making, 123–24, 197–99
  definition, 214
  dynamics of, 198–99, 222
  empowerment, 211–14
  evolution, 215–17
  facilitators, 198, 220, 222–23,
    237–39
  forming, 214–15
  information needs, 54
  in matrix organizations, 47–48
  motivating, 224–25
  performance evaluation, 222,
    223–24, 262
  potential problems, 223, 239
  problem-solving, 218, 220
  problem-solving tools, 123–26
  recognition and reward, 224–25
  self-directed work groups,
    46–47
  training for, 214, 220, 237
  types, 218–19
technology. *See also* computers
  changes in, 72–73
  use in training, 247–48
testing, nondestructive, 100, 308
Theory X managers, 65
Theory Y managers, 65
Toffler, A., 209
tolerances
  design, 137, 175–77
  statistical, 177–78
Tompkins, J., 4, 211, 219
tooling and equipment standards, 33
tools
  continuous improvement (CI), 123
  continuous process improvement
    (CPI), 126–34

  control charts, 137–42
  decision-making, 123–24, 143–45
  planning, 86, 143–45
  problem-solving, 123–26
  project performance, 264–70
  quality control, 123–43
  quality function deployment
    (QFD), 146–48
  quality management, 143–45
  scheduling, 145, 265–70
  seven, of quality, 315
  statistical, 167–71
  training, 245–48
top management. *See* management
total productive maintenance
  (TPM), 186
total quality control, 2
total quality management (TQM)
  definition, 317
  differences from traditional
    methods, 6
  history, 2
  holistic approach of, 8
  implementation failures, 3–4, 8, 9
  management commitment needed,
    8–9, 317
  model, 7
  terminology, 7–8
  in United States, 2–3
  value, 3
TPM (total productive maintenance),
  186
TQ (total quality) organizations
  management roles, 46–47
  structures, 6–7
TQM. *See* total quality management
training
  alternatives to, 243–44
  Baldrige Award criteria for,
    233–34
  Body of Knowledge topics, 292
  compared to education, 230–31

training—*continued*
customizing, 230
effectiveness, 233
evaluating, 244–45
for facilitators, 238
ISO 9000 requirements, 234–35,
241–43
just-in-time, 240
for managers, 229–30, 236
needs analysis, 231–33, 240–44
on-the-job, 247
potential problems, 245
for quality function staff, 100
in quality standards, 241–43
self-development, 246
sources of, 235–37
staff, 205, 208–9, 236–37
for teams, 214, 220, 237
timing of, 239–40
tools, 245–48
tree diagrams, 144–45
trend analysis, 162–63
trend control charts, 317
type I errors, 317
type II errors, 317

U
u charts, 142
UCL (upper control limits), 287,
317
United Airlines, 94
United States, history of quality
management, 1–3
U.S. Department of Defense (DOD),
1, 153
U.S. Food and Drug Administration
(FDA), 29
U.S. Senate Award, 27, 35
upper control limits (UCL), 287,
317

V
validity, definition, 167
value-adding processes, 317
variables
control charts, 286
data, 318
definition, 7
in experiments, 172
measuring, 13–14
variables control charts, 140
variation
causes, 10
common causes, 10, 297
definition, 8, 318
in measurement, 164–65
measuring, 9–10, 11
piece-to-piece, 175
reducing, 11, 13–14, 155, 171
special causes, 10, 315
structural, 10, 316
tampering as cause of, 10, 316
theory of, 9–11
time-to-time, 175
within-piece, 175
vendors. *See* suppliers
visions, 79, 81
vital few, useful many, 318

W
warranties, 72, 110
Waterman, R., 22
WBS. *See* work breakdown structure
Welch, Jack, 59
Wescott, Mason E., 318
Whiteley, R. C., 103, 105
work breakdown structure (WBS), 255
world-class quality, 318

Z
zero defects, 318

READER FEEDBACK
Fax to ASQC Quality Press Acquisitions: 414-272-1734

Comments and Areas for Improvement:
A Review of Managing Quality and a Primer for the Certified Quality Manager Exam

Please give us your comments, feedback, and suggestions for making this book more useful. We believe in the importance of continuous improvement and in meeting your needs. Your comments will help determine what improvements can be made in all ASQC Quality Press books.

Please share your opinion by circling the number below:

Ratings of the book	Needs Work		Satisfactory		Excellent	Comments
Stucture, flow, and logic	1	2	3	4	5	
Content, ideas, and information	1	2	3	4	5	
Style, clarity, ease of reading	1	2	3	4	5	
Held my interest	1	2	3	4	5	
Met my overall expectations	1	2	3	4	5	

I read the book because:

The best part of the book was:

The least satisfactory part of the book was:

Other suggestions for improvement:

General comments:

Thank you for your feedback. If you do not have access to a fax machine, please mail this form to: ASQC Quality Press, 611 East Wisconsin Avenue, P.O. Box 3005, Milwaukee, WI 53201-3005   Phone: 414-272-8575